# THE MUSIC/RECORD
# CAREER HANDBOOK

# THE MUSIC/ RECORD CAREER HANDBOOK

BY JOSEPH CSIDA

Typography & Design by Mary Jane Merrill

BILLBOARD PUBLICATIONS/NEW YORK

This book is for
Carol, Joe, Jr., Bob,
Greg, Chris and Jennie
with love

and with the hope that
the recital of these experiences
and these suggestions will help
some people of their generations
along the way

Copyright © 1973 by First Place Music Publications, Inc.

First published 1973 by First Place Music Publications, Inc.,
12754 Ventura Boulevard, Studio City, California 91604

Published 1975 by Billboard Publications, Inc.,
1515 Broadway, New York, N.Y. 10036

**Library of Congress Cataloging in Publication Data**
Csida, Joseph.
    The music.
    1. Music as a profession. I. Title.
ML3795.C76          1975          780'.23          75-16394
ISBN 0-8230-7580-X

Manufactured in U.S.A.

First Printing, 1973
Second Printing, 1975
Third Printing, 1977
Fourth Printing, 1979

# CONTENTS

# INTRODUCTION

# PART I

## THE CREATIVE CAREERS

### SECTION ONE - Songwriter

### SECTION TWO - Musician

### SECTION THREE - Conductor/Director

### SECTION FOUR - Group Member Or Leader
### Band Member Or Leader

### SECTION FIVE - Singer

*I have found power in the mysteries of thought,*
*exaltation in the chantings of the muses; I have*
*been versed in the reasonings of men; but Fate*
*is stronger than anything I have known.*
Euripides, 406 B.C.

# 1. THE INTENT

This book is for people who believe they want to begin a career in the Music/Record Business — or who are presently engaged in the Music/Record Business, and feel they may be able to use some practical suggestions as to how they may develop their careers more successfully.

"The Music/Record Business" is, of course, a ridiculously broad term, which would embrace the activities of a young guitar player, getting five dollars for sitting in with a new group at the Twilite Cafe, and Frank Sinatra, who recently decided not to come out of retirement because the potential, for him, in the Alan Jay Lerner-Fritz Loewe musical, *The Little Prince* missed by a million or two dollars what Sinatra thought he should get. It would include the salesman, who just went to work this morning for the RCA distributor in Pittsburgh, and Clive Davis, the president of Columbia Records.

It would cover the functions of all practitioners on the creative side as well as on the business side of Music. Right here, however, I should stress that I am narrowing this area down to the Commercial and Popular phases of the Music/Record Business (by Popular, I do mean so-called Pop music *plus* Rock, Contemporary, Middle of the Road, Country & Western, Folk, Soul and/or Rhythm and Blues, Jazz). And I mean these categories in every area from the creation of the song through its performance and promotion in the record, motion picture, television, radio, night club, theatre and concert areas.

The record industry, and careers within it, are covered with some thoroughness for the obvious reason that (unlike motion pictures, television and the other entertainment arts) music constitutes 99% of what's on records, and thus records and music are inseperable.

I am not attempting to cover, in any way, the classical or operatic phases of the music business for the simple reason that I know almost nothing about them. I also will not deal with such important areas as Instrument Manufacturing and Repairs; Music in the Military; Recreational Music; Music as Therapy, etc. Again for the simple reason that I know little about them.

In the area of composing/arranging/conducting I am most fortunate in being able to present (in addition to my own notions) the thoughts and recommendations of one of the most able practitioners in the field, my partner, Dick Grove.

And because many persons who wish to get into the Music Business are interested in working as Music Educators, and because today so many Music Educators work so closely with professionals in jazz and other commercial music areas, I have prevailed upon my good friend, Jack Wheaton to write a special section on building a career as a Music Educator.

Jack, among many other important functions, serves as Chairman of the Music Department of Cerritos College in Norwalk, California (one of the best college Music departments in the country) and is President of the National Association of Jazz Educators. He knows as much or more about the Educational Phases of Music as I know about the Commercial and Popular phases.

I hope we may be able to give some meaningful help to anyone seeking a career or anxious to further a career in the areas of the music business in which we have knowledge and background.

*I should not talk so much about myself*
*if there were anybody else I know*
*as well.*

Henry David Thoreau

## 2. CREDENTIALS

It will occur to the intelligent prospective reader of this book to ask:

How can a writer presume to tell me anything authentic, useful or practical about composers, lyricists, arrangers, copyists, musicians, singers, producers, engineers, commentators, disk jockeys, music publishing jobs, record company functions, distributors, personal managers, booking agents, press agents, attorneys and accountants in more than a half dozen areas of commercial music?

The best way one could do this, and do it well, would be to have spent many years working successfully at a number of the occupations mentioned, and to have worked intimately over a period of years with people in all the other occupations.

So, credentials:

In February, 1934 I went to work for *The Billboard*, today the leading tradepaper in the popular music and record industry. I worked there from that date till 1949. During that stretch I was Music Editor, and then, Editor in Chief for a good many more years.

I wrote reviews of hundreds of records, singers, bands in every medium. And news stories and editorials covering scores of major music industry developments. I developed close

relationships with literally hundreds of people both on the
creative and business sides of every conceivable kind of music
business operation.

For example, I hired Jerry Wexler as a music reporter.
Jerry today is executive vice president of Atlantic Records, a
perennial "Record Man of the Year" and a millionaire. I was
instrumental in creating the Record Industry Association of
America.

I served a term as President of the New York Chapter of
the National Academy of Recording Arts and Sciences (NARAS).

When I left *Billboard* I went to work for the Radio Corporation of America, initially as number two man to John West,
vice president for Public Relations and Advertising, then as head
of the Artists & Repertoire Department of RCA Victor Records.

In those capacities, naturally, I worked with singers, bandleaders, their agents and managers, music publishers of every description, recording engineers, arrangers, songwriters and uncount-
ed dozens of other people on the business side of the television,
radio, record and music industries. At RCA I signed Eddie Fisher
to his first record contract and produced the largest collection of
Big Band albums ever released in a single package.

Following a run with RCA I went into business for myself
for the first time, initially in partnership with a father and son music team, George and Eddie Joy. We were in music publishing and
talent management. Bob Merrill wrote *Doggie in the Window* and
all kinds of other hits for us in that period. And later a string of
successful Broadway musicals. I left the Joys and set up in talent
management, music publishing, record and show production on
my own. All this while I was writing a column called *Sponsor
Backstage* in a television/radio tradepaper called *Sponsor*.

Broadcast Music, Inc. (BMI) and its top executives, Carl
Haverlin, Bob Burton, Bob Sour, Thea Zavin, Russ Sanjek were
largely responsible for my being able to set up as an independent
practitioner.

At that point I managed Eddy Arnold, who had just left
Tom Parker . . . and later Bobby Darin . . . and a very hot guitar
team called Santo & Johnny, and a bright young man named

Jim Lowe, whose "Green Door" was one of the biggest hit records of all time. (We also published "Green Door" and produced the record). And a girl singer named Betty Johnson, who almost made it. And Norman Leyden, musical director for the Arthur Godfrey radio show and many others.

Some dozen years after setting up my three-pronged operation, I sold out and became Vice President in Charge of Eastern Operations for Capitol Records. Among other duties I supervised the acquisition of Broadway Show Original Cast album rights and had the pleasure of working with major talents like Richard Rodgers, Hal Prince, Steve Sondheim, Meredith Willson and many others.

During my Capitol phase I took over and completely reorganized the entire Capitol Singles Record operation, which necessitated my having complete control (for Singles) of not only the creative side, but all the business aspects — sales, merchandising, promotion, etc. of the business.

I left Capitol and became President of a publicly-owned company, Recording Industries Corporation. And put together that operation from the ground up, from office boy through vice-presidents.

Along the way I was Executive Producer of the Eddy Arnold TV Film series (one of the earliest ever made featuring a singing star), and later Producer of the John Gary 90 minute syndicated television show.

And finally went back into my own business once more, to manage John Gary, and take him from a room at the West Side YMCA in New York (which he couldn't afford) to $400,000 a year and two national television shows of his own. And to run a number of publishing companies at the same time. I left Gary after seven years, and went into the Educational Music Publishing business, forming an organization called First Place Music Publications, Inc. with the aforementioned talented composer/arranger/conductor, Dick Grove.

In the almost forty years which have passed since I began my own multi-faceted career in the Music Business on *The Billboard* I have learned something about almost every job of any consequence in the popular commercial music industry.

6.

This seems a good time to pass on as much of it as I can, in as honest and straightforward way as I can, to young people who are planning careers or struggling to develop careers in this fascinating business.

*Lots of times you have to join a parade*
*in which you're not really interested*
*in order to get where you're going.*

7.

Christopher Morley

# 3. THE GOOD AND THE BAD

Before getting into your own individual place in the
music business let's take a quick look at its present state and its
future. Thanks largely to some exciting technological developments in recorded music (longplaying 33 rpm and 45 rpm speeds;
tape cartridges, cassettes, etc.); spreading of music generally,
and all its styles through wars (which sent young people from
their home towns to other areas all over the country and the
world), and particularly thanks to television every phase of the
music business has reached huge proportions.

The record business hit just short of a billion and three
quarters dollars in 1970. In less than five years, from 1966 to
'70 tape and cartridge sales went from $40 million up to over
$500,000,000. The American Society of Composers, Authors
and Publishers (ASCAP) took in a record $72,000,000 plus for
its publishers and writers; Broadcast Music, Inc. (BMI) did well
over $34,000,000. (I still remember writing the story of BMI's
birth for *Billboard.* It's entire catalogue, for a while, was
*Jeannie with the Light Brown Hair.)*

And the business can get nothing but bigger. Upcoming
is quadrasonic records and tapes and quadraphonic players. Upcoming is videocassettes, and Community Antenna Television.
Not really upcoming, already here, of course. But with great

promise for continued growth in the music business.

However the business is not unpopulated. ASCAP has almost 13,000 songwriter members, and a large percentage of them don't make a living writing songs. Another 21,000 songwriters belong to BMI. That's 34,000 songwriters, which is a lot of words and music. At the last count some of these 34,000 writers copyrighted almost 90,000 songs in a single year.

The American Federation of Musicians had 305,202 members in 1971. And most of them were not earning their daily bread as professional musicians.

In 1934 for all practical purposes there were three record companies (RCA, Columbia and Decca — and Decca had just started with Bing Crosby, Guy Lombardo and the Andrews Sisters). Today there are literally hundreds of companies, scores of them highly successful.

Yes, the business is heavily populated, but there are probably more opportunities in it today than there ever were. I saw many men — the aforementioned Jerry Wexler, Randy Wood (Dot), the late Glenn Wallichs (Capitol), Herb Alpert (A & M) become millionaires.

Among the music publishers Lou Levy sold his Leeds group to MCA for three or four million; Tommy Valando, ex-song plugger sold his Valando-Sunbeam firms to Metromedia for a few million. Writers like Merrill, Fred Ebb and others with whom I worked reached great heights.

And I saw many performers, Arnold, Darin, Gary become rich and famous. Some stayed right up there; others blew it.

I also saw some very capable men (performers, composers, administrators) come on strong, go quite high and then reach the point where they had to drop out of the music business and go into other fields.

If you think the business is exciting, glamorous, rewarding, you're right. It is.

It also has its full share of finks and phonies, and its own adequate quota of trials and travail for anyone who wants to make progress in it. There is indeed, as Jack Anderson has recently insisted in several columns, payola. Groups do sue their managers and vice versa. Manager/Producer Terry Knight is suing the Grand Funk members, and they are suing him. Altogether some fifty million dollars is involved. Terry Melcher, who, of course, is Doris Day's son, is suing her. She's not suing him. Two quite prominent record company executives were recently indicted by the Federal government for income tax evasion. One, while sales manager of a major record company, is said to have bought back unsold records from distributors, who then gave the executive large kickbacks. He didn't declare his income on those kickbacks.

There are bootleggers, who illegally press hit records and sell them to dealers off the back of a pickup truck, cash on the line, tax-free. Sometimes the bootleggers are record label owners who bootleg their own hit records. There are tape duplicators, who duplicate hit tapes and sell them to retailers and claim that this is perfectly legal as long as they pay the publisher's royalty for the songs on the records.

About twenty years ago I went to what was the second disk jockey convention. A big "do" in Miami Beach. Scandalous headlines popped. "Booze and Broads" were being used to persuade the jockeys to favor certain records and companies.

Recently, a broadcasting-chain-owned record company introduced an important new rock act to disk jockeys and the press in San Francisco. Scandalous stories about drugs and broads being used to seduce disk jockeys resulted.

All this is true. But there is also the *Concert for Bangladesh* which George Harrison (ex-Beatle) and friends (engineered by ABKCO head, accountant-personal manager-record-film-publishing executive Allan B. Klein) put on to raise somewhere between $5,000,000 and $15,000,000 for UNICEF, hassles or no hassles. You may not admire some episodes in Sinatra's career, but it is a fact that he has done hundreds of benefits in which he's raised millions of dollars for worthy causes (not including the dinner for Spiro Agnew).

And similarly, scores of entertainers, dozens of music/record industry organizations such as the National Academy of Recording Arts and Sciences, the National Association of

Record Merchandisers, etc. have created funds and scholarships for all kinds of deserving causes.

You no doubt will, in your own career in the music business, march to your own drummer, whatever the beat. Whatever the beat, there are certain definite approaches and steps you can and should take to get into the business, and to progress in it. Let's take a look at some.

*The race is not always to the swift,*
*nor the battle to the strong, but that's*
*the way to bet.*
                    Damon Runyon

## 4. LEARN & GET IN

If you're already in the music business in any way at all,
we'll come to you in a while. If your father is president of a
record company, music publishing firm or whatever you have no
difficulty getting in, and we'll come to you later too. If you're
not in the business now, what can you do to get in, where, when,
how?

To begin with, if you're presently in school, *and learning*
stay there. I know a lot of successful people in the music business
who have had minimal formal educations. There seems to be a
general tendency these days to put down formal education.

If you're concerned about the practical value of much
formal education you may take comfort from the fact that, in
some cases, formal education seems to be moving toward achieving more immediate practical results.

There is a strong movement to revise school curricula in
the direction of preparing young people for careers at early
stages in their education. Dr. Sidney Marland, United States Com-
missioner of Education, speaking before the Manpower Institute
and the National Academy of School Executives in Washington
recently had this to say about a new approach to career education:

"The new program includes motivation toward a career
in early childhood. Adolescent years, and sometimes beyond,
are spent in orienting the student's talents, aptitudes and interests

to information about career possibilities. This includes giving students actual experience in the world of work. It means doing even more in the area of cooperative work experience which places more responsibility on business and industry, as well as on unions."

A trend toward realism and modernism in education seems to be developing.

At Lake Park High School in Chicago, for example, in history, they now not only cover the American Revolution, they cover *all* revolutions. They don't study revolutions from the purely American point of view, but from *all* points of view. Were the British right? Was George Washington a washout as a general, and a traitor? A traitor to Britain, that is?

Geographically and culturally, instead of the emphasis on Greece and Rome, there is today a big concentration on Africa and China, in many schools.

In a high school in Vancouver, Washington, three years ago music educator Jack Francis started a Rock Lab. Now all three high schools in the district have Rock Labs, and they're fully accepted parts of the curriculum. In the Perkins public schools in Sandusky, Ohio James M. Gray, director of Music teaches melody writing and uses tunes like *Light My Fire, Close To You* and *Proud Mary* (current rock hits, of course) as examples.

Today there are approximately 18,000 to 20,000 stage bands (or contemporary or jazz bands) in America's high schools and colleges. Five years ago there were less than 10,000. Figuring approximately 16 young people per band that would be between 288,000 and 320,000 into current contemporary music. And probably another quarter to a half million kids in swing and show choral groups.

If you choose carefully you certainly can get a most useful education for a music career through established channels. And right now it seems to be getting easier to get into the nation's top schools than it has been for years.

For the first time in years leading colleges and universities are out hustling for potential freshmen instead of turning them away. UCLA, for example, in the 1971-1972 period, had

25,500 students on its General Campus, a drop of a full 10%
from the 1970-1971 year. And many schools are making drastic
and most revolutionary changes in their curricula.

In the music/record business a certain amount of career
education activity is carried on by trade organizations, individual firms and unions, about all of which more in individual career
chapters.

But, I repeat, if you're in school *and learning*, stay there.
Note, please I stressed *and learning.* If you're *not*, you're wasting
your time, and the time of a lot of teachers.

If you have the opportunity to, and can afford to get
into the right kind of school, by all means do.

My point is that — whatever area of the music business
you want to work in — the more you know the better. And
there are obviously just two ways to learn: Studying, formal or
otherwise; and Experience.

If the teachers in your school are good, and know their
subject, and can impart their knowledge to you, it would be
most difficult for you to find any better way of learning, short
of actual experience. If the teachers are not good, you'll be
much better off learning some other way.

And obviously there are many other ways. Some are:
Private Teachers;
Correspondence Courses;
Books;
Seminars;
Workshops;
As with schools and teachers, some of these are good and
some bad. Some expensive, some free. I've had considerable experience with many of them, and will cover them for each individual area as we come to each, since the educational requirements, opportunities, and such for a songwriter or singer are
obviously quite different than those for a promotion man or a
disk jockey.

The ideal structure for the acquisition of knowledge for
pursuing any music business career, of course, is the *combination*
of education and experience. And, indeed, many of the most successful people I know in almost all areas are people who more

or less combined, and continue to combine *learning* with *daily practical work.* Thus, I know a number of successful musicians, who continue to study with private teachers, take Courses such as the Dick Grove Improvisation Course, attend Workshops and Seminars, etc.

   *But back to getting into the business, if you're not now in:*

   Where you are *geographically* is important in determining your approach. If you live in New York, Los Angeles, Chicago, San Francisco or possibly any one of a half dozen of the other larger metropolitan areas in the country, you obviously have a far greater opportunity to get into the business than if you live in a smaller town.

   In these cities, and particularly New York and Los Angeles there are numerous record companies, music publishing firms, management offices, agencies, record distributors, television and radio stations, night clubs, theatres, etc.

   Most fortunately for thousands upon thousands of would-be music-industryites recent years have seen the development of literally scores of smaller cities and towns as extremely active music/record centers.

   Nashville, of course, has long been famed as "Music City, U.S.A." and many of the most brilliant talents in every area of the business developed and operate from there. Indeed a substantial number of erstwhile New Yorkers and Angelenos have moved their operations to the city.

   Memphis (the home of Elvis Presley) is another Tennessee city, which has developed into a substantial music center. The American Federation of Musicians Local 71 there is one of the most progressive in the nation. Stax Records, headed by Al Bell, is one of the most successful and active of the independent record operations. They record Isaac Hayes of *Shaft* fame, and produced Melvin Van Peebles' sound track album of *Sweet Sweetback's Badasssss Song* and his Broadway hit, *Don't Play Us Cheap.* Sam Phillips, who first recorded Presley and sold his contract to RCA, still operates a most successful studio and record operation there.

   Atlantic Records has studios and much activity in Miami

Beach, Florida. Atlanta, Georgia, sparked to a large degree by record company-music publisher-manager executive Bill Lowery is "heavy" on the scene. And in Muscle Shoals, Alabama people like producer Rick Hall, studio executives like Ronnie Ballew, Bill Coffield, Joe Wilson and others have put that city on the music map. Performers like Aretha Franklin, the Rolling Stones, Sonny & Cher, The Staple Singers and many others have cut sides in Muscle Shoals.

Many other cities (Dallas, Houston, Las Vegas, Reno, Boston, Philadelphia, etc.) have considerable action. And foreign capitals (London, Paris, Tokyo, et al thrive musically.)

So if you're in any one of these music-active cities your chances of getting started in the music business should be good. If you're in a city or town which does not have a great deal of commercial music activity you may still break into the field, though it may be a little more difficult.

The first and most important step (surprise!) is to *get into the business.* Any way you can! In any job or function! What I mean is if you want to be a singer, don't concentrate entirely on trying to get started as a singer. Sure, work at that in every way possible (and those ways will be discussed in the appropriate section of this book), but if you can't break through as a singer, get into the business in some other way:

As a promotion man for a local record distributor; as a sales clerk in a music store; as a gofer at a radio or television station; as an usher in the local concert hall. *Any way at all!* The important thing is to get in, become a part of the business. And then, watch for, and/or where possible create, your own opportunities.

Sonny Bono was a record promotion man, and so was Isaac Hayes, before they became singers. I have a friend who wanted to be an Artist & Repertoire Man and Record Producer. His name is Paul Robinson. He started out as a promotion man for Columbia Records and worked his way into production for RCA, then as an independent producer.

A man who worked for me at Capitol, Manny Kellem, started with a record distributor in Philadelphia and wound up with Artist & Repertoire jobs with Capitol, Epic and RCA in

New York.

Again, the *important thing is to get in!* Naturally, if you can connect in the job or area you're specifically aiming at, finé If not, get in, any way.

# 5. THE TRADE PRESS

One important way to help you get in, in the most advantageous possible situation, is to subscribe to, and begin reading regularly and carefully, as many of the tradepapers as you can afford.

The three most important publications in the music/record field are:

1. *The Billboard.* In 1934 the music department of my *alma mater* consisted of one full page, edited by a nice man named Mousie Shapiro. Today it is a weekly newspaper, which covers every conceivable area of the music/record/tape, etc. industry exhaustively. It also publishes many special issues and special sections each year in which are given the names and addresses or record and tape manufacturing companies,distributors, studios, music publishers, personal managers, agents, producers, et al.

Its music editor and executive editor is one of the most knowledgeable and best loved men in the industry. His name is Paul Ackerman, and to show you how experienced he is, he started on the paper about two months after I did in 1934.

The subscription rate is $40.00 per year. The address is: One Astor Plaza (1515 Broadway), New York, N.Y. 10036.

2. *Cash Box.* Many years ago the employees of *The Billboard* in New York, members of the New York Newspaper

Guild went on strike. When the strike was settled one of the employees, Joe Orleck, left the paper and was given a substantial amount of severance pay. With this, and in partnership with an advertising agency man named Bill Gersh, he started a publication called *Cash Box*. Initially it concentrated quite heavily on the juke box and other coin machine business, since that was Orleck's and Gersh's special area, but in the passing years it grew into a music/record tradepaper. It, too, is a weekly and costs $35 per year. Address: 1780 Broadway, New York, N.Y. 10019.

     3. *Record World.* A year or two after I started on *The Billboard* in 1934, the Indoor Editor and General Manager of the New York office, where I worked, was a man named Eli Sugarman. One day a young Encyclopedia salesman named Bob Austin managed to get an appointment with Sugarman, and his pitch was so persuasive that instead of purchasing the Encyclopedia, Sugarman hired him as an advertising space salesman for *Billboard*. After *Cash Box* was launched Austin joined them. Several years ago he left *Cash Box,* and with Sid Parnes, one of the *Cash Box's* early editors, started a music/record tradeweekly called *Record World.* It has done well. Its subscription price is $30 per year. Its at 200 West 57th Street, New York, N.Y. 10010.

     If you can afford it, I would recommend you subscribe to all three of these publications. If not, one will do. If you read them thoroughly and carefully each week they'll give you a running familiarity with what is going on in the music/record business which you can acquire in no other way. In addition to enabling you to absorb the ebb and flow of the industry at large, you'll frequently find ads and stories which will tell you about job openings, events you should attend, etc.

     As a matter of fact I consider tradespapers such an invaluable source of essential information that, if you can afford it, I would recommend as regular-as-possible reading and study of several other trade publications, not exclusively music/record papers.

     These are:

     1. *Variety.* This "bible" of showbusiness has a good music/record department, but not as extensive as the aforementioned three papers. On the other hand it deals exhaustively and

authoritatively with other phases of showbusiness in which music is important in a way none of the other three do. This applies to coverage of motion pictures, television, radio, night clubs, theatres, etc. It's a weekly and its subscription rate is $20 per year. Address: 154 West 45th Street, New York, N.Y. 10036.

2. *Daily Variety.* Published on the West Coast, it covers motion pictures and television primarily, some music and record news, on a *daily* basis, but often has ads and stories important to music/record people. Particularly valuable to L.A. people. Yearly subscription, $30; address: 6404 Sunset Boulevard, Hollywood, Ca. 90028.

3. *Hollywood Reporter.* Covers same areas, generally speaking, as *Daily Variety.* Also daily. Also particularly useful to Los Angeles people. $30 per year. 6715 Sunset Boulevard, Hollywood, Ca. 90028.

4. *Broadcasting.* A weekly which covers the television and radio fields most thoroughly and knowledgeably. This excellent publication has recently begun to run music stories (as they apply to the broadcaster) fairly regularly. 51 issues per year, $14. Address: 1735 DeSales Street, N.W. Washington, D.C.

5. *Downbeat.* For musicians, contemporary composers, arrangers, etc. the best in the field. Emphasis on jazz, blues and rock. Publisher Chuck Suber constantly strives to spread contemporary music gospel, increase its use in schools, etc. Published biweekly except monthly during January, July, August and September. Subscription rate, $9. per year. Address: 222 West Adams Street, Chicago, Ill. 60606.

6. *Pro/Ed Review.* A new 4-times per year newsletter-digest dealing with Contemporary Music education in high schools and colleges, and emphasizing the effective ways in which professionals and educators work together. This writer is Editor/Publisher. Per copy price, $1.; Subscription price, 4 issues annually, $3.50. Address: First Place Music Publications, Inc. 12754 Ventura Boulevard, Studio City, Ca. 91604.

There are many other publications which would be helpful to people interested in specific areas of the field, i.e. in the Educational areas: *Music Educators' Journal, The Instrumentalist, School Music News, State Educator publications;* — in the

20.

area of musicianship, union papers, national and local, *The Guitar Player, Clavier,* etc.

In the retailing, sales and merchandising areas *Sales Management, Merchandising Week,* and many others.

I'm sure that persons getting into those specific areas will find out about the publications in due time. The basic point holds true. Trade publications can be most helpful to people breaking into an industry, as well as to people already in, who want to keep alert to trends and developments in their field, and opportunities for getting ahead.

In general there are, of course, ways of breaking into the music field other than via trade publication leads. If you're in school, for example, various faculty members and/or even some of your fellow students may be able to steer you into an opportunity. Whether you're in school or not you can go after a job in the specific career area for which you are aiming, or if you can't find an opening in that area, you may go after any entreé into the music business.

I think it will prove more useful and practical if these approaches are discussed in the Sections of the book dealing with specific careers.

Here I might simply add that, generally, joining groups or organizations active in any music and/or record/tape area may be most advantageous. I, for instance, landed on *The Billboard* in 1934, by the pure and happy coincidence that I met a man named Leslie Anderson at various meetings and functions of a group of advertising men called The Advertising Association of New York. Anderson was then Eastern Advertising Manager of *The Billboard* and he hired me as a clerk in the advertising department. That's how one music business career began.

It's stating the obvious, of course, to say that once you've developed your leads and opportunities to get into the business in any area, the way you follow up those leads should be determined by your own evaluation of your own strengths. Thus, if you have a scintillating, irresistible personality your emphasis should be on trying to gain your entree *in person.* If you're better on paper, by all means, write first.

A second, equally obvious suggestion for career opportunities and development in the music business (as well as any other) merits a short chapter of its own.

Contacts is what I'm talking about.

*Nothing is there more friendly to*
*a man than a friend in need.*
**Titus Maccius Plautus**

## 6. FRIENDS & RELATIONS

In days of yore when monarchs ruled supreme there was, of course, constant angling to arrange marriages between the king of this land and the princess of that. And if all the people who have married the boss's daughter were stacked on top of one another, the mound would probably be taller than the Empire State Building.

Presumably, one of Richard Nixon's reasons for cultivating the friendship of Mao Tse-Tung, Chou En-Lai and Leonid Breszhnev is that he will be able to make more advantageous deals for our nation.

The music business is no different.

One of my own very best friends is an attorney named Richard Jablow. Dick is counsel for the National Academy of Recording Arts and Sciences and the Writers' Guild, for Tom Jones and Englebert Humperdinck and Billy Taylor and I don't know how many other important and highly successful groups and personalities in the music and allied businesses. Dick introduced me to John Gary and arranged for me to handle Gary as personal manager. Dick had already made a record deal for Gary with RCA.

Another of my good friends is one of the most successful personal manager/producers in the business. He has very strong feelings about friendships and contacts in the business.

He strictly forbade his wife to make social engagements for him with doctors, plumbers or other non-music business, non-show business people. His attitude was that he simply was not interested in people in any areas alien to his own business. *Dedication!*

Another good friend of mine started on his road to millionairedom in music as a song plugger, working for the same George Joy whom I joined in my first venture as a music publisher. This was Tommy Valando. In Tommy's early days Perry Como was one of the most important and influential people in the popular music field, since a record by Como could earn a songwriter and publisher several hundred thousand dollars. Tommy, an excellent golfer, cultivated his relationship with Como to the point where they played golf (one of Perry's favorite pasttimes) several days a week.

Tommy and Perry were such good friends that Perry went into the publishing business with Joy, and then later with Valando.

As Valando's own career as a publisher blossomed he got into the area of publishing the scores of musical comedies and dramas, a highly profitable phase of the business. At that stage Tommy played golf very frequently with George Abbott, legendary Broadway director/producer, and developed almost precisely the same kind of complete and intimate friendship with Mr. Abbott as he had previously developed with Como.

As mentioned elsewhere in this book, Tommy eventually sold his publishing companies to the Metromedia Broadcasting group for several million dollars. This was a reasonable price because by that time Tommy's catalogues contained the scores to such shows as *Fiddler on the Roof, Cabaret* and many others.

Marriage, naturally, is frequently an even more effective relationship in the evolution of a career. One of my colleagues at Capitol Records told me one day that he wouldn't, under any circumstances, consider marrying a woman who was not only beautiful, but also wealthy and held the potential of having a beneficial effect on his career.

At that point he had been married twice previously, once to a woman who only had a moderate amount of money and no connection with showbusiness; the second time to a once-important girl singer. Shortly after our conversation he did indeed marry a girl who was beautiful, wealthy and had many close relationships with a large number of the highest placed people in the music, theatre and motion picture worlds.

An additional titillating touch to this tale is that the lady's fortune derived from a divorce settlement she had made with her previous husband, one of the most successful musical comedy writers of all time.

It surely did no harm to Eddie Fisher's career to have married Debbie Reynolds and Elizabeth Taylor.

One of my oldest friends, and a man who was once my partner, is Lee Eastman, without question one of the most successful men in the entire history of the music business. Lee is an attorney (about which more later) and he was already vastly successful long before his daughter, Linda, a talented photographer, married Paul McCartney, after the breakup of the Beatles. But it surely did not hamper Lee's involvement with a number of music enterprises, in which The Beatles were at one time active, to have Paul in the family. Nor did it hurt Lee's young son, John, who is partnered in the law business with Dad.

There is certainly no reason to feel that one should reject a friend or a fiance simply because that person may be helpful in furthering one's career. It is indeed as easy to love a wealthy person as a poor one. Or as easy to love a smart and gregarious person as a dumb recluse. Easier.

Again, the effects of your personal relationships on your career in music will depend on the drummer's beat you hear, your own philosophy and fate.

So, on to specific careers.

# PART I

## THE CREATIVE CAREERS

Songwriter
Musician
Conductor/Director
Group member or Leader
Band member or Leader
Singer
Arranger
Producer

# PART I

## SECTION ONE

### Songwriter

## 8. SONGS & EARNING POTENTIALS

Grace Slick is a songwriter. And so is Richard Rodgers. And Stephen Sondheim. And Isaac Hayes and Boudelaux and Felice Bryant. And Smokey Robinson and Kris Kristofferson and Carole King. And Bob Merrill and Bob Russell and Harlan Howard and Howard Dietz. And Frank Loesser and Marvin Moore. And Paul Anka and Paul Simon. And Sheldon Harnick and Jerry Bock and Mel Tillis and Cindy Walker and Bobbie Gentry. And Jimmy Webb and Webb Pierce. And Burt Bacharach and Hal David and David Gates and Paul McCartney and John Lennon and Yoko One and you and me.

Sometimes it seems like everybody is a songwriter or wants to be. There is no doubt that there are almost as many different kinds of songs and writers as there are people. If there is any one career in the music business of which it may be said that you may come from big town or small, country or city; you may be a kindergarten dropout or a Julliard graduate, young or old, black or white, there's no reason you can't get to be a successful songwriter. If you have some talent, will work hard, keep studying and learning, and most of all keep writing.

It's not too likely, but there may be a reader or two who is unfamiliar with the ways in which a writer earns money from his songs. For this minority, a brief rundown:

1. *Performances.* Writers get paid for public perform-

ances of their songs by television and radio stations and networks, night clubs, concert halls and/or promoters, night club
and hotel dining room operators, merry-go-round operators and
all other users of music for public performance for profit, excepting juke box operators.

The 1909 copyright law exempted the juke box operators of that day (the boxes obviously were quite different from
today's machines) from paying for the right to perform music
for profit. The law is still in effect and exempts juke box operators today. The juke box lobby, abetted by some Congressmen
one can only view with suspicion, have outmaneuvered the publisher and writer group lobbies down through the years and kept
new copyright legislation from passing. The music people keep
trying, however, and one of these days the juke box exemption
may be discontinued.

If you write a song and it is performed, say on the radio,
you won't be paid for that performance unless your song is
licensed by one of the Performing Rights organizations. The oldest of these is The American Society of Composers, Authors and
Publishers (ASCAP) formed in 1914 by Victor Herbert and some
friends. Broadcast Music, Inc. (BMI) came into being in 1939,
through a set of circumstances which deserve and will get a little
more discussion in a moment. SESAC is another performance
rights organization, about forty two years old, owned by a
family named Heinecke. It is far smaller than either ASCAP or
BMI.

For writers (and others) interested in detailed information on these Performing Rights organizations, the organizations
themselves will happily supply information – or if you prefer,
you may get much pertinent data in an excellent book called
*This Business of Music* by Sidney Shemel and M. William Krasilovsky (two music business attornies) and published by Billboard
Publications, Inc. at $15.00 per copy.

If you are not a member of one of these organizations
you will probably not be paid for any public performance of
your songs. But then again, if you're not a member of one of
these organizations, you probably haven't reached the point
where any of your songs are being performed anyway.

2. *Mechanical royalties.* These are, for the most part, royalties paid by the record companies to the publisher (who, in turn, is supposed to pay half to the writer) on any records sold of songs belonging to said publisher.

3. *Royalties from printed music.* This would include royalties from sheet music, song folios, published arrangements and other printed versions of your song.

4. *Synchronization and other special fees.* This would be earnings from special payments made to you for songs written on assignment, and or songs purchased by a user for a special purpose, i.e., motion picture and/or television usage, etc.

5. *Foreign earnings.* All the aforementioned sources of income apply around the world, in one form or another these days.

Incidentally, the aforementioned *This Business of Music* is highly recommended for detailed information in all these areas for the writer as well as the publisher, and even the recording artist, agent, producer, et al.

In our book, of course, we're dealing with the question of how you get started and develop your career as a writer. Toward that end you may find it interesting, and possibly even useful to read a brief presentation of your recent heritage as a potential or currently practicing songwriter. It may even give you a little inspiration to realize how lucky you are to be trying to make it as a songwriter today rather than in the thirties or even the early forties.

# 9. SONG PLUGGERS & BIG BANDS

In those days there was only one performing rights
Society of any real consequence, the aforementioned ASCAP.
It was quite difficult to get into ASCAP either as a publisher or
writer. Lyricists, for the most part, wrote slick and sophisticated, frequently frothy treatments of one theme: l-o-v-e, dreamed
of, unrequited, sometimes ecstatically fulfilled (but delicately).

When Richard Rodgers and Oscar Hammerstein wrote
*Oklahoma,* in 1943, it was hailed as a helluva piece of realistic
musical theatre.

Few songs became hits in that period. The general procedure was this: A major publisher decided which song would
be his "plug" song for a period of two, three, four months. His
songpluggers would present that song to each of the few record
companies, and for the most part, the artist and repertoire directors of the record companies would dutifully record the song,
each with one of his leading artists.

The same song pluggers would take the song to the big
band leaders (Harry James, Tommy and Jimmy Dorsey, Glenn
Miller, Guy Lombardo, et al) who played in swank hotel dining
rooms and supper clubs, whence the radio networks piped their
music across the nation in what used to be called "remote broad-
casts." Those radio network performances were worth a great
deal of performance money to publishers and writers, and it was

not uncommon for a songplugger to indulge in a little plain or fancy payola to get a song put into a "remote" program line-up. One night I sat with a top bandleader and a songplugger at a table in the Cafe Rouge in the Hotel Pennsylvania in New York. The bandleader indicated great reluctance to put the plugger's current tune in the line-up.

"I'll bet you a hundred dollars you can't drink that glass of water," said the plugger to the leader.

The leader picked up the glass of water and drank it.

"I'll be a sunofagun," said the plugger and handed the leader two fifty dollar bills.

The song got on the program.

Under these circumstances few writers of very few songs thrived in the music business. Those who did, thrived mightily.

Almost to a man (and an occasional woman) they were refined, disciplined ultra-establishment writers, both lyricists and melody writers. Only the wildest rebel would have dreamed of writing a song that wasn't precisely thirty two bars long, and followed a specific ABAB, or AABA or some other precise format. They didn't call it junemoon time for nothing.

Of course, here and there, on farm or in prison camp somebody, usually black, was writing songs about real people and real problems and hardly ever coming up with thirty two well-notched measures or tinkling inner rhymes. But nothing much happened to those songs, and nobody paid much attention or money to or for them.

The performers of the songs, for the most part, bands and/or singers fitted neatly into the same precise and plastic pattern.

Sammy Kaye and Guy Lombardo and Blue Barron and others dispensed uncomplicated, syncopated syrup. Benny Goodman, Tommy Dorsey, his brother Jimmy, Artie Shaw and a handful of others swung in their fashion and tried to introduce elements of jazz, but if they got too far away from the pop formula they risked box-office decline and decreasing record sales.

The singers were equally polished and pop. Sinatra and Dick Haymes and Como, and the girls Helen Forrest, Dinah Shore, Helen O'Connell, et al invariably sang on key, with beautiful and precise intonation, deadly clever phrasing and flawless articulation. Of course they sang with feeling, but formula feeling. It was the style of the day.

How Louis Armstrong's gravel-sound penetrated is a mystery, and the great blues, jazz and folk singers toiled in relative obscurity for the most part.

Upper teenagers and young adults did the Lindy to the big bands. Lower and sub-teeners listened to children's records unless a freak pop like *Mairzy Dotes* broke through.

Then a small group of men, the ASCAP Board of Directors, changed the entire course of popular music in America, maybe most of the world — or at least played a key part in changing it. They set the economic stage for the vast change to come. (And as you pursue your career in the music business, if financial success is a major goal, always keep an eye on those economic stage sets.)

*Success covers a*
*multitude of blunders.*
George Bernard Shaw

31.

## 10. FROM JEANNIE TO ROCK

In mid-1939 the National Association of Broadcasters
went into negotiations with ASCAP for the renewal of their
Performance Rights contract, which was to expire at the end of
1940. I don't remember the numbers, but the broadcasters, of
course, were already by far ASCAP's biggest customer, paying
its publisher and writer members tens of millions of dollars
for the right to perform their songs.

ASCAP requested an increase in the broadcaster license
fee which jolted the radio men. They refused to pay it. Negotiations continued and got nowhere. Expiration date (December
31, 1940) came and there was no deal, and the broadcasters
could not legally play any ASCAP song on their airwaves.

But the radio people had anticipated this stalemate
in the fall of 1939 and formed their own music performing
rights organization called Broadcast Music, Inc.

The only problem was they had no music to license.
This was the period in which the deceased and great songwriter
Stephen Foster (long since in the public domain) got his greatest exposure. As I mentioned earlier, *Jeannie with the Light
Brown Hair* was played endlessly, while BMI frantically scrambled to entice everybody who could write or find a song to create
playable material.

A gentleman named Herman Starr, since deceased, was
then head of the vast Warner Brothers music publishing empire,

and probably the most important member of the ASCAP board.
Late in January of 1941 Herman said to me:
"They'll come crawling to us on their knees, begging to
pay what we ask, in six months."
Wrong!
What they did wasn't crawl, but run like crazy, all around
the country, trying to find songs, songwriters, publishers and
others who could develop music material. ASCAP had virtually
every so-called pop songwriter (including, of course, motion picture and Broadway show writers) tied up, so the BMI pioneers
went into the areas ASCAP had not only neglected, but scorned.
Paradoxically enough, two European gentlemen named Jean
and Julian Aberbach, who speak with Teutonic accents to this
day, spearheaded a move into the country music areas. If I recall correctly their arrangement was that they would get $200
for every song on which they secured a record. They secured a
hundred or more songs which they had recorded in Nashville
and vicinity. Today they operate a multi-million dollar music
publishing empire.

There were men like Herman Lubinsky, who had been
making what were then called "race" records (later called
rhythm and blues) for years. Herman got a BMI publishing deal,
and delivered scores, nay hundreds of r & b copyrights.

Naturally a hassle between a powerful group of "in"
publishers and songwriters and an equally powerful group of
broadcasters could not change the course of American music all
by itself. There would, obviously, have to be significant sociological developments, occurring simultaneously.

The good Lord's timing, in this respect, was uncanny.
You would almost believe that He was determined to spread the
earthier musical forms such as country and western, and "race",
at any cost.

In the fall of 1939, as I've said, the broadcasters formed
BMI. On September 1 of that year Hitler invaded Poland and
two days later Britain and France declared War on Germany,
and we were off on a holocaustic six year journey that would
take deep south blacks who grew up on "race" music, into war
plants in eastern, northern, midwestern and western cities here

and all around the world. Their white country cousins, who flew in their formative years with *The Great Speckled Bird,* spread their own simplistic song gospel far and wide and developed new afficionados by the millions.

The merging of the many musical forms into the popular mainstream didn't happen all at once, of course. It happened rather gradually and many music men were oblivious to its happening and consequently fell by the wayside. Again, from a career standpoint, it's essential, particularly as a writer, that you keep up with trends and developments. Some of the milestones along the way were:

The aforementioned *Oklahoma* in 1943, with which Richard Rodgers and Oscar Hammerstein rather bar-mitzvahed the musical theatre in America.

In 1954 Bill Haley, a young country band leader, who had gotten into rhythm and blues, wrote and recorded a song called *Rock Around the Clock.* It was a bomb, and lay unheard for almost a year. Then somebody sold it to the producers of a movie called *The Blackboard Jungle,* in which it was used in the main and end titles as well as throughout the film. In this context the record and the song became a kind of rallying cry for the rebellious young, and set up strong adult screams of protest.

In those quaint times, many adults insisted that the word "rock" meant the act of sexual intercourse, and objected to it with the same strenuous fervor as an earlier generation objected to the word "jazz", for the same reason. Today, of course, the more explicit four letter word for the act is used rather openly. (I state this as an observational aside, neither lauding nor denouncing it.)

*No man but a blockhead ever
wrote except for money.*
Samuel Johnson

## 11. ELVIS & THE COLONEL

About that same time, Sam Phillips, an astute and talented record producer, studio owner and manufacturer in Memphis, Tennessee recorded two songs called *Mystery Train* and *I Forgot to Remember to Forget* with a young truck driver, Elvis Presley. The record didn't do too much, but it did sell well locally, and found a place in the top 10 on the regional best selling charts.

*(To show you how fleeting fame may be for a songwriter, neither of those two tunes are included in David Ewen's voluminous work, American Popular Songs, covering 4,000 American popular songs, and I don't remember who wrote them myself.)*

About that time a man named Oscar Davis was working for Tom Parker. Today's Colonel was then managing Eddy Arnold, and also promoted country concerts, notably *The Eddy Arnold Show,* through another company he owned called Jamboree Attractions. Davis was in Memphis to promote an Arnold concert, and heard about Presley. He was at radio station WMPS, cutting some promotion spots for his concert, and he asked the station's top disk jockey, Bob Neal about Presley. Neal later became Presley's manager, and Oscar Davis originally called Tom Parker's attention to Presley. In due time Parker bought Presley's contract from Neal.

Presley, of course, was a fierce fan and student of Bo
Diddley and other race artists, and loved country music, and his
work blended the two into what was then, and is still frequently
called rockabilly. And another musical style was on the way to
blossoming. (It could have died aborning, however, were not Tom
Parker the astute talent manager he is. But more about that
in the section on Managers as a music career).

About this time, in England, two young men in their
mid-teens had a group called the Quarrymen, and were just getting into songwriting. They were John Lennon and Paul McCartney.

36.

*A bare assertion is not necessarily
the naked truth.*
George Prentice

## 12. KNOCKIN' THE ROCK

And in November, 1953, about a year before Haley and
Presley broke through, 33 members of ASCAP, including some
fine songwriters like Alan Jay Lerner, Ira Gershwin, and Arthur
Schwartz, filed an anti-trust suit against BMI, seeking an award
of $150,000,000. Approximately 18 years later (in the spring
of 1971) a Federal Judge signed an order dismissing the suit
with prejudice and declaring that none of the defendants need
pay any cost. By that time seven of the original thirty three
plaintiffs had died, and presumably only a small handful of attornies had profited from the long conflict. (One example of
how profitable a career as an attorney in the music business may
be. About which, too, more later)

I have indicated the desirability of trying to keep up
with musical trends.

I should add here that this is frequently easier said than
done. In the long course of the ASCAP-BMI hassle many expressed their opinions of the emerging country and western,
rhythm and blues, rock and other musical styles which were
evolving.

You probably would have known better than to listen
to a Congressman on songwriting. About the mid-fifties New
York Congressman Emanuel Cellar was chairman of an anti-trust
subcommittee of the House Judiciary Committee. He said at the

time that, in his opinion, rock and roll pandered to bad taste.

"That bad taste," he said, "is exemplified by the Elvis Presley *Hound Dog* music, with his animal gyrations, which are certainly most distasteful to me, are violative of all I know to be in good taste."

He further remarked that if BMI were permitted to continue he felt we would never hear "serious" or "good" music like songs by Kurt Weill, Deems Taylor, Aaron Copland and Carlo Menotti.

You might have said, "Different strokes for different folks, Mannie."

What does a Congressman know about music. But you could not have been blamed for paying heed to the words of somebody like the top singer of the day, Frank Sinatra. About that time Sinatra said about what he called "rock and roll": It is sung, played and written, for the most part, by cretinous goons and by means of its almost imbecilic reiterations and dirty lyrics it becomes the martial music of every side-burned delinquent on the face of the earth . . ."

But even the denunciation of an expert like Sinatra could not stem the tidal wave of rock.

*A rolling stone gathers no moss
but it gains a certain polish.*
Oliver Herford

## 13. DULA & DYLAN

Other musical elements evolved and flowed into the mainstream to become a part of the popular whole. In 1958 a young man named Dave Guard found an old mountain folk tune named *Tom Dula*, the lyrics of which told about a 19th century North Carolina murder. He arranged it into *Tom Dooley* and the group of which he was a member (with Bob Shane and Nick Reynolds), the Kingston Trio recorded it on Capitol. Smash! And folk music entered the scene as a dominant force.

An idea of how great a force may be derived from this fact: In one year in the early 60's when I was vice president of Capitol Records, the Kingston Trio record sales accounted for fully 14% of the total popular sales of the entire company. Again the ultimate super-success and development of the Trio was due in substantial part to their manager, Frank Werber. Years later, after the Trio retired from the music business, Frank was busted on a rather serious drug charge.

But the Kingston Trio was the musical ancestor of another young man, who played a major part in the direction of American music and songwriting. My son, Joe, who was about seventeen or eighteen at the time (somewhere around 1960) had taken to hanging out in Greenwich Village in New York. He played some guitar and was quite heavily into the folk scene. One day he told me about a new young singer, who had just arrived in town and was working at some of the Village spots for cokes and cakes.

The young man's name was Bob Dylan. Joe predicted he would be a giant, and about a year later, one of the music critics of the New York Times, Bob Shelton, said the same thing.

John Hammond, Sr. vice president in charge of Talent Acquisition at Columbia Records (whose son, John, Jr., by the way, is quite a talented musician-singer himself) signed Dylan, and shortly thereafter came his first album, and *Blowin' in the Wind.* About that time Dylan appeared as a guest on one of the panels I was conducting for the National Academy of Recording Arts and Sciences.

He was shy and somewhat vague, but if you followed him closely you knew he was a free spirit. In 1964 he wrote *The Times They Are a-Changin'*, and then switched in 1965 to electric instrumental backing and folk-rock.

In the later sixties he went country with a vengeance, as you have heard in his albums *John Wesley Harding* and *Nashville Skyline.* Dylan writes and sings purely to the beat of his own drummer, and if you have the talent and stay with it, you have as good a chance of making it that way as any other.

When Dylan moved over to the rock side, he was severely criticized in many quarters, but that was the way he felt he had to go at that time.

*Would you have your songs endure?*
*Build on the human heart.*
Robert Browning

## 14. LOVE & HONKY TONK WOMEN

While all this was going on Paul Mc Cartney and John Lennon in 1957 (15 and 17 respectively) wrote a tune called *Love Me Do*. Nothing much happened with the song until five years later, when it was released as one of their sides in England. In the meantime the boys and their partners changed the name of their group from the Quarrymen to, ultimately, the Silver Beatles, scrambled around England and the Continent, working where they could.

It wasn't till 1961 that a salesman in a record shop in London, Brian Epstein, got curious about the group, and searched them out in a club called The Cavern. Epstein took over as their manager.

By the end of that year they were beginning to be recognized as a top group, at least in Liverpool. In 1962 Epstein got them a record deal. By 1963 their records (now as The Beatles) were beginning to catch on in England, but it wasn't until the beginning of 1964 that *I Want to Hold Your Hand,* written, of course, by Lennon and McCartney, hit number 1 in the United States and the Beatles were on their way to changing not only the face of popular music around the world, but the hair styles and mode of dress of a substantial part of the population of the developed countries of this planet.

An ironic sidelight about the emergence of The Beatles,

and one that demonstrates a truism about your career in the music business (and any other business for that matter) is this:

A giant conglomerate in England, Electrical & Musical Industries, Ltd. (EMI) had bought Capitol Records some years before the Beatles arrived on the scene. EMI also owns record companies in many other countries around the world, and it was their policy to permit each of the companies they owned to operate virtually autonomously. But when The Beatles got hot in England in 1963 they urged Capitol to release some of their singles in the United States. The Capitol people in charge of selecting foreign associates' records for release in America saw no value or potential in The Beatles' sides.

Thus, if you check the tradepaper files of the day, you'll find a number of Beatles records released in the United States on labels other than Capitol before their first release on that label. (The *EMI - Capitol arrangement was such that Capitol had first refusal on EMI product, but if Capitol turned down a record, EMI could strive to have it released on any other label with which they could make a deal).*

Finally EMI became exasperated with Capitol's stubbornness and simply issued a direct order that Capitol release The Beatles in America!

Who knows what would have happened with the Beatles if EMI had not issued that ultimatum. You'll find such accidents of fate playing a part in your career in music, whether as a writer, performer or whatever. As I've said, it's a pattern of life not exclusive to the music business. What you've got to do is roll with the punches. Don't get shook up unduly over the bad breaks. Don't get unduly cocky and mindless over the good ones.

It's interesting from a songwriting standpoint to note that The Beatles earlier song successes, like the writers of the thirties and forties dealt largely with l-o-v-e. Lyrically they were not drastic or revolutionary, until sometime later (1967) when they recorded songs like *Lucy in the Sky with Diamonds* (which some claimed was a reference to LSD) that they got into less orthodox themes. But their melodies were often fascinating departures from the formula.

The Rolling Stones, on the other hand, didn't do love songs. Where the Beatles were clean, neat and adorable, the Stones (particularly their leader, Mick Jagger) were dirty, low-down and rough, rough, rough. They went back to the earthiest of the blues and got earthier. *Honky Tonk Women* ("I met a gin soaked, barroom queen in Memphis. She tried to take me upstairs for a ride"); *I Can't Get No Satisfaction* (I can't get no girl with action) didn't deal with handholding or other of the gentler forms of romance.

*What experience and history teach is this:*
*That people never have learned*
*anything from history, or acted upon*
*principles deduced from it.*
                    Georg Wilhelm Hegel


# 15. A WAR OR TWO ALONG THE WAY


About 1960 a young and vastly talented black man in Detroit, Berry Gordy started a label called Motown. Working initially with a brilliant young songwriter-producer named Bill (Smokey) Robinson, Gordy built one of the great record labels of the day, utilizing the Detroit sound, which was largely r & b, gospel based.

In short the spreading and the merging of the musical styles, pop, country, race, jazz, blues, rock went on through the decades. Music was a pond in a steady rainstorm. Each heavy raindrop fell into the pond and a growing ring of circles rippled out to join other growing rings of circles caused by other heavy raindrops.

And the changes in music were, all the while, abetted by sociological circumstance. World War II ended in 1945, of course. But Cold War I got underway pretty quick and hundreds of thousands of the boys continued to sing and play their songs in far off lands.

And in June of 1950 North Korean troops crossed the 38th Parallel in that land and on June 27, the United States rushed to the aid of the South. And more American boys from every corner of the country got together, lonesome and home-sick, and to get their minds off their misery, played their music for each other.

Korea didn't run too long. An armistice of sorts was signed at Panmunjon in July, 1953, but then, less than a year later, March 24, 1954 President Dwight Eisenhower said, for all the world to hear, that the defeat of Communist aggression in Indo-China was of vital importance to the United States.

And on June 16, 1961 the United States agreed to increase the 685 man U.S. military advisory group in South Vietnam, and to assign training specialists to the South Vietnamese army and to send American officers into the field to "observe troops in action."

*Where Have All the Flowers Gone* sang the Kingston Trio during their heyday. Pete Seeger's song said, "Where have all the young men gone? Long time ago . . . They're all in uniform . . . Oh, when will they ever learn."

Many, indeed were. And more to come.

On other musical fronts we traveled from *Oklahoma!* to *Jesus Christ, Superstar,* to *Hair!* and *Tommy!* and *The Godspell* and *Oh! Calcutta!* But Lawrence Welk is the biggest band in television.

And now ASCAP has an office in Nashville and courts the country writers and not too long ago about ninety seven rhythm and blues writers, all out of the largely black Jobete Music stable joined ASCAP, and today BMI, which started out with a catalog of country and race tunes (though still big in those areas) has the best Course on writing for the Musical Theatre (which in the forties was ASCAP's private preserve.) More on this later.

We have come from two or three thousand little girls dancing in the aisles, (some paid by a sharp press agent named George Evans) screeching and fainting as Frank Sinatra lays his gliss on them at the Paramount Theatre to maybe half a million boys and girls dancing (and doing other things) in the meadows at Woodstock, New York to the pied piping of a long string of uninhibited rock acts. And another multi-hundred thousand festival at Altamont, California featuring The Rolling Stones and a murder.

And with today's musical emphasis on electronics, on

Moog synthesizers and other uncanny mechanical devices who knows where we're going.

What had happened, so far, was this: - - -

Because a handful of radio men thought they were being ripped off by a handful of music publishers and songwriters, and because Adolf Hitler decided to take a shot at all the marbles, and things kept getting messed up around the world, we have the most diversified, fascinating conglomeration of popular music the earth has ever known.

Grace Slick and Richard Rodgers and Stephen Sondheim and Isaac Hayes and Boudelaux and Felicia Bryant write it. And so do Kris Kristofferson and Smokey Robinson and Carole King. And the Bobs Russell and Merrill and the Pauls Simon and Anka and McCartney and Lennon and Yoko Ono and Bobbie Gentry and Cindy Walker and Frank Loesser and Marvin Moore and Burt Bacharach and Hal David and Harnick and Bock and Mel Tillis and Howard Dietz and Harlan Howard and Jimmy Webb and Webb Pierce and you and I.

So let's take a look at how some of them do it, and how you may do it most effectively.

*It took me fifteen years to discover
I had no talent for writing, but I couldn't
give it up because by that time
I was too famous.*
Robert Benchley

## 16.  SAGA OF ONE SONG

My own career as a songwriter was a seldom and sometime thing. I go into it here because it gives me the opportunity
to pass on some thoroughly practical tips every songwriter should
know, and will indeed, sooner or later, discover.

The first song I ever wrote (or at least a song for which
I wrote the original lyric) was a very big hit. It is *Here in My
Heart,* and (as of this writing) I got my last royalty check from
the publisher for the period ending December 31, 1971. The
check was for $56.43, but since I have been collecting royalties
on the song since 1952, when I wrote it, that amount is not too
puny. When you consider my share of the royalty on the song
is only 10%, it becomes even more interesting.

Here is the story of *Here In My Heart:*

I was Editor of *The Billboard* in 1952 and among my industry friends was a music publisher named Bobby Mellin. Bobby
and I would have dinner every couple of weeks. One evening,
Bobby told me he had acquired the publishing rights to a lovely
foreign melody and asked me whether I would like to try to
write a lyric for it. I'd never tried one, and the idea intrigued me.
Bobby gave me a demo record of the melody, played on piano,
and I sat up most of that night, playing it over and over, until I
had written a lyric entitled *Here In My Heart.* I was pleased with

it, and turned it in to Bobby the next day.

A couple of days later Bobby called me and asked if I would mind if he gave the lyric to Pat Genaro for a little rewrite. I didn't mind at all. Pat was a mutual friend, and more or less, a working songwriter. He dabbled in real estate on the side or vice versa. He had written the lyric to *You're Breaking My Heart (Because You're Leaving)* to an Italian melody for Bobby, and Bobby had secured a Vic Damone record and the tune turned out a smash, and was incidentally a major factor in establishing Damone as a singer.

The second line of *Here in My Heart,* as it eventually was recorded was (and is), "I'm alone and so lonely." It was only one of the lines in the rewrite to which I objected. I considered it then, and do now, a bad, redundant line. There were other lines to which I objected, but not strenuously, since I had no ambitions to become a songwriter. I merely asked Bobby to leave my name off the song.

Some time passed and I was busy with other pursuits, and then a record of *Here In My Heart* was released. It was by Al Martino on a label called BBS. It was, for some time, the number one record in the country, and it made Al Martino a star for a while. I knew Al slightly, but I knew his manager, Bill Borreli even better. Bill and Al were both from Philadelphia, and Bill would occasionally come by *The Billboard* office to tout his singer.

In time I got my contract on the song, and I discovered that there were three other writers on the song: Pat Genaro, Bill Borreli and a man named Lou Levinson. I don't remember why either Bill or Lou were on the song. At the time I wasn't concerned, and I'm not that concerned now. Maybe they both did rewrites after Pat did his rewrite.

But from the standpoint of building a career as a songwriter, there are several interesting and useful tips here:

1. *Get into the business.* Be around publishers, managers, singers, anybody in the business, any time, as much of the time as you can. If I weren't seeing Mellin regularly, possibly if I didn't know Borreli, I certainly would not have had the opportunity to write the first lyric.

2. *Don't worry about - - - at least in the early stages of your career as a writer - - - how many co-writers you acquire.* As I say, I don't know why Bill Borreli was one of the writers of the song. Maybe he did a rewrite on Pat Genaro's rewrite; or on the melody; or maybe the fact that he was Al's manager and had a voice in which songs Al would record, had something to do with it. Whatever it was, it was certainly all right with me. And if I had intended to pursue a career as a songwriter, I surely had been given a good send-off.

2. *Don't be a prima donna.* If a smart publisher wants to change your lyric or melody, let him do so. Even if you don't think the change is an improvement on your work. The commercial songwriting business is not the place to lay down your life for a line of your deathless prose or a measure of melody. Later, when you're a big success, and rich and powerful, you can stand pat on your every word or note.

Two interesting sidelights on the Al Martino episode. Al became an "overnight" star, and a group of very rough men, not dissimilar from the characters in *The Godfather,* took over the managerment of the young singer. Al, of course, plays the pop singer in the current motion picture.

After *Here in My Heart* Al didn't have another hit for about ten years. One day I ran into him in the office of our mutual friend and accountant, the late Lew Lebish. I was managing Eddy Arnold, among other people at the time, and told Al I felt country and pop were merging at a rapid rate and suggested he try recording one of the country hits Eddy had recently done. He did, and it was his second big smash record. I wish I could remember the name of the tune, but I can't.

It's odd, because I do remember the big smash which evolved about 1962, when Ray Charles blended his soulful rhythm and blues vocal genius with Don Gibson's poignant country words and music in a song called *I Can't Stop Loving You.*

But we've started in this chapter, with some songwriting *do's* and *don'ts.* Let me wind it up with a couple of elementary, but essential *don'ts.*

If you write lyrics only, DON'T waste your time and money sending them to any of the people who advertise that they will write music to your lyrics, unless you want to do so to satisfy your own ego. The chances of such people writing anything melodically, which will give your song any chance for commercial success, is almost nil.

The same DON'T applies if you write melodies. DON'T send your melodies to some assembly line operation which writes lyrics. The simple fact is that if you can't write both lyrics and melody yourself you are at a disadvantage to begin with, in pursuing a songwriting career in the '70s. But if you write only lyrics or melody, your best bet is to search out a good co-writer in your own area, with whom you can work in person. It's hard enough to create a good, usable commercial song when you're working intimately and regularly with a co-writer. It's almost impossible to do it by mail, with a person or firm, who are interested only in getting a fee from you. I have never heard of a single case where any song written by an individual in collaboration with a so-called lyric or melody writing service ever amounted to anything.

A second elementary DON'T, (a practice which literally thousands of would-be songwriters follow is this:

Don't send lead sheets and/or demonstration records, unsolicited, to record artists, singers and/or musicians in general, personal managers, record companies, music publishers, television shows, or any other professional persons or organizations in showbusiness. I have received, in the mail, literally hundreds of such lead sheets and demo records, in the various functions in which I've served.

In certain situations, i.e., in most record companies and/or publishing companies, the policy is that all such material goes directly into the wastebasket, unopened. Any such material sent registered mail, return receipt requested, is refused.

In the several situations in which I did have occasion to open and look at and/or listen to such songs they were invariably impossibly amateurish and hopeless. It's possible that the writers of some of these songs have the talent to develop into successful songwriters, but what they needed urgently was guidance as to ways of learning their craft, be it lyric or melody writing.

50.

We will get into that. The point here is: DON'T waste your time and money sending your songs indiscriminately through the mails.

*In order to compose, all you need*
*to do is remember a tune that*
*nobody else has thought of.*
        Robert Schumann

**51.**

## 17. IT TAKES ALL KINDS

There are several highly pertinent facts to be considered in contemplating or attempting to develop a songwriting career today. The first we have already stressed: *That virtually any style of music is acceptable, and a writer may concentrate on any one or any combination of them.*

The second fact is equally evident: *Today more song-writers than ever before in the history of popular contemporary music are also performers. They either play or sing their own tunes.*

Carole King is one of today's top selling artists and her songs and records virtually swept the 1972 Grammy Awards. Carole has been writing for well over ten years, and in 1963 a performance of one of her songs, *It Might as Well Rain Until September,* sung by herself was released and hit the top ten on the best selling charts. But Carole didn't like performing, or didn't feel ready for it, and went back to the relative anonymity of writing till years later. James Taylor, however, persuaded her to go back to performing, and she has, obviously, with great success.

Nine of the 107 most performed songs in the BMI repertoire for the year 1971 were written by members of the Beatles: 4 by George Harrison; 2 by John Lennon and Paul

McCartney; 2 by McCartney with his wife Linda; 1 by Ringo Starr. And the majority of the other hundred and two were written by performer-writers.

There are several reasons for this, but one of them surely is the fact that technical vocal and musical perfection in a performance has become increasingly less important, and genuine feeling and emotion (which can often be expressed by the writer of the song far better than many more polished interpreters) increasingly more important.

This development is both good and bad for the modern songwriter. It's good for the writer who is a performer with a record contract, a television show or some other platform for exposure of his tunes. It's bad for the writer who is not a performer, and is incapable of being or doesn't care to be, because such a writer has fewer avenues of getting his songs heard than at any time before. Obviously with large numbers of singers, groups, et al doing their own tunes, unaffiliated writers have a difficult time getting a hearing. It's also difficult for the writer who *is* a performer, but still has no record deal or other means of substantial exposure. We will get into some of the ways to overcome this situation later in this book.

The natural first step a writer should take is to determine what kind of songs he wishes to write. The literary and musical knowledge and background necessary to write a rock tune about how your baby turns you on are not the same as those required to write a complete score for a Broadway musical. Background, literary and musical talent requirements vary, of course, with the style in which a writer wishes to work, and with the goals he sets for himself.

A study of the careers of any random selection of writers will quickly reveal what should be a most encouraging fact to any and all would-be writers: *Good and successful writers have emerged from almost every conceivable kind of background, and have had widely varied educational and career histories.*

William "Smokey" Robinson of the Miracles and Motown fame was born in the ghetto area of Detroit (the Black Bottom). No luxuries, but musical groups by the hundreds on every block.

Smokey started saxophone lessons when he was 8. By the time he met Berry Gordy, who started Motown, and gave Smokey invaluable tips on writing, Smokey already had over a hundred songs scribbled into his school composition book. He and Berry wrote *Getta Job,* and later he had his first million seller record *Shop Around.* No formal education, but basic playing-singing-writing.

Frank Loesser came from a highly cultured, prosperous New York city family of classical music lovers. He hated classical music. Played piano by ear, and broke in as a music publisher (Leo Feist, Inc.) staff writer. Went to Townsend Harris High School in New York, and dropped out of City College of New York after his first year. Later wrote all kinds of hit songs and musicals, including of course, *Guys and Dolls, Most Happy Fella,* etc.

Country star-songwriter Buck Owens (Alvis Edgar Owens, Jr. on his birth certificate), who today just about owns Bakersfield, California was born in Sherman, Texas. His father drove a truck. But Buck's mother taught him to play guitar, and he then proceded to teach himself mandolin. He played lead guitar for singers like Sonny James, Tommy Sands and others. Along the way he also learned to play steel guitar, saxophone, piano and drums. So far he's won 24 BMI songwriter awards, in addition to being one of Capitol Records major sellers.

Isaac Hayes, who wrote the score for *Shaft,* was born in country music territory, Covington, Tennessee. In his earliest days country songs were all he heard, except for the music he heard in church. His mom and dad were very active in the local church and thus Hayes picked up on gospel. Later he got into black blues and jazz. He started out as a singer, and the greatest influences on his singing style were Billy Eckstine and Nat Cole. Musically he concentrated on studying Charlie Parker and Miles Davis.

The late and great Hank Williams was from Montgomery, Alabama, had little formal education, was taught guitar by a local Negro singer in Montgomery. Jimmie Rodgers, often called the father of country music, also learned to play banjo and guitar from the blacks on the work gangs in the railroad yards

in Meridian, Mississippi. Bobby Russell, one of the business's
best country-pop writers *(God Didn't Make Little Green Apples,
Honey,* et al) had a rock band at Hillsboro High School in Nashville where he grew up.

With virtually no formal musical training Melvin Van
Peebles has written some of the most exciting musical theatre
(and films) we've ever seen. Ven Peebles wrote, directed, scored,
edited and starred in *Sweet Sweetback's Baadassss Song,* a movie
which will gross better than $10,000,000 before it's through.
Van Peebles also wrote *Ain't Supposed to Die a Natural Death,*
and *Don't Play Us Cheap,* both important Broadway productions.

Van Peebles, now still under forty, was born on the
South Side of Chicago. He made it to Ohio Wesleyan, but dropped out. For a time he was in the Air Force. He took one shot
at Hollywood years ago, but got nowhere, so he made his way
to Paris. He continued to educate himself, and eventually made
his way back to Hollywood and the success of *Sweet Sweetback.*
Van Peebles still can't read or actually write music.

Possibly at the opposite end of the pole of educational
opportunity and background is Richard Rodgers. Rodgers was
born of well-to-do parents in New York City in 1902. He went
to Townsend Harris Hall High, De Witt Clinton High School,
Columbia University and the Institute of Musical Art (Juilliard).
In 1953, Deems Taylor wrote a book *Some Enchanted Evenings,*
about Rodgers and his lyricists, Lorenz Hart and Oscar Hammerstein II.

Rodgers told Taylor, then, "What I am doing today is
what I have wanted to do all my life." At the age of ten, Rodgers
was writing tunes. It was difficult to get him away from the piano.
At 15, in 1917, he wrote his first complete score for a musical,
performed for a boys' athletic club in aid of a New York Sun's
Fund for American Soldiers in France. Rodgers conducted the
five piece orchestra, which played the show.

True, Rodgers had the educational opportunity to become a great songwriter, but he had more: He had the attitude,
and the desire and he worked, worked, worked. It is hard to believe that one man, in one lifetime could have achieved what
Richard Rodgers has achieved. There is a hard cover book called

*RICHARD RODGERS Fact Book,* published in 1965 which details his works to that date.

The book contains 582 pages, and lists the 39 musical comedy/drama stage scores he wrote (28 with Hart; 9 with Hammerstein, 1 with Stephen Sondheim and one by himself). It also details the play he wrote with Hart and Herb Fields; the 9 motion picture scores (8 with Hart, 1 with Hammerstein); 3 television scores (1 with Hammerstein, 2 major background music scores); 1 complete night club score (with Hart) and 1 ballet score. This does not include the countless individual songs he has written.

What Rodgers has obviously done is dedicate himself to the single function of writing the very best songs he could possibly write. He dedicated himself to learning everything he could about the craft through every means available to him. And then he moved into the business as directly as he could, and wrote and wrote and wrote. And, as this is written, in 1972, still writes.

It is interesting to note, from a lyricist's standpoint, that the three lyric writers with whom Rodgers has worked, also had extensive formal educations.

Lorenz Hart also went to De Witt Clinton High School; Weingart Institute; Columbia Grammar School; Columbia University and the Columbia School of Journalism.

Oscar Hammerstein II went to Hamilton Institute, Columbia University and Columbia Law School.

Stephen Sondheim (now writing both words and music for his own hits such as *Company)* went to the George School and Williams College.

It's entirely conceivable you don't care to adopt a Richard Rodgers attitude or work that hard. There are, of course, other work styles and they have been successful in their fashion. John Carpenter, well known rock writer-editor/producer/manager/disk jockey, did an interview with various members of the Jefferson Airplane for *Words & Music* magazine (a relatively new publication, combination fan-magazine/trade paper, which you should read regularly). This is how some of the writer-members of that highly successful group talked about their songwriting:

*Grace Slick:* "I can write just all the time, lyrics,

whatever. Music is more plodding for me than lyrics . . . I change them all around, rhythmically, to fit whatever. The meaning stays the same, but, if say, you end a phrase with a word that doesn't sing right you change it to something else . . . I don't write with Paul (Paul Kantner). We just steal from one another. We never sit down and say 'Hey, let's put this here.' . . . We just go through each other's material and put in this here and this here . . ."

*Joey Covington:*(Joey tells Carpenter this story about his drumming background . . . "I played with the Bucky Carter Trio. All the VFW halls in the world. $8.00 a night. Sometimes I'd back up strippers . . . They're really good for drummers. There was this place called the Sky Club, and I went in there and I had to back up this spade stripper with like a 35 minute drum solo to *Caravan.* There was a mirror and she would watch herself work, then work with the drums. She got so crazy she fell of the stage.")

And, Joey, in answer to Carpenter's question: "How do you write for the Airplanes?"

"Whatever comes out. Sometimes you'll just be walking down the streets and this really dirty tune will come up . . . Let me tell you about *Pretty As You Feel* (a hit Joey wrote for the group) . . . just to show you how far out fate is, and she's a mean chick. Just like a woman, always the unexpected. Everybody thinks its a cosmetic song. They all have their interpretation. Incredible. It's gotten some really nice reviews. One said that it was like the ultimate tribute to a woman. This girl wrote that it was a high compliment to pay a lady, and that makes you feel good . . . more than royalties and that stuff . . . I guess I've had that song all my life . . . You just have to stumble around 'til you find it. *Pretty As You Feel* came off a jam. One night, Jorma (Kaukonen), Carlos Santana, Jack (Casady) and I had nothing to do, so I sang."

*Papa John Creach:* When Carpenter said to the great blues/jazz fiddler, "You write music . . . ", the answer was, "Yeah, I scratch 'em out."

And indeed he does, from a bottomless background of blues and jazz listening, playing and experience.

And Paul Kantner told Carpenter how the songs get recorded:

"Jorma has some songs, Grace has some songs, Joey has some songs, and so do I. We just play them. There is more of a definition. We decided to divide the album evenly, like Jorma has a section now which he never had taken or gotten before because he didn't write that much before . . . "

Yes, indeed, there are all kinds of music styles and all kinds of approaches to writing songs, and the style you choose and the approach you take is entirely up to you. If you care to, and have the means to acquire a total formal education in writing words or music that's certainly a most sound approach.

If you don't care to or haven't the means to make it to Juilliard, there are countless other ways to prepare yourself: *Experience, help from professionals, studying* and *learning through books, correspondence courses, workshops, seminars,* and many of them are relatively inexpensive or free.

One thing is true: Unless you *do* study and work at it, in whatever fashion, you're not likely to get too far as a songwriter. So let's look at some of the ways you may learn and develop.

*In composing, as a general rule, run your
pen through every other word you have
written; you have no idea what vigor
it will give your style.*
Sidney Smith

## 18. HOME-MADE WRITER'S WORKSHOP

If you're a budding Richard Rodgers and have the desire
and wherewithal for a maximum formal education in playing
and/or singing and writing (remember, for a songwriter it's highly
desirable to be a performer, too) you really don't have a problem,
and don't need much help. In elementary school in some cases,
and certainly in high school many music teachers are oriented
to the contemporary music scene enough to steer you to the
proper and most effective areas of higher music education in
your own community. An increasing number of stage band directors and choral directors in the schools are most eager to help
young people find effective ways into the popular music industry.
(I should insert here, parenthetically, that . . . on the
other hand . . . there are too many situations around the country
in which the music programs in the schools are being drastically
curtailed or entirely eliminated, and it is most important that
everyone interested, in any area of music, fight such trends
wherever they exist. Chicago . . . as this is written . . . has just
dropped the Music, Arts and Physical Education programs in its
public schools for lack of funds).
An excellent source for finding the best Colleges for music training is the New York Times 1972 Guide to College

Selection by Ella Mazel.

If you don't care to, or can't afford higher music education and training there are still literally scores, if not hundreds of effective ways in which you may pursue a career as a songwriter. It is impossible to set forth any comprehensive, let alone all inclusive list of sources of such education and training.

I will discuss all sources, in general terms, and go into specific detail about those with which I am thoroughly familiar, and which I heartily endorse. But before proceeding, once more, a few words of caution:

Among the huge numbers of learning sources available to people who feel they can write songs, there are a substantial number of worthless ones. Some are worthless because they are created by people who know very little about songwriting or music and are intended only to extract a little money from the unwary and gullible. Others are worthless, even if well-intentioned, merely because the people who create them lack sufficient practical background and experience.

Before you adopt any course of study, whether a book or a complete Course in any form, investigate it thoroughly, check out the backgrounds and reputation of its creators and merchandisers. Discuss it with the most knowledgeable people you know. It's not a bad idea to make a final check with your local Better Business Bureau if you don't have enough friends to check out the more elaborate and expensive Courses yourself.

In short, be careful.

I will assume that you accept what I have said about the desirability for a songwriter to be a performer, and that you are learning to play and/or sing in whatever manner is most practical for you.

In this section of the book we will concentrate on methods of learning to become as proficient a songwriter as possible.

In my opinion the most effective method of all is also the simplest method of all. Once you have determined what kind of songs you want to write, *immerse yourself in that kind of song.* Get hold of every successful record of that song style you can. Listen to radio disk jockey shows, which feature your chosen music style. If you can afford it, get a tape recorder and put as many of such songs as possible on tape so that you may play them over and over. Follow the careers of the top singers, musicians or groups doing your kind of song. Catch them on television, go to their live concerts.

*BUT don't just listen and observe.* Listen and observe *analytically.* As you're listening and watching ask yourself questions like these:

1. How much of the success of this given song is due to the performance itself as separated from the song? How much is due to the performer's voice, style, stage presence, magnetism or whatever?

2. How much of the success of the song is attributable to the song itself, as separated from the performance?

3. How much to the lyric of the song, its idea in words?

4. How much to the melody of the song?

5. How much to the arrangement?

6. The rhythmic patterns?

7. Are the songs you're writing anywhere nearly as good as the ones you're hearing and analyzing?

It's difficult, but you *must* be objective in answering that last question. You *must* develop an attitude wherein you analyze your own songs as objectively and as critically as any other song by any other writer.

Fortunately, for any songwriter trying to improve his skills, there is available a goldmine of working material for the purposes of making these analytical studies of successful songs, *beyond* listening to them and observing performances of them. And this working material is available at relatively low cost.

I'm talking about the many books or folios of songs published these days. The best, and one I believe every songwriter should have and study, is *The New York Times Great Songs of the Sixties,* edited by Milton Okun with an introduction by Tom Wicker. Published by Quadrangle Books, Inc.,

Chicago, $5.95. It has 82 songs arranged for voice, piano and guitar. It embraces virtually every song style, whether straight pop as exemplified by Broadway show tunes or movie songs; rock, folk, jazz, et al. It has a brilliant analytical introduction by Milt and a penetrating overview of the sociological developments of the period by Wicker.

You'll find words and music to such outstanding tunes as *Alfie, What the World Needs Now Is Love* and *Raindrops Keep Fallin' on My Head* by Burt Bacharach and Hal David; *Blowin' in the Wind* and *The Times They Are A-Changin'* by Bob Dylan; *Yesterday, I Want to Hold Your Hand, Eleanor Rigby* and *Hey, Jude* by John Lennon and Paul McCartney; *Honky Tonk Women* and *I Can't Get No Satisfaction* by Mick Jagger and Keith Richard of the Rolling Stones.

This particular folio, as I've said, will give you a beautifully comprehensive overview of the songs which have been important coming into the seventies. If you'll supplement an intensive study of that book and other general collections of its kind, with similar studies of folios or songbooks by the leading artists (singers or groups) of the style in which you're most interested, you cannot fail to make great strides as a writer (within the bounds, of course, of your own talents and capabilities.) What you will be doing is carrying on your own continuing hit song Workshop.

In the category of folios of songs featured and recorded by specific singers or groups you will find performers of virtually every style represented. Here are just a few typical examples:

*Carole King Tapestry,* which features the twelve songs from Carole's album of the same title: *I Feel the Earth Move; So Far Away; It's Too Late; Home Again; Beautiful; Way Over Yonder; You've Got a Friend; Where You Lead; Will You Love Me Tomorrow?; Smackwater Jack; Tapestry;* and *You Make Me Feel Like a Natural Woman.*

This is published by Screen Gens-Columbia Publications, P.O. Box 488, Miami, Florida 33138 and sells for $3.95.

*McCartney,* a matching song book for the twelve tunes

from that album by the ex-Beatle, including *The Lovely Linda;
That Would Be Something; Valentine Day; Every Night; Hot
As Sun; Junk; Man We Was Lonely; OO You; Momma Miss
America; Teddy Boy; Singalong Junk; Maybe I'm Amazed;
Kreen-Akrore.* It's got photos of McCartney, taken by his wife,
is produced by McCartney Productions, c/o McCartney's
father and brother in law, Eastman and Eastman, 39 West 54
Street, New York, N.Y. 10019 and sells for $3.95.

    *The Rolling Stones Hot Rocks, 1964-1971* is a book of
their tunes, with words and music to *Brown Sugar; Wild Horses;
Gimme Shelter; Honky Tonk Women; I Can't Get No Satisfac-
tion; Paint It Black; Jumpin' Jack Flash; Street Fighting Man;
Midnight Rambler; You Can't Always Get What You Want;
Let's Spend the Night Together; Mother's Little Helper; 19th
Nervous Breakdown; Ruby Tuesday; Get Off My Cloud;Play
With Fire; Time Is On My Side; Heart of Stone; Under My
Thumb; Sympathy for the Devil* and *As Tears Go By.*

    The Stones book is published by ABKCO Music, Inc.,
which they own with Allan Klein, their manager. 1700 Broadway, New York, N.Y. 10019, and it too, sells for $3.95.

    In the general folio area, among innumerable others,
there are: *Hansen's Top 40 Song Album,* which includes the
following:

| | |
|---|---|
| AMAZING GRACE | HERE COMES THE SUN |
| THE CANDY MAN | I AM . . . I SAID |
| CHANTILLY LACE | I GOTCHA |
| (THEY LONG TO BE) CLOSE TO YOU | LEGEND IN YOUR OWN TIME |
| COLOUR MY WORLD | LOVE SONG |
| DOUBLE LOVIN' | (WHERE DO I BEGIN) LOVE STORY |
| THE DRUM | ME AND BOBBY MC GEE |
| FOLLOW ME | (THE) MASTERPIECE |
| FOR ALL WE KNOW | MY HANG UP IS YOU |
| FOR THE GOOD TIMES | MY SWEET LORD |
| HAVE YOU EVER SEEN THE RAIN? | ONE LESS BELL TO ANSWER |
| | PROUD MARY |
| HE AIN'T HEAVY . . . HE'S MY BROTHER | PUT YOUR HAND IN THE HAND |

(I NEVER PROMISED YOU A) ROSE GARDEN
SNOWBIRD
SOMEDAY NEVER COMES
SOMETHING
SONG SUNG BLUE
SPEAK SOFTLY LOVE (LOVE THEME FROM "THE GODFATHER")
STAND BY YOUR MAN
SWEET CAROLINE
THAT'S THE WAY I'VE ALWAYS HEARD IT SHOULD BE
THEME FROM LOVE STORY
TILL LOVE TOUCHES YOUR LIFE
WITHOUT YOU
YOU SAID A BAD WORD
(THE) YOUNG NEW MEXICAN PUPPETEER
YOU'RE MY MAN

And another Hansen book, *Easy Listening - 50 Swinging Sounds,* in which you'll find:

AND THE GRASS WON'T PAY NO MIND
CAN'T STOP LOVING YOU
CHELSEA MORNING
(THEY LONG TO BE) CLOSE TO YOU
COME SATURDAY MORNING
CRACKLIN' ROSIE
DO IT
DOES ANYBODY REALLY KNOW WHAT TIME IT IS?
FOR THE GOOD TIMES
FORGET TO REMEMBER
GAMES
(THE) GREEN GRASS STARTS TO GROW
GYPSY WOMAN
HE AIN'T HEAVY . . . HE'S MY BROTHER
HEY, GIRL
I AM . . . I SAID
I DON'T KNOW WHY
I THINK I LOVE YOU
IF
I'LL GET BY
ISN'T IT A PITY
IT DON'T MATTER TO ME
JULIE, DO YA LOVE ME
LONG AS I CAN SEE THE LIGHT
LOOKIN' OUT MY BACK DOOR
LOVE YOU FUNNY THING
LOWDOWN
MAKE IT EASY ON YOURSELF
MAKE ME SMILE
ME AND YOU AND A DOG NAMED BOO
MY SWEET LORD
NO MATTER WHAT
ONE LESS BELL TO ANSWER
ONE MAN BAND
PASTURES GREEN
RAIN IN MY HEART
(I NEVER PROMISED YOU A) ROSE GARDEN
SEE ME, FEEL ME
SILVER MOON

| | |
|---|---|
| SNOWBIRD | THEME FROM "LOVE STORY" |
| SO CLOSE | 25 OR 6 TO 4 |
| SOMETHING | UP ON THE ROOF |
| STAND BY YOUR MAN | WHERE DID ALL THE GOOD |
| THAT'S WHERE I | TIMES GO? |
| WENT WRONG | WOODSTOCK |
| YOU'VE GOT A FRIEND | |

The Hansen books are $2.95 each, and if you can't find them in your music store, the address is: Charles Hansen Music and Books, 1860 Broadway, New York, N.Y. 10023.

Warner Bros. Music, 488 Madison Avenue, New York, N.Y. 10022 has one called *The Big 75 Song Book*, which sells for $3.95. It includes:

| | |
|---|---|
| ACROSS THE UNIVERSE | FOR WHAT IT'S WORTH |
| AIN'T SHE SWEET | FREIGHT TRAIN |
| AIN'T WE GOT FUN | GAMES PEOPLE PLAY |
| ALABAMA JUBILEE | GET BACK |
| AL DI LA | GIVE PEACE A CHANCE |
| ALL YOU NEED IS LOVE | GREEN GREEN GRASS OF |
| AND I LOVE HER | HOME |
| ARE YOU FROM DIXIE? | HEY JUDE |
| AUTUMN IN NEW YORK | HIGH AND THE MIGHTY, THE |
| BAND OF GOLD | I DIG ROCK AND ROLL MUSIC |
| BEAT GOES ON, THE | IN-A-GADDA-DA-VIDA |
| BLOWIN' IN THE WIND | I ONLY HAVE EYES FOR YOU |
| BYE BYE BLACKBIRD | INTO THE MYSTIC |
| CINNAMON GIRL | I SHALL BE RELEASED |
| COME TOGETHER | IT ONLY HURTS FOR A |
| DAY IS DONE | LITTLE WHILE |
| DAY TRIPPER | IT'S ALL IN THE GAME |
| DAYS OF WINE & ROSES | LADY WILLPOWER |
| DEEP IN MY HEART, DEAR | LEAVING ON A JET PLANE |
| DOWN BY THE RIVER | LES BICYCLETTES DE BELSIZE |
| EARLY MORNIN' RAIN | LET IT BE |
| ELEANOR RIGBY | LET THE REST OF THE WORLD |
| EVERYTHING IS | GO BY |
| BEAUTIFUL | LONG AND WINDING ROAD, THE |

LOVELAND
LOVE MINUS ZERO
NO LIMIT
LOVE OF THE COMMON
PEOPLE
MA BELLE AMIE
MACK THE KNIFE
MICHELLE
MISS OTIS REGRETS
MR. BOJANGLES
MY ELUSIVE DREAMS
MY OWN TRUE LOVE
(BASED ON TARA
THEME FROM "GONE
WITH THE WIND")
NEVER MY LOVE
NIGHT AND DAY
OB-LA-DI, OB-LA-DA
OHIO

PUFF (THE MAGIC DRAGON)
RIDE CAPTAIN RIDE
SECRET LOVE
SPIRIT IN THE DARK
SUMMER ME, WINTER ME
(PICASSO SUMMER)
SUMMER PLACE, A (THEME
FROM)
SUSPICIOUS MINDS
THOU SWELL
TURN AROUND, LOOK AT ME
WALK A MILE IN MY SHOES
WHAT NOW MY LOVE
WITH A LITTLE HELP FROM
MY FRIENDS
YAMA-YAMA MAN, THE
YELLOW SUBMARINE
YESTERDAY
YOU ARE TOO BEAUTIFUL
YOUNG GIRL

And if you want to keep up with the lyrics *only* on current hits and near hits, you'll find magazines like *Hit Parader* and *Song Hits Magazine* on your newsstand.

But to repeat, *listen* to the records of these songs, over and over and over. Catch them being performed as frequently as possible, in every possible medium, television, live, wherever, whenever possible.

Separate performance contribution from song (lyric, melody, rhythm, arrangement) contribution in analyzing the record's success.

But there's an obvious and essential corollary to all this: - - - *If you don't know what you're listening for - - - if you don't understand how to construct a good lyric, if you don't know why a melody is a good melody, how it is constructed, what chord progressions, what harmonies, what rhythmic patterns are being used and why, all the studying in the world isn't going to help you too much.*

**66.**

So let's examine some of the ways, other than via formal music education, you may be able to learn the fundamentals of lyric writing, melody writing, songwriting.

*Knowledge is of two kinds. We know*
*a subject ourselves, or we know where*
*we can find information upon it.*
Samuel Johnson

67.

## 19. SOME BOOKS & COURSES

In 1966 I was President of the New York Chapter of the National Academy of Recording Arts and Sciences and I tried very hard to put together, in conjunction with the New York University School of Continuing Education and Extension Services a Course in popular songwriting, and another in the production of popular records. For one reason and another we weren't quite able to get the Courses going that year, but since that time the NARAS Chapters around the country have managed to launch some effective programs along these lines.

For example, in the fall of 1971 the Los Angeles Chapter conducted a week long Course on music and records. It was attended by 42 high school students and eight teachers. A & M Records studios were used as the classroom. All during the week key professionals in the field lectured on various phases of the business. Virtually all the other Chapters of the recording organization (New York, Chicago, Nashville, Atlanta) have educational programs of one kind and another, many of which are valuable to songwriters.

In California, too, an "experimental college", called The Sherwood Oaks Experimental College in Hollywood runs seven week seminars, with such successful and established professionals as Phil Spector, Bones Howe and Jerry Fuller conducting classes.

In Nashville this summer (1972) the Nashville Songwriters' Association set up a course in the fundamentals of
songwriting to be given at the University of Tennessee. The
faculty consisted of successful country and pop/country writers, including Eddie Miller, Harlan Howard, Dallas Frazier, Kris
Kristofferson, Mic McAlpin, Buddy Mize, Clarence Selman and
Mickey Newberry. The course ran for six weeks, with one two
hour session each week.

I mention Courses of this kind only because, as far as I
have been able to determine, very few (if any) accredited
colleges offer Courses in songwriting. The University of California
at Los Angeles summer extension section, for example, does
offer such Music classes as *Choral Workshop for Conductors and
Singers; Song Interpretation,* dealing with traditional and contemporary art songs in German, French and English; *Music Cultures of the World,* which surveys the role of music in society
and its relationship to the other arts; *The Afro-American Musical
Heritage,* which is a study of Afro-American rhythm, dance,
music, field hollers, work songs, spirituals, blues and jazz.

With the possible exception of the last-listed of these
Courses none are too likely to be of any great practical aid to
the contemporary songwriter. What it really comes down to is
that the writer should make it his business to canvas every possibility for help in playing, lyric writing, melody writing, harmony
and theory in his own area. Here again the suggestion I made
earlier regarding subscribing to music/record tradepapers is
pertinent.

In addition to carrying news of the specialized Courses
I have mentioned above, the tradepapers will also keep the
writer alerted to extraordinary and special opportunities for
Scholarships and other music/record educational opportunities.

For example in June, 1972 the Record Industry Association of America, under the chairmanship of Henry Brief, sponsored a luncheon in honor of Paul Ackerman, music editor of
*The Billboard.* Ackerman was presented with a well-deserved
award for distinguished service to American music, and the funds

raised through the luncheon went toward fifty scholarships in the Scholarship Fund of the Third Street Music School, the oldest community music school in the United States.

In addition to Courses there are,of course, hundreds of books on songwriting. Many of them are totally worthless, although I suppose a novice writer could conceivably learn *something* from any of them. Again, in the purchase of books, I would urge great care, and consultation with friends or acquaintances who have some knowledge and experience.

For background information there are various books covering just about any music style in which you choose to work. Most of these books don't attempt to teach writing as such, but all serve the admirable purpose of giving the songsmith exhaustive background knowledge of the areas in which he's working.

In the rock field, a few years ago, Lillian Roxon put together a *Rock Encyclopedia,* in which she tackled the gargantuan task of writing biographies on over 1200 rock performers (including, of course, all the stars); listing 22,000 records and albums complete with release dates. Anyone working in Rock should have the book. It's published by Grosset & Dunlap, New York, and sells for $9.95

Another good rock book is *The Story of Rock* by Carl Belz, published by Oxford University Press, New York, $6.95. Belz's book details, quite authoritatively, the latest sounds and trends in rock music, and covers all the new groups. It also has an exhaustive discography.

There are two good books on so-called Soul (rhythm & blues, race, whatever you wish to call it - - - black music primarily, I guess): One is Arnold Shaw's *The World of Soul,* and the other Phyl Garland's *The Sound of Soul.* A most informative and entertaining book on country music is *The Nashville Sound* by Paul Hemphill.

As I've indicated, these are excellent background books, but more directly useful to the songwriter are a couple of others recently published: One is Alec Wilder's *American Popular Song - - - the Great Innovators 1900-1951 - - -* Oxford, $15.00

If you're writing in the "middle of the road" vein,

mined in the last half century by such as Irving Berlin, Richard Rodgers, Cole Porter, Arthur Schwartz, Jimmy Van Heusen, Hoagy Carmichael, Ray Noble, Johnny Green, Duke Ellington, Jimmy McHugh, etc. this book is an absolute *must*. Wilder, a talented songwriter himself, not only discusses the work of these craftsmen, but *analyzes* approximately three hundred of their songs. Since Wilder is primarily a melody writer, his emphasis is on the music side of the analysis, and tends to treat the lyric aspects somewhat lightly. But a reading and re-reading, a careful study of this book will be invaluable to the average popular writer.

This past season (winter of 1972) I attended a couple of classes conducted by Lehman Engel on writing for the musical theatre. This Course, sponsored by BMI, is by far the best available to lyricists, melody writers or librettists who wish to write for the Stage. Unfortunately only a relatively small number of people are permitted to take the Course (one must have produced some work, even if unproduced, for the musical stage), but Engel has put his Course into book form. The Macmillan Company, New York has just published the book, *Words With Music,* at the truly bargain price of $7.95. (If it sounds like I'm touting the book, it's only because I am.)

Engel has a substantial background in the professional Broadway theatre. He was musical director for many shows including *L'il Abner, The Cradle Will Rock* and a dozen others.

He wrote the incidental music for Margaret Webster's Shakespearean productions, and for such distinguished works as *Streetcar Named Desire* and *Murder in the Cathedral.*

Although he covers, in the most thorough manner possible, the ingredients which go into a successful musical, as to book, lyrics, music, he nevertheless stresses the one essential fact, which anyone hoping to work in the theatre must recognize and adjust to:

That a musical is a co-operative effort which involves the work of not only writers, but musicians, singers, dancers, lighting directors, costume designers, set designers, stage managers, director and producer. Rarely has a more helpful book been

written on any phase of writing. If you have eyes to write musical comedy or drama at all, you *must* study this work.

There are two other books I know would be valuable to
songwriters. Both, I hasten to point out, are published by my
company, First Place Music Publications, Inc. So obviously I am
prejudiced. However I have no hesitancy in saying that these two
books will help any writer willing to study them.

For beginning writers, especially, I recommend a new
book by Jack Smalley called *A Simplified Guide to Writing and
Arranging Songs for the Swing and Show Choir and Small Instrumental Groups.* I edited Jack's book and I found it the most
lucid, well-organized, no-nonsense work on writing melody and
lyrics, taking songs off records, writing arrangements that I have
ever encountered.

The book also contains two complete small group arrangements of two of Jack's own tunes, with a step-by-step explanation of how the arrangements were created. It sells for $9.95.

The second book which I heartily recommend, I recommend *only to writers who are fairly knowledgeable musicians.*
It is actually two books, Volumes II and III of the Encyclopedia
of Basic Harmony & Theory Applied to Improvisation on All
Instruments by Dick Grove. As the title states, the books are
Harmony and Theory works, intended *primarily* for musicians,
but elements of the second and third volumes are invaluable to
writers.

Volume II, for example, contains a study of all Musical
Styles and their related Major and Minor Chord families, along
with the Scale Sources which run through them. Covered are
Popular/Show, Rock, Country & Western, Folk, Jazz, Swing,
Dixie and Modal.

Volume III has a number of Lessons on 119 Chord Progressions, and the manner in which they are used in all musical
styles. There are three long playing records on which Dick plays
and lectures on these progressions. Let me stress again that
these volumes are not meant for the untutored songwriter with
little or no technical musical knowledge. The two Volumes are
actually the text book versions of the Dick Grove Improvisation

Course, which almost four hundred musicians study via correspondence, and which is taught in a number of high schools and colleges.

The books are expensive: $24.95 each, plus $15 for the three records which accompany Volume III. So please don't buy them unless you are an advanced-enough musician to be able to use them effectively. First Place's address is: 12754 Ventura Boulevard, Studio City, California 91604.

But whether you study your craft through books or a course or a combination of both, or by working with other writers or however, continue the practice I suggested earlier in this Chapter:

Listen to, observe and analyze every possible successful song in the style in which you're working. Analyze and study a dozen, a score, a hundred, a thousand, the more the better. You'll find that home-made hit Workshop really pays off.

And as you learn, more and more write. Write and keep writing. Let nothing discourage you.

And now let's assume you're at least a fairly competent writer, with at least a few - - - 2, 3, 10, 50 good songs - - - to show and/or play for singers, groups, record producers, publishers, whoever.

Next steps - - - !

*The gent who wakes up and finds himself a success hasn't been asleep.*
Wilson Mizner

## 20. SANTA & THE GREEN DOOR

In the beginning I said the essential factor for building a career, any career, songwriter or otherwise, in the music business, is to get in. Get into the business. If you can't get in as a song-writer, get in in any way you can. Any way that will enable you to meet and demonstrate your sincerity and your talent to people who may be able to help you.

If you're a capable enough musician and/or singer as well as a writer, try to get with a group, the best and most active, (although if you're in school, get with the school group) professional rather than amateur, the busiest group possible. Joey Covington probably wouldn't have gotten *Pretty As You Feel* recorded by the Jefferson Airplane if he was still playing drums with the Bucky Carter Trio.

If you're not a musician, try to get a job with a music publisher, in a music store, at a radio station, a television station, a theatre or auditorium where music acts play, a record shop, any business where groups, singers, musicians, managers, agents, other writers come and go.

Without unduly bugging people try to find out what kinds of material they're seeking, try to come up with that kind of material. Here's how that type of awareness works:

Shortly after I set up my own publishing company,

Trinity Music, I had dinner with one of the artist and repertoire men at RCA Victor. His name was Henri Rene. Henri mentioned that the company had just signed Eartha Kitt, and he had been assigned to produce her first session.

It was late summer so music men were already beginning to think in terms of Christmas songs.

"I would love to," said Henri, "find a sexy Christmas song for Eartha."

The idea struck me as a good one. I went back to the office and called a new songwriter with whom we had just begun to work, a young lady named Joan Javits (the niece, incidentally of New York Senator Jacob Javits). Joan was a lyricist and I had been struck by the freshness and cleverness of the words and ideas in some of her songs.

I told Joan about Henri's idea for a sexy Xmas song for Miss Kitt, and it appealed to her. The next morning she called me and read me the lyric to *Santa, Baby*. I thought it was great, and that day Phil Springer, the melody writer with whom she worked, came in and she and Phil completed the song. I took it over to Henri, he liked it, so did Eartha, and in November *Santa, Baby* was the hit song of the Christmas season.

One of the most effective approaches I know, as a matter of fact, to achieving success as a songwriter is to establish a reputation with producers, publishers and/or artists for being able to write well on specific assignment. Fred Ebb (who with melody writer John Kander has written major hit Broadway musicals, such as *Cabaret, Flora, the Red Menace,* etc.) sharpened the skills, which enabled him to write those musicals, by coming up with one competent song after another *on assignment.*

In addition to operating Trinity Music, we were then managing a singer/writer (today a top disk jockey and commercial television announcer) Jim Lowe. Jim did a great job singing novelty songs. One day we asked Fred to write a song based on an old joke:

An inveterate gambler went to Las Vegas and soon lost all his money at the roulette wheel. As he was leaving the Casino he heard a mysterious, disembodied voice.

"Play number seven," the spooky voice said. The player got into his Cadillac, his sole remaining possession, to begin the drive home, but the voice kept urging him, over and over, to play number seven. He pulled into a used car lot, sold his Cadillac for $2500, went back to the Casino, and put the entire bundle on number seven. Number eight came up, and the voice said: "How about that!"

If you want to see how far you've developed as a songwriter, try writing a song called *Play Number Seven,* which Fred did, and Jim recorded. It wasn't as big as *Green Door,* but it was a profitable record and song.

The story of *Green Door,* incidentally, illustrates another truism about the music business, and about songwriting in particular, which every writer, publisher, artist and producer learns sooner or later. And which points up an important moral for the budding writer.

At Trinity one of the teams of writers we had under contract was Marvin Moore and Bob Davie. They were prolific, and particularly good at writing on assignment for the various artists our talent management firm, Csida-Grean Associates handled. One day they came in quite excited about a new tune they had written for Jim Lowe.

It was called *The Little Man in Chinatown.* And it was indeed, an intriguing little novelty, good pseudo-Oriental sound gimmicks, funny lyrics, a really good possibility. Jim liked it too, and we decided to record it. A day or so before the session was scheduled we were still searching for at least one more decent tune for the flip side of our anticipated *Chinese* hit.

Marvin and Bob finally came in with a song they said they thought was pretty fair, and worth doing. It was *Green Door.* Outside of Jim Lowe, my then partner Charlie Grean, Moore and Davie, and possibly Randy Wood, then head of Dot Records, who bought the master from us, I doubt if anyone in the world remembers that the song on the back of the three million (world wide) selling record *The Green Door* by Jim Lowe was *The Little Man in Chinatown.*

A similar story is told about one of the great copyrights

of all time, *Rudolph, the Red Nosed Reindeer.* Gene Autry
wound up a record session with five or ten minutes to spare and
songwriter Johnny Marks persuaded him to cut *Rudolph* as
long as he still had the time. I was head of artists and repertoire
at RCA Victor at that time, and I virtually had to force Dennis
Day to record the song. Although Autry's record was the hit,
Dennis did fairly well with the record, and conceivably could
have done better had he put his heart into making the record.

The Green Door — Rudolph moral is, of course: Keep
writing, one song after another. No matter what anybody,
alleged expert or otherwise, says about your song, nobody really
knows. Nobody in the music business is, or ever was, right one
hundred percent of the time about songs.There are those who
will tell you they have been and are, but they're liars.

Probably the most talented of all the assignment writers
I have ever worked with was Bob Merrill. When I started Trinity,
with George and Eddie Joy, they had Merrill under exclusive
contract. He wrote *Doggie in the Window,* specifically for Patti
Page. Eddie Joy operated as a talent manager, too, and his male
singing star was Guy Mitchell. Merrill ground out hit after hit
after hit, on specific assignment for Guy. You may remember
*Pittsburgh, Pennsylvania, Feet Up, Pat 'Im on the Popo, Truly,
Truly Fair* and *Sparrow in the Tree Top.* Bob also wrote *If I
Knew You Were Comin' I'd 'ave Baked a Cake, Candy and Cake,
Love Makes the World Go Round,* many of them on specific
assignment. Merrill, incidentally, picked out his melodies by
playing them on a toy xylophone.

It was that kind of training, (not the xylophone, the
assignments), which enabled Merrill to become, eventually, one
of the most active of the Broadway Show writers. He did *Funny
Girl* (with Jule Styne), *Take Me Along, New Girl in Town* and
a number of others.

If you are not a performer yourself, and have no inten-
tions of being one, or feel you lack sufficient talent in that direction, the next best approach is to find one or more singers
and/or musical groups and aim your writing at them. Write the
kind of songs that specific singer or group does. (Obviously, in

this connection, it's advisable to select - - - if you can find one
- - - a singer or group, who don't write their own songs).

Burt Bacharach and Hal David are highly talented writers,
of course, and hardly need a specific singer for whom to write,
but the songs they've done for Dionne Warwick (which, incidentally, they produce as well as write) have been an important
element of their writing careers.

So those are some of the essential approaches to developing a career  as a songwriter.

1. Get where the action is.

2. Aim your songs at a specific singer and/or group.

3. Try to develop a reputation for writing on assignment,
writing the kind of material specific artists or producers are
seeking.

*Early to bed and early to rise*
*and you'll meet very few*
*of our best people.*
George Ade

## 21. MEET THE PEOPLE

One way to get into the business, of course, other than finding a job is to join any one or more groups, to which other writers, performers, producers, belong. It's even more advantageous, obviously, to have the job, and belong to a number of groups.

Naturally the first group to which you should belong for the good, simple and sufficient reason that it's the only way you can collect performance earnings on your songs is one of the Licensing Organizations. As indicated earlier, the three most active are ASCAP, BMI and SESAC, with the latter much smaller than the first two. All three of these organizations have eased their requirements for membership in recent years, but the best thing for you to do before joining any one of them is to find out what their current requirements are. At the same time that you do this, you may also find out whatever you wish to know about how they log their performances, how they pay, and any other pertinent details with which you should, or care to concern yourself.

I am listing here their offices and representatives. If they do not have an office or representative in your town, the intelligent thing to do, of course, would be to write one of the two main offices, either New York or Los Angeles. If you do live in a town in which they have offices or representatives, you may find out what you wish to know on the phone or in person.

(Parenthetically, I should say here that many writers I have known tend to check the performing rights organizations by asking friends, other writers, publishers or whoever, about them. I strongly advise against this. Too many writers, and even some publishers, only have the vaguest and often inaccurate notion about what the individual licensing organizations do, how they operate, what services they have for members, etc. Performances of your songs, and everything dealing with them are much too important to approach casually, or to be informed about loosely. And besides, the organizations, particularly ASCAP and BMI have many activities and services of great value to writers, other than their collection and distribution efforts . . . I have already mentioned the excellent Lehman Engel BMI sponsored course on writing for the Musical Theatre.

Here, then, are the organizations and their branches and representatives:

AMERICAN SOCIETY OF COMPOSERS, AUTHORS & PUBLISHERS (ASCAP), 575 Madison Ave., New York, N.Y. 10022. Tel: (212) 688-8800.

Branches:

Hollywood, Calif., 6430 Sunset Blvd., Suite 1002. Zip: 90028.

San Francisco, Calif., Equitable Life Bldg., 120 Montgomery St. Rm. 1020. Zip: 94104.

Denver, Colo., 1330 Leyden St., Rm. 136-138. Zip: 80202.

Miami Beach, Fla. 1025 Kane Concourse, Suite 206, Bay Harbor Island. Zip 33154.

Atlanta, Ga., 1223 Fulton Nat'l. Bank Bldg. Zip: 30303.

Chicago, Ill., 200 E. Ontario St. Zip: 60611.

New Orleans, La., International Trade Mart Bldg., Suite 910-911. Zip: 70130.

Baltimore, Md., 1 E. Redwood St. Zip: 21202.

Boston, Mass., Park Sq. Bldg., 31 St. James Ave. Zip: 02116.

Detroit, Mich., 821 Penobscot Bldg. Zip: 48226.

Minneapolis, Minn., 1434 Midwest Plaza Bldg. Zip: 55402.

St. Louis, Mo., 130 S. Bemiston Ave. Zip: 63105.

Syracuse, N.Y., State Tower Bldg., Suite 618. Zip: 13202.

Cleveland, Ohio, 715 Hanna Bldg. Zip: 44105

Portland, Ore., 617 Pacific Bldg. Zip: 97204.
Jenkintown, Pa., The Benson-East, Suite 223-B. Zip: 19046.
Pittsburgh, Pa., 515 Grant Bldg. Zip: 15219.
Nashville, Tenn., 700 17 Ave. S. Zip: 37202.
Dallas, Tex., 1700 Tower Petroleum Bldg. Zip: 75201.
International branch: Puerto Rico.
ASCAP has affiliations with performing rights and licensing organizations in a number of foreign countries. In these countries such organizations collect for performances of ASCAP songs, and ASCAP in the United States periodically pays such foreign earnings to its writers and publishers. The countries with which ASCAP has such affiliations are:
Argentina, Australia, Austria, Belgium, Brazil, Canada, Chile, Czechoslovakia, Denmark, Finland, France, Germany, Greece, Hungary, Iceland, Israel, Italy, Japan, Madagascar, Mexico, Netherlands, Norway, Paraguay, Peru, Philippines, Portugal, Puerto Rico, South Africa, Spain, Sweden, Switzerland, UK, Uruguay, Yugoslavia.
BROADCAST MUSIC, INC. (BMI)
589 Fifth Ave.,
New York, N.Y. 10017
Tel: (212) 759-1500.
Branches:
Los Angeles, Calif., 9720 Wilshire Blvd., Suite 802, Beverly Hills 90212.
San Francisco, Calif. 680 Beach St. Zip: 94109.
Miami, Fla., 150 SE Second Ave. Zip: 33131.
Chicago, Ill., 230 N. Michigan Ave. Zip: 60601.
Syracuse, N.Y., 217 Montgomery St. Zip: 13202.
Nashville, Tenn., 710 16 Ave. S. Zip: 37203.
International branch: Canada.
International affiliates: Argentina, Australia, Austria, Belgium, Brazil, Chile, Czechoslovakia, Denmark, Finland, France, Germany, Greece, Iceland, Israel, Italy, Japan, Liechtenstein, Mexico, Netherlands, New Zealand, Norway, Philippines, Portugal, Spain, Sweden, Switzerland, South Africa, UK, Yugoslavia.

SESAC INC.
10 Columbus Circle,
New York, N.Y. 10019
Tel: (212) 586-3450
Branch:
Nashville, Tenn., 1513 Hawkins St. Zip: 37203.
International affiliates: Argentina, Australia, Austria, Belgium, Brazil, Canada, Colombia, Denmark, Finland, France, Germany, Iceland, Israel, Italy, Japan, Mexico, Netherlands, Norway, Portugal, South Africa, Spain, Sweden, Switzerland, UK.

If you prefer not to make your own investigation of the Performance rights organizations, the best source I can recommend to you for an explanation of their functions and modus operandi is one I mentioned earlier, the book *This Business of Music* by Sidney Shemel and M. William Krasilovsky.

Once you join one of these organizations, you'll have natural opportunities at membership meetings and other events to meet other writers and other people in the music business. In addition to joining ASCAP, BMI of SESAC you should join as many other trade organizations as appeal to you, and as you're able to.

If you're a musician-writer the chances are you'll join your own local of the American Federation of Musicians. If you're a performer-writer you may also join the American Federation of Television and Radio Artists (to work in radio and/or television, of course), or the American Guild of Variety Artists (if you work in night clubs, theatres, etc.)

Two national and important song writer organizations are the American Guild of Authors and Composers and the west-coast based Composers & Lyricists Guild of America. The latter group consists mainly of motion picture and television writers, the former of writers in all fields. In addition to these two organizations there are a number of local organizations to which writers may profitably belong. Among these are the Nashville Songwriters' Association and Memphis Music, Inc.

There are also many other organizations, whose membership consists of writers and other people in the business, who are important to and work with writers.

Outstanding among these are the National Academy of Recording Arts and Sciences and the Country Music Association.

If you are currently in the retail area or the one-stop or rack jobber/distributor area of the music business, the trade organizations representing these groups are most active, although their relationship with the creative aspects of the industry such as writers/performers is, of course, oblique and secondary. Dealers are banded together in the National Association of Music Merchants (NAMM) and rack jobbers in the National Association of Record Merchandisers (NARM).

Pertinent data on these, and other organizations of possible interest to the writer follow:

American Federation of Musicians
641 Lexington Ave.
New York, N.Y. 10022
Tel: (212) PL 8-0600.
American Federation of Television & Radio Artists (AFTRA)
1350 Ave. of the Americas,
New York, N.Y. 10019.
Tel: (212) 265-8062.
American Guild of Authors & Composers (AGAC)
50 W. 57th St.
New York, N.Y. 10019
Tel: (212) 757-8833.
Hollywood, Calif. 6331 Hollywood Blvd. Zip: 90028.
American Guild of Musical Artists (AGMA)
1841 Broadway
New York, N.Y. 10023
Tel: (212) CO 5-3687.
American Guild of Variety Artists (AGVA)
1540 Broadway
New York, N.Y.
Tel: (212) 765-0800
Composers & Lyricists Guild of America Inc.
6565 Sunset Blvd., Rm. 419
Hollywood, Calif. 90028

Country Music Ass'n. Inc.
700 16th Ave. S.
Nashville, Tenn. 37203
Tel: (615) 244-2840

National Ass'n. of Rec. Mdsrs. Inc. (NARM)
703 Trianon Bldg.
Bala Cynwyd, Pa. 19004
Tel: (215) TE 9-7900

Nashville Songwriters' Ass'n. (NSA)
P.O. Box 1556
Nashville, Tenn. 37202
Tel: (615) 254-8066

National Academy of Recording Arts & Sciences (NARAS)
Offices:
Hollywood, Calif., 6430 Sunset Blvd. Suite 503. Zip: 90028.
Atlanta, Ga., P.O. Box 9687. Zip: 30319.
Chicago, Ill., 25 E. Chestnut St., Suite 4G. Zip: 60611.
New York, N.Y., 21 W. 58th St. Zip: 10019.
Nashville, Tenn., 1905 Broadway. Zip: 37203.

Memphis Music Inc.
P.O. Box 224
Memphis, Tenn. 38101
Tel: (901) 525-2741

It's not only important that you join as many of these organizations as deal, either directly or indirectly with your work as a songwriter, but that you make it your business to learn as much about their functions and activities as you can. If you know these functions and activities, and select and participate in those which best coincide with your own mode of operation, you will find that the contacts you make will prove extremely valuable; the knowledge you acquire will be of great use.

*I am really an average man, but*
*by George, I work harder at it*
*than the average man.*
Theodore Roosevelt

## 22. GETTING YOUR SONG HEARD

Now you've picked the specific artist or type of artist
or group of artists (singer, groups) and you're in the business
- - - either in some kind of job or as an active member of one
or more organizations, and you've got some good songs you
want to submit. (Again, if you're a performer, yourself, we'll
cover that in the section dealing with performer careers). But
here we're assuming you're a songwriter.

If you play and sing well enough to demonstrate your
own songs, that's the ideal. And don't worry about how badly
you sing, just so long as you can carry the melody and give
some real expression to the lyrics. Fred Edd, whom I mentioned earlier, had a terrible singing voice, so did Bob Merrill
and Frank Loesser and most other song writers I've heard
demonstrate their songs, but that didn't stop them from
making effective presentations of their material.

Which leads me to insert that one quite important
characteristic a successful songwriter should possess is
*chutzpah,* a total lack of shyness and a generous amount of
aggressiveness. Almost every successful songwriter I have
known over these many years has been aggressive in pushing
his songs - - - to get them performed and recorded, and indeed
to promote them after they were recorded.

But back to getting those first important hearings for your tunes. As I said, if you can demonstrate your own songs, live, singing and playing piano or guitar (for instance) that's the ideal way, since you'll frequently be able to get an immediate personal reaction from your listener. If you can't demonstrate your own songs, you'll have to make arrangements with someone who can.

In either event the first prospect to whom to try to submit your song, in most cases, is the artist himself (or the key members of a group). This is frequently difficult, of course, until you have developed some acceptance and reputation for your work. But it is the way to try to go. If you can't get to the artist, there are several secondary, but still highly important, other ways to go. (As a matter of fact, in some cases, these "secondary" personages, may be the decision-making element, rather than the artist himself.)

If you can't get to the artist, perhaps you can get to his manager. If you can't get to the artist or the manager, you might try his record producer, whether that producer is an independent producer (of whom there are many these days) or whether the producer is a member of the artist and repertoire staff of a record company.

If you can't get to the producer, consider this possibility: Many artists (and/or their managers) own their own music publishing companies, and these music publishing companies are frequently operated for the artist by an individual, who might be a one-man music operation, or general manager of a somewhat larger and more active music publishing operation. Bobby Darin, for example, has a music publishing company, which is operated for him by a young man named Steve Burton, son of one of my partners, the late Ed Burton, in the days when we were managing Bobby.

If you can't get to the artist, the manager, the record producer, maybe the artist's music man is the one to get to. He's constantly looking for songs for the firm, for the artist who owns it, or for any other good songs for any artist he might be able to influence.

You can keep going down the line in this way. If you can't get to the artist's music man, maybe you can connect with his press agent, or a man in the booking agency which books him, or a promotion man, who works for him. Depending on your own particular situation in the industry - - - where you're working, if you're working; which organizations you belong to; what your contacts and connections are, you'll take one or another of the above approaches to getting your songs heard.

This points up one more essential in a successful songwriter's list of skills and data required:

Obviously the more you know about any given artist's entire operating structure, the better are your chances of getting your song to the right place at the right time. I have known artists who listen to almost no one, when it comes to selecting the songs they will record. I have known some who will record only what their managers tell them to record; some who swear by their record producer; some who swear at him, and will listen to nothing he says.

Two other elements, human nature being what it is, complicate this situation even further:

Some people must make themselves seem important, no matter what. Thus, you may encounter a manager who will tell you that his artist does exactly what the manager tells him, while in reality the artist may hardly listen to a word the manager says.

Or the artist may, at one time, have paid great heed to what a producer told him about songs, but having had a hit or two, may no longer listen to any one, about songs or anything else.

That, as you'll find out if you haven't already, is life and not unique or exclusive to the music business. But if you're going to make it as a songwriter, it's something you should be aware of - - - and constantly study.

You may also discover as you go along that, on occasion, it may help you get a song accepted and launched if you will accept a co-writer. This could be the artist himself, the

manager, the producer, or almost anyone significantly involved. Sometimes such a co-writer may actually make a contribution to improving your song, by suggesting an A$^\#$ instead of a
natural A on the first half note in the third measure or changing the lyric word "girl" to "gal". Whatever the contribution
such a co-writer may or may not make keep in mind the
practical idea that it is better to be one of two writers on a
recorded song, a successful song, than 100% exclusive writer
on a song which exists only on your own lead sheet.

It's a simple case of being proud but poor, or com-
promising for a chance to make it. If that kind of compromise
is the most severe one you'll ever have to make in the music
business (or any other that I know of), you may indeed consider yourself fortunate.

But back to the simple, physical mechanical aspects
of getting a hearing for your song: - - -

If you can't perform your song live, and in person, for
the artist or other key people, the second best procedure, of
course, is to make (or have made) the cleanest, most professional possible looking lead sheet of the song and make the best
possible demonstration record of it. In this situation, again,
the desirability of being as accomplished a musician as possible,
is highlighted. If you can write your own lead sheets and make
your own demos, you'll obviously save a great deal of money
in preparing your songs for submission. If you can't you'll
either have to get a musician friend and/or player/singer to do
it for you for free or pay for it.

In some cases, of course, where an active established
music publisher accepts a song from a writer, the publisher
will pay for the preparation of whatever lead sheets and demonstration records are necessary. But, of course, you've got to have
the song in some kind of physical form, to submit it to the
publisher in the first place - -- but this may be an amateurish
scribbling of the notes and words on a brown paper bag.

At any rate, as I've said, if you can't get to play your
song live and in person the next best procedure is to submit
a lead sheet and demo record.

The demo can be utterly simple; you playing (piano, guitar, whatever) and singing the song on a home tape recorder (and you may try to play or submit the tape or cassette) - - - or the demo may be as elaborate as you like or can afford. I've known of quite a few demos, some made by writers, some by artists, some by publishers that were actually released as finished records. And some of these have been quite successful records.

But no matter what kind of lead sheet and demo you make for submission, remember again that it's essential that you know as much as possible about who makes the decision as to whether the song will be accepted and recorded. If you're submitting lead sheets and demos it may even be more important, because they both cost money, and not too many artists, managers, publisher or record companies around the music business bother to return lead sheets and demos. Some don't even bother if you enclose return envelopes, postage, and say pretty please.

Try, as you pursue this phase of your songwriting career (submitting songs, demos, etc.), to learn as much as possible about each submission. Who actually listens to the song? Who makes the decision? How long do they hold a song? How reliable are they? If they tell you, they're going to record it, do they actually come through? *Etc., ad infinitum.*

I set up a system when I started Trinity Music, which I, and my associates found most helpful in keeping track of our songs, and most educational in developing our knowledge of the artists, managers and others with whom we dealt. You might find it useful to set up a similar simple system.

Make up a sheet in a loose leaf note book for each song you write. Head the sheet, of course, with the name of the song and the date you wrote it. Then in columns across the page, show the following:

| Submitted To | Date Submitted | Date Response Received | Reaction |
|---|---|---|---|
| *(Here you would list whether leadsheet, demo or both were submitted and the name of the person and/ or company to whom submitted)* | *(Obviously just write in date you gave that person or firm the song)* | *(Naturally if you played the song in person you would be likely to get a response immediately - - - but if you submit lead sheets or demos it may take from an hour to a year before you get a response)* | *(Here, it's quite important that you list the most thorough and honestly objective report you can unearth. If ten listeners to the tune in succession tell you they like the melody but don't think the lyric makes it, you've obviously got a strong message to do a new lyric to the tune - - - This kind of data should be noted in addition to whether the tune is being rejected or accepted.)* |

You may extend this form to include pertinent data on songs you get recorded, i.e., by whom, what label, release date, promotional efforts and by whom made, earnings, etc. Some writers like to keep all kinds of data on their works, and others don't bother at all. Whether you do or not is relatively unimportant and entirely up to you. It's far more important that you keep studying and writing and creating more and better songs all the time - - - and developing and spreading your contacts.

In submitting your songs it's naturally desirable not to bug the artist or manager or whoever to the point where they will simply refuse to have anything to do with you. But it's almost equally fatal to be so timid that you never attempt to get a straight answer on whether or not they like your tune and expect to use it. Faint heart ne'er got a record.

Hit that happy medium. Be persistent, but lovable. And one last suggestion: Wherever possible, if your listeners are turning down a tune of yours, for whatever reasons, but they indicate they like your work, try to find out what kind of material they're looking for. Try to get a specific assignment, maybe even throw some ideas at them - - - lyric-wise, sound-wise, whatever. Remember what I said earlier about assignments.

Everything I've said here, of course, applies only in the event you are trying to place and promote your own songs. If you turn the songs over to an established publisher almost all of the previously described functions are primarily his responsibility. I go into such detail because the great majority of new writers will find it most difficult to get legitimate, established music publishers to accept their songs.

And also because even if a publisher is handling your song, it is well to work with him to the fullest possible degree to do as many of the previously described functions as you can. The chances are the publisher is working on a number of songs, and consequently you cannot always be sure he is making an all out effort, or trying every available source to move your song along. Successful writers follow the cliche that if you want something done right, do it yourself. True, they bug their publishers mercilessly to try to persuade or force them to do everything possible with and for their songs, but they never quit doing whatever they can on their own.

The same principles apply to promotion of the song. About which, a few words coming up.

*There are two kinds of men who
never amount to much: Those who
cannot do what they are told; and
those who can do nothing else.*
**Cyrus H.K. Curtis**

91.

## 23. BEYOND THE WRITING

There is nothing that says that to be a successful songwriter you need do anything more than write great songs. Theoretically you could spend your life sitting in your little room,
turning out great songs one after another, dropping them in the
mail to presumably interested parties, and become a successful
songwriter. Theoretically, *believe me,* ONLY!

Practically you had better do a substantial number of
the things I have already suggested, and do them consistently
and well if you really want to make it as a songwriter.

Theoretically, too, if you do all those things and write
good songs, and get them recorded, you may sit back and consider your work as a songwriter well done. Some writers do
that. Not too many of the most successful ones, however.

It is true enough that once a record of your song is
made by a recognized, or even a new artist on a legitimate,
fairly well established record label, a substantial number of
people and companies become responsible for promoting *your*
song. The artist and his manager are surely interested in having
the song become a success. So are the record company, and
(if there's a music publisher involved) so is the music publisher.
You should be able to count on one or more of them to have
their promotion men, publicity men, contact men, advertising

and merchandising men, their distributors' sales and promotion people all working to make the record of your song a big success.

But again, the realistic view is that the probability is that the record company, the publisher, the distributors, et al are working on a number of records other than yours at the same time, maybe three others, maybe a half dozen, maybe a dozen. If your record is not by one of the best selling and most successful artists on the label, the chances for getting promotion attention are not great. Record companies and their distributors and their personnel generally find the same appeal in strolling down the path of least resistance, which most humans do. So they tend to work on the hit artists because the hit artists present the least problem in getting airplay, good reviews, etc. and have the strongest chances of coming up with yet another hit record.

But what about the artist who made the record of your song, no matter who he is? Does it not behoove him and his manager, promotion man, press agent, et al to work on that record? Indeed it does. But the record has two sides, and it may be the artist and his entourage decide their best chance for a hit is to work on the song on the other side, not on your song. In such an event it is true that you would collect exactly the same amount of mechanical (record) royalty as the song on the other side, even if that song were a smash hit and yours disappeared into obscurity. However you would not collect on all the other vastly lucrative areas (outlined in Chapter 8) in which hit songs become goldmines, and obscure songs earn nothing.

Most of the successful songwriters I have known, consequently, work just as hard promoting their songs as they do writing or placing them for publishing and/or recording.

I have known writers who have been told by the artist and the record company *not* to promote a song, because the artist and record company wanted to work on the song on the other side, feeling it had the greater potential. They ask writers to lay off in such cases, because they do not want to dissipate the promotion effect by having airplay split between the two tunes on the record. And in every case, the most successful writers I know, work on their tunes anyway. Surreptitiously if they have to, but they work on them.

And I have known dozens of cases where the side the artist and record company was pushing died, but the writer achieved hitdom for the record, by stubbornly working on his own side.

The methods writers use to promote their songs via records are, of course, substantially the same as those used by all others involved in the promotion of records and/or songs. (Much of this, of course, is covered in detail, in other Chapters of this book).

In broad terms, writers promoting their records:

1. Try to get their side of the record played by as many disk jockeys, on as many stations as possible. The more influential the better;

2. Try to persuade tradepaper critics and reviewers to give them rave reviews, and to select their side of the record as potential hits;

3. Try to con people on tradepapers that their record is selling big, and should be on the best selling charts;

4. Try to get entertainers to perform the song on television, preferably high rated network shows, but local shows if necessary. (Of course if the artist who recorded the song is working on it, he'll perform it himself at every opportunity, without any prompting from the writer.)

5. Try to get the song performed in any and every other entertainment medium - - - night clubs, concerts, etc.

6. Try to get other records of the same tune.

If it seems unfair or unattractive to you that a good songwriter should also have to be a good promotion man, keep in mind that in the very course of working to promote your song, you are opening up all kinds of new opportunities for your further and continuing success as a writer. For one thing, artists, their managers, publishers, record companies, all the people and firms involved, generally appreciate all the help they can get in promoting their product. Given two songs of equal merit, one by a writer who also works hard at promotion, the other by a writer who refuses to participate in promotion, record men, artists, et al will invariably go with the promoting writer's song.

And it is inevitable that as you pursue the promotional side of a writer's career, you will be expanding your contacts, increasing your chances for picking up specific assignments to do tunes, possibly even finding a compatible artist who digs you so much he wants you to do most, if not all, of his material. And there is always, also, the possibility, that your efforts as a thoroughly well-rounded, active-in-all areas songwriter will lead you into successful record production, administrative work with publishers and/or record companies or whatever. In the music business, careers are frequently and happily, profitably interchangeable.

If you aspire to a career as a songwriter exclusively this total participation approach will bring you the maximum amount of commercial success. And if you want to expand into areas beyond writing, this total approach is by far the soundest way to achieve such expansion.

Whichever way you go, good luck. That, too, we all need.

# PART I

## SECTION TWO

Musician

*Do the best you can*
*with what you've got.*
Dandy Don Meridith

95.

## 24. NO ROAD TO RICHES


In an overview of the music business earlier in this book it was pointed out that in 1971 there were 305,202 musicians who were members of the American Federation of Musicians. Recently *all* of the members of the AFM in the United States and Canada who were active in recording were sent a new AFM-Record Company labor agreement for ratification. The number of members who received the request for ratification was a little over 3800. In other words 3800 out of the 305,000 members in the musicians union were active in recording.

In the other areas where respectable earnings may be achieved, television and motion pictures for example, even fewer musicians were active.

New wage scales were recently set by the AFM. A musician working a Cocktail Lounge (11 a.m. to 6 p.m. - - - and he must work a 2 hour minimum) gets $16.00. Of course the leader gets 1½ times that or $24. And the overtime rate is all of $3.50 per half hour before 6 p.m. and $4.50 per half hour after 7 p.m. I will not run down through the scales for other types of live work, such of it as there is. Suffice to say that plumbers, electricians, sanitation department workers and any number of practitioners in other fields not only earn more money than musicians, but also have considerably more work available.

There are those who would say that this is a sad state of affairs, and that we are inevitably heading for the day when young people will realize the futility of becoming musicians and the sounds of music will vanish from the planet.

Fear not.

The simple human truth is that there are, and hopefully always will be, huge numbers of us who will pursue an art or craft because we love it, with only secondary consideration of the economic consequences. And thus it is with most musicians.

A certain school of career counsellor makes a careful presentation of the economic facts of life concerning a given occupation, and if the potential for earning fame and fortune seems limited and remote, advises sternly against a person pursuing that career. I am not of that school. I firmly believe that every person should, to the greatest degree possible, pursue the career or combination of careers he will enjoy most, as long as he can make a living at it.

I will not belabor this because it is clearly evident from my own long and personal intimate experiences with literally hundreds of musicians of all shapes, sizes and scales of skills, and from the activity in music education across the land today that people are pursuing careers as musicians, almost all reasonably happily, many making modest to excellent livings, some even becoming rich and celebrated.

Even though we find music programs in many elementary and secondary schools and indeed in colleges and universities seriously threatened by budget inadequacies, we also note that more and more colleges and universities are introducing more contemporary music education programs. More and more high schools and colleges are organizing what are called stage bands, rather than jazz or rock or jazz/ rock bands, which they really are.

At present there are almost two hundred High School and College Jazz/Rock Festivals held annually around the country, with well over 60,000 young musicians participating in them. And these 60,000 young musicians are only the top of the iceberg of young musicians. But more about educational requirements and opportunities later. There will be musicians to spare, and good ones, for a long, long time to come. And if you want to be one of them, don't falter. There's room, and opportunity. But one thing you should do, early in the game, is decide what kind of a musician you want to be.

98.

*If I learned from all my mistakes
I'd be a genius.*
Charlie Waters
Cornerback, the Dallas Cowboys

## 25. WAYS TO GO

Chet Atkins, Howard Roberts, Joe Pass, Al Viola, John McLaughlin, Santo and Johnny Farina, Jose Feliciano, Eddy Arnold, and John Gary all play guitar. And so did Jimi Hendrix. Chet, of course, is country and western oriented, although he plays fine guitar in many styles. He is also a vice president of RCA Victor, and one of the most successful producers in the record business.

Roberts, Pass and Viola are three of the most accomplished jazz oriented pickers in music. All three are active studio musicians on the West Coast, and Roberts and Pass write guitar books, participate in Workshops and Clinics and are quite active in music education. Roberts, as a matter of fact, conducts workshops in five cities around the country each year.

John McLaughlin, of course, is the organizer and leader of the widely hailed Mahavishnu Orchestra, purveyors of spectacular improvisational jazz with a strong Indian religioso-spiritual base.

Santo and Johnny Farina are a couple of Italian brothers, whom few may remember, but they had one of the biggest selling records of all time in a song called *Sleep Walk.* It featured Santo's steel guitar, and Johnny's acoustic guitar.

In the period when their hit records created a demand for them in live performance, they worked various clubs around the country, saved their money, married sweet young ladies and settled down in modest homes on Long Island to raise decent and wholesome little families.

Feliciano, Arnold and Gary, as you know, are singing entertainers primarily, and Eddy and John play just enough chords to fake their own accompaniment when necessary, but Jose is a fine guitarist. Feliciano is from Puerto Rico, Arnold from Tennessee and Gary from upstate New York.

Of Hendrix it is hardly necessary to say anything except that he was an astonishing musician, and chose a life style you would do well to avoid.

Papa John Creach and Jerry Goodman both play violin. Papa, of course, is an older black with decades of deep roots in country and western, rhythm and blues and jazz, and lends an invaluable sound and drive to the Jefferson Airplane. Goodman fiddles with McLaughlin and the Mahavishnu, is of today's young generation, but makes both modern and electrified sounds as well as classical sounds with his violin.

Dave Brubeck, Billy Taylor, Herbie Hancock, Roger Williams and Liberace are, of course, all piano players. And Eddie Harris and Boots Randolph both play saxophone. Boots is a happy-go-lucky country boy, and Eddie spends a good deal of his time, when not blowing, writing excellent music education books and directing the growth of Black Star, his black musicians' union in Chicago.

Ray Brown is possibly the best bass player in the history of the music business. He works more major motion pictures, television shows and record dates than you can count, but he also wrote and publishes an excellent Bass method book, manages people like Quincy Jones, and still finds time to serve as a member of the Board of Local 47 of the AFM in Hollywood.

I could run down through the entire catalogue of instruments and point up again and again the simple, obvious fact that your career as a musician may take a thousand and one different forms. Consequently, then, there are two matters you should decide to set the course for your own career as a musician:

1.   What type of music (or what combination of types and styles) do you want to work in:  Jazz, rock, country and western, rhythm and blues, pop, show, classical or whatever.

2.   (And this is equally important from the standpoint of your career) - - - What areas, if any, other than playing, do you want to get into.

An earlier Chapter noted that relatively few musicians make their total income from playing alone.

There are any number of directions in which you can go, beginning with the simple choice of deciding you want to be so talented and proficient a sideman, that you can earn your living by doing nothing other than playing. Or you may decide you want to be an instrumental star, and work as a single; or you may want to build and lead a group or band; or you may want to develop to the point where you are a musical director in television or motion pictures; or you may want to teach and become active otherwise in music education.

All these avenues and more are open to you, of course. But before we get into the question of getting a start in each of those activities, let's consider the degree and kind of education and training you should have.

*Learn all the rules, every one of them,*
*so that you will know how to break them.*
Irvin Cobb

# 26. WAYS TO LEARN

I suppose it is true enough that there has been an occasionally gifted person who has become a great musician with almost no formal training or education. I have encountered a number of young people whose attitude is that they will simply teach themselves their instrument, listen to and play only the music they enjoy, and only when they feel like it. Thus, they argue, they will develop their own feelingful, emotional natural style, untainted by square, establishment rules and regulations.

*Nonsense!*

Even if you are gifted with natural musical talent there is no question in my mind that you will develop that talent to the greatest possible degree in almost direct ratio to the amount of learning and practicing you are willing to pursue. The greatest musicians I have known, in any field, country through jazz, are those who never quit studying and practicing and never will. There is so much to be learned about music, about playing any instrument or any group of instruments so that no man's lifetime is long enough to learn all there is to know, or to play as excellently as an instrument may be played.

One of the most talented players I ever met is Bill Perkins. Bill is what I choose to call a *pure* musician. That is, he does not wish to become an instrumental super star; lead a group or a band; produce sessions; direct in television or films. He wants to play.

And does! He plays alto, tenor, soprano, baritone and bass saxophones; C flute, alto flute, bass flute and piccolo; clarinet, bass clarinet and contra bass clarinet. He has played with major big bands like Stan Kenton and Woody Herman. He is one of Hollywood's most in-demand studio musicians. He plays countless top record sessions, is generally in the band of one of the major network television shows and playing on film sound tracks.

Yet he will play scale gigs in jazz clubs to keep his chops up. And he practices at least two to three hours a day every day of his life. He improvises some of the best solos you'll ever hear, on almost any of the long list of woodwinds mentioned. Yet he is studying the Dick Grove Improvisation Course because he feels there is much that he does not know about improvisation.

Of course there is also the Jim Dandy Mangrum kind of musician. Jim Dandy plays washboard and does the lead vocals for the relatively new group called Black Oak Arkansas, which got some rave reviews when they played the Long Beach Auditorium recently. It is entirely possible that Black Oak Arkansas will become a major rock group, and that Jim Dandy will become as rich and famous as Mick Jagger.

It really gets down to what kind of a musician you want to be, and where you want to go. The important fact is that there are all kinds of educational and training opportunities available to young people who want to become musicians today.

As previously mentioned, in spite of budget problems, more and more high schools and colleges have stage bands, jazz or jazz/rock groups of one kind and another. More and more colleges are instituting studies in Contemporary music. *Downbeat* publishes a directory of such schools, which I'm sure you can get from them by writing Chuck Suber, the publisher, at 222 West Adams Street, Chicago, Ill. 60606.

In addition to orthodox secondary schools and colleges

and universities, there are, of course, music schools like
Berkelee in Boston, Massachusetts.

There is also an ever-increasing number of professional
musicians with great skill and years of practical experience,
who are getting into the music education scene and passing
their knowledge on to young musicians. Among these are Roy
Burns, noted young drummer with a substantial background of
playing for top big bands, who conducts scores of clinics each
year; Clark Terry and Doc Severinsen, who do trumpet clinics
and workshops; Howard Roberts, who is expanding his annual
Guitar Workshop. Roy and Howard also have a number of books
on their instruments available to would be drummers and
guitarists.

The Stan Kenton and Woody Herman bands have insti-
tuted combination Concert/Workshop events for high schools
or colleges. The band not only plays for a paid concert, but the
leaders and key members of the band do Clinics on their own
areas of expertise. One obvious problem here is that because of
the size of the bands, and their box office values, the cost is
prohibitive for the great majority of schools.

My partner, Dick Grove and I have been instrumental
in attempting to correct this situation. Dick has a big band of
top players, from which he's put together a Quintet consisting
of Dick, himself on piano; the aforementioned Bill Perkins or
Lannie Morgan on alto saxophone; Jay Daversa or Buddy
Childers on trumpet; Norm Jeffries or Joe Porcaro on drums;
Gene Cherico or Jim Hughart on bass. All these palyers have
paid their dues with top bands such as Kenton, Herman, Louis
Bellson, Bud Shank, Gerald Wilson, Charlie Barnet, Maynard
Ferguson, Benny Goodman and others.

The quintet plays a Concert (generally with an all-star
participating school band) and Dick does improvisation and
arranging clinics, while each of the players does a clinic on his
own instrument.

There are, of course, literally hundreds of other Clinics
and Workshops, carried on all around the country, all year long
including summer. Instrument companies sponsor many of the

Clinicians at these Workshops, with Rogers Drums of the CBS family sponsoring Roy Burns; Getzen sponsoring top music educators like Rich Matteson as well as Doc Severinsen, and many others.

Many young musicians, of course, prefer to and do study with private teachers. If this is what you want to do it's obviously important that you select a teacher who is truly expert on his instrument, and has the credentials to prove it. A bad teacher may well be worse than none at all. Young musicians in areas such as New York, Los Angeles, Nashville and other cities where there is a great deal of professional music activity, have the advantage of being able to go to top working professionals, many of whom teach on the side. But here again the student should proceed with caution. There are some musicians who are good players, but have no talent for teaching. With care, and by trial and error, however, the young musician will find the teacher who may be of the most help to him.

Where good teachers are not available, of course, there are always correspondence courses and books. In these areas, most of all, the prospective musician must investigate and choose with great care. Correspondence courses range all the way from the U.S. School of Music, where at extremely nominal rates they will teach you to play piano, guitar, or any number of other instruments to quite expensive in-depth courses such as our own Dick Grove Improvisation Course.

The best way for a young student to evaluate the comparative merits of such Courses is to get the advice of other musicians who are familiar with the Courses. If no such advice is available the Courses should be checked with local music teachers, and even, in the final analysis with the local Better Business Bureau.

There are so many Courses on virtually every instrument that it would be impossible to list even a small number of them. The best are advertised in musicians' magazines such as *Downbeat*.

When it comes to instrumental technique and method books the picture may be even more bewildering. There are literally thousands upon thousands of such books, many of them quite valuable and helpful. Here again, checking with other musicians and/or music teachers is advised, although you may be sure that books by top established professionals, such as those mentioned, by Roy Burns, Joe Pass, Carole Kaye (bass) and others are bound to be legitimately helpful.

This is not to say that books by contemporary music educators may not be every bit as useful (sometimes even more so) as books by working professionals. My company, for example, publishes (among many other books) one by Jack Wheaton, formerly president of the National Association of Jazz Educators and currently teaching at Cerritos Community College in Norwalk; California State College at Long Beach and Saddleback College in Mission Viejo. Jack's book *Basic Modal Improvisation Techniques for Keyboard Instruments* is a most useful work for teaching that phase of keyboard work.

It really gets down to precisely what you wish to learn, and a thorough investigation of the best available ways to learn it. In addition to orthodox schools, special workshops, clinics, correspondence courses and books there are also available to interested young persons a number of Courses run by music industry firms and organizations.

One example is the week long Course on music/records given last summer by the Los Angeles Chapter of the National Academy of Recording Arts and Sciences. Forty two high school students and eight teachers attended this Course in Los Angeles. Herb Alpert and Jerry Moss's A & M Record company contributed it Studio A as the classroom. This Course dealt only to a limited degree with playing as such, dealing rather with an overall presentation of record production and promotion. Nevertheless it was valuable to a musician interested in the vital recording areas of the business. The other Chapters of NARAS, in New York, Nashville, Chicago, etc. also offer courses. (More about all these Courses will be found in the Producer and other Sections of this book.)

One of the most interesting of all educational programs for young musicians was inaugurated by Local 47 (the Los Angeles local) of the American Federation of Musicians last summer.

This was the Young Sounds Program. Musicians between the ages of 14 and 21 were invited to participate. The union announced the purpose of the program as follows: " . . . to inform, educate and train young musicians who are interested in becoming knowledgeable professionals in today's world of music."

Satisfactory participation in the program leads to full membership in the union. The program, said Frank Sorkin, member of the National Apprenticeship Committee of the Federation will "supply the basic concepts necessary to start a career in music."

There is indeed a wide choice of ways of learning to be whatever kind of musician you want to be. Perhaps the most effective of all is one of the most obvious, the one most musicians instinctively and automatically follow. But it should be mentioned:

Listen to every performance, live or recorded, in concert or on television or wherever of every musician you admire and respect in your own chosen area. And don't just listen, but listen with a trained ear, listen and analyze. At one stage of your career you may find yourself unconsciously copying one or more of your favorites, but eventually you will evolve your own style. The listening and analyzing may easily be the most effective part of your training. That and constant playing and practicing.

So let's assume you've decided what kind of musician you want to be, and you've studied and practiced, and are ready to begin your career as a musician. Again, as stressed in the very beginning of this book, the important thing now is for you to *get into the business* - - - as a musician of the type you want to be. Or if that's impossible for the moment, get in any way you can.

*Where the willingness is great,*
*the difficulties cannot be great.*
Nicollo Machiavelli

107.

## 27. THE SIDEMAN

The Young Sounds Program of Local 47 of the American Federation of Musicians (the Los Angeles Chapter) indicates, of course, that one of the most immediate and effective ways to get into the music business as a musician is to join the Union. There are well over 600 Locals of the American Federation of Musicians in the United States and Canada. The national AFM publishes a book called LIST OF LOCALS, BOOKING AGENTS-MANAGERS AND SUB-AGENTS.

This book lists every local. If you are going to look up your own local in the telephone directory, keep in mind that you may not find the listing under American Federation of Musicians, since each local has its own name. Typical are:

Fort Dodge Musicians' Association, Local 504, Fort Dodge, Iowa;

Musicians' Protective Union, Local 495, Klamath Falls, Oregon;

Professional Musicians' Association, Locals 464-615, Beaumont-Port Arthur, Texas.

In other words, look up your local under M, first, since most of them are titled Musicians' something or other. If they're not listed that way, they're frequently listed under the name of the city, as the above Fort Dodge Example. If you have any trouble finding your local, your music teacher or another musician, playing in a club, or the local newspaper will certainly be able to help you.

Presumably the effectiveness of your joining the union will vary from local to local, but the important point is that you'll be meeting and developing relationships with other musicians.

This is obvious, but vital. I do not know of any other single group of people in the music business who are so willing to help each other as are musicians. If you haven't discovered this already, you surely will.

If you're in school it goes without saying that you should play with your school band or one or more of the groups in the school. Even if you do, you should also play, as frequently as possible, with outside groups, amateur or professional. As in any creative work the more you work at it, in addition to continuing to study and practice, the better you'll get. If you can join a professional band or group, that's naturally your best initial step.

If you're studying with a professional who also teaches, he may be your entree' into professional work. He may find a place for you with one of the bands he plays with, or he may have you substitute for him on an occasion when he can't make a gig.

The point is to be ready when the opportunity comes. This may be a good place to mention that it is highly desirable for a sideman to double, triple, quadruple or whatever on as many instruments as possible. The Bill Perkins rundown I gave you in the previous Chapter is a good, but extreme example. You'll discover, if you haven't already, that virtually all top sidemen play a number of instruments. Bob Hardaway, for example, plays tenor sax along with Bill in the Dick Grove Big Band, and is also one of the most in-demand of all Hollywood studio musicians. Bob plays the same long list of woodwinds as Bill, except for contra bass. On the other hand Bob also plays two other instruments Bill doesn't play, English Horn and oboe.

Another essential for a successful sideman is that he be

a good fast reader, and even more important that he be able to improvise effectively when there is a call for it. These elements cannot be stressed too strongly. And while we're describing qualifications for professional musicians we might insert here some of the rather obvious essentials:

1. Be reliable and prompt. Show up for the gig well ahead of time;

2. Be friendly and cooperative. Get along with the other sidemen, and do anything reasonable the leader and/or employer requests;

3. If you have the knowledge and talent, be helpful where you can . . . *if you're asked.* If there's a musical problem and you think you can help out by making a suggestion, do so. But don't be unwarrantedly aggressive. If you don't know the answer to a given problem, don't pretend you do.

But back to getting into the business:

Some cities have services or organizations other than the Union through which musicians may find out about groups or bands looking for sidemen. One such is the Musicians' Contact Service in Hollywood. Many local groups tell the MCS when a sideman drops out, and the service makes this information available to subscribing musicians for a small fee.

In the beginning of this book I stressed the importance of reading the tradepapers to keep informed about the business in general. Almost all the tradepapers from time to time, carry news items and advertisements about groups and/or bands looking for players. These should be watched.

Under certain circumstances it might even be advisable for a musician looking for a spot as a sideman to run an ad himself. The AFM *International Musician,* published monthly, carries many ads by musicians looking for gigs, and groups and bands looking for players. Classified ads or small display ads are not too expensive, and frequently get results.

Earlier in this Chapter I mentioned the AFM book listing the locals. You will have noted from the title that the book also lists agents, managers and sub-agents. Although most agents and managers, under normal circumstances, are not too concerned with placing sidemen with groups or bands, they do occasionally find the need to help out one of the units they book or manage by suggesting players to fill a vacancy. Thus, it might be wise for a young musician to make the rounds of the agents in town and leave his name and a resume, giving his musical training, background, experience, etc.

Again, as suggested earlier in the book, in connection with any kind of a music career — It is important to get into the business, even if you cannot get in immediately in the specific career for which you're aiming. Thus, if you can't get in as a musician right away, don't be discouraged. See if you can get some kind of a job, even if part time, with a company or a location where musicians consistently work.

For example, you might try for a job in a local recording studio, or a local rehearsal hall used by groups or bands, or a local club which plays groups and bands, or at the local concert hall or auditorium where travelling and local musical organizations play. If you're on the scene, in any way at all, your opportunity will come sooner or later.

And when it does, and you're a professional sideman, the rest is up to you. If you study and practice, you'll inevitably get better and better, and be more and more in demand. But remember that only a relatively small percentage of the 305,202 members of the AFM make their livings as full time musicians. Remember that the absolute ultimate for you as a sideman is to be a so-called studio musician in major centers such as Los Angeles or New York, or to a lesser degree Nashville, Chicago, and a handful of other cities.

Bill Perkins once told me, kidding of course, that the way to get the important gigs as a studio musician is to "sleep with the Contractor." The Contractor is a musician, who is called upon by record producers, tv and film producers, et al, to assemble a band as the needs arise. What Bill was getting at, of course, is that in addition to having to work fairly hard at becoming a good musician, you needed to be in good standing with the busiest Contractors.

But the important point to remember is that to

successfully compete for the relatively small number of gigs as a studio musician you have to play as well as or better than the Bill Perkinses and the Bob Hardaways. Are you willing to study that hard; practice those countless hours every day of every week of every year; become proficient on a number of instruments; practice on them all, all the time? If you are, fine. And good luck.

If you want to go into a career as a musician beyond being a sideman, read on.

*In the long run men hit*
*only what they aim at.*
Henry David Thoreau

## 28. VARIED SUCCESS STORIES

Take two drummers, Buddy Rich, let's say, and Roy
Burns. Buddy has pursued a commercial pop/jazz big band
career relentlessly down through the years, and today is at
one of his peaks. His concerts are consistently successful, and
his RCA Victor albums are winning wider and wider audiences.

Roy, after launching a spectacular big band drummer
career (with Woody Herman, Benny Goodman, Lionel Hamp-
ton and others) decided on a most interesting career switch.

He gave up playing with the top big bands to become
a representative for Rogers' Drums, a CBS subsidiary, and now
does drum clinics for dealers and in schools around the country.
Here's a sample section of one of Roy's recent tour schedules:

Latter portion, 1972: Nov. 18, Corona High School
Jazz Festival, Corona, Cal.; Nov. 25, Terry Gibbs Music Store,
Canoga Park, Cal.; Nov. 27, The Music Shop, West Los Angeles,
Cal.; Dec. 2 - 4, New York State School Music Association
Convention; Dec. 5, The Music Supply Shop, Red Bank, New
Jersey; Dec. 9, University of Pennsylvania, Stockton, Pa.; Dec.
13 - 16, National Association of Music Merchants Convention,
Potsdam, New York.

Early, 1973: Jan. 25, Marshall University, Huntington,

W. Va.; Feb. 3, Sam Houston University, Huntsville, Texas;
March 10, Hammond, Louisiana Jazz Festival; April 12 - 14,
Music Educators' Association West Virginia Conference,
Charleston, W. Va.; May 3, 4, Greater Southwest Music Con-
ference, Amarillo, Texas.

As he has pursued his new career as top pro drummer/
educator Roy has written the following drum books:
DRUM SET ARTISTRY
A book that analyzes all of the drum parts and drum solos. (With
accompanying record album.)
ROGERS INTERMEDIATE DRUM METHOD
(With Saul Feldstein)
Excellent junior high percussion method. Special section with
pictures and explanations of how to play traps, exercises to develop skills.
ROGERS ELEMENTARY DRUM METHOD
For the beginning school drummer. Emphasis on hand position,
reading, counting and beginning technique.
FINGER CONTROL
(With Lewis Malin)
Advanced special technique book for developing left hand speed
and all around sensitivity for both hands.
CYMBALS IN THE STAGE AND DANCE BAND
Complete instructions on playing, cleaning, care of and selection
of cymbals for the drum set.
ELEMENTARY ROCK AND ROLL DRUMMING
(With Howard Halpern)
A basic step-by-step method and study for the young player.
Includes hand and foot independence, easy rock beats and rock fill-ins.
ADVANCED ROCK AND ROLL DRUMMING
A complete method that includes dexterity studies to develop
hand and foot independence, standard rock beats, Latin-American rock
rhythms, Chelsea rhythms, and advanced West Coast "hip" rock and roll
rhythms.
ELEMENTARY PERCUSSION SOLOS, INTERMEDIATE PERCUSSION
SOLOS, and ADVANCED PERCUSSION SOLOS
(With Saul Feldstain)
A collection of solos exploring the tonalities and musical proper-

114.

ties of the snare drum.
DRUM SET MUSIC
(With Saul Feldstein)
A collection of solos exploring the tonalities and musical properties of the entire drum set.

As this is being written Roy is working with Dick Grove on the production of a new jazz/rock album starring Roy with the Dick Grove Big Band. This album, too, will be accompanied by a book, and the charts in the album, most of them arrangements of originals by Dick Grove, will be available to high school and college stage bands.

In short, where Buddy chose to build his own commercial band, Roy decided he could get greater satisfaction out of playing as a Clinician and working with young drummers than by continuing as a commercial big band musician and/or leader. Interestingly enough Roy says he plays more as a Clinician than he ever played in his busiest days as a top commercial pop/jazz sideman or leader.

Many musicians, of course, go into music education in a formal way, joining the Music Departments of elementary or secondary schools or colleges and universities. This is an area obviously quite removed from the commercial areas as such, so as indicated, we have included a section on formal music education as a career by Jack Wheaton.

Here let us continue our exploration of the commercial career avenues and combinations open to musicians. Let's take three trumpet players, at random:

Danny Davis, Bill Chase and Don Ellis.

When I first knew Danny he was a record producer, a so-called A&R (artist and repertoire) man on the staff of MGM Records. He then switched to RCA Victor, still as an A&R producer, in their New York headquarters. He produced many successful singles and albums. Ultimately he wound up in RCA's Nashville offices, and there once again picked up his horn and organized a group called the Nashville Brass. Danny's new brass group had a couple of hit singles and albums, became a successful night club and concert act, and while Danny is still with RCA he's now the leader of a Nashville-based, heavy horn group. How is he making out? Well, he and his brother John recently purchased a motel on Cape Cod in Massachusetts. Danny told Red O'Donnell, who writes *Record World's* Nashville Report column: "All I can tell you about it is that I can't afford to stay there. Room and board is $140 per day."

Bill Chase concentrated on the classical music field in his earliest years. Then, in the 60's, he took a chair with the Woody Herman band. Now he leads *Chase,* one of the most successful newer jazz/rock groups in the business. Chase's Epic records are big sellers, and the four trumpet-nine man group is one of the top college attractions in the country.

Ellis possibly is the outstanding example of the many directions in which a musician may go, depending on his willingness to study, practice, work and make sacrifices. Don went to Boston University, where he got a Bachelor of Arts degree in Composition. In the 50's, in his late teens and early twenties Don played with bands like Maynard Ferguson and Charlie Barnet. He got into the Army, where he worked with top musicians like Eddie Harris.

He finally put together a couple of groups of his own and worked jazz spots in New York's Greenwich Village. Early in the 60's he played with George Russell, talented composer and creator of the famous Lydian Chromatic Concept of Improvisation. In the mid-sixties Don put together his Big Band. He used his extensive musical training and background to experiment with odd time signatures, and with various unusual instruments and electric and electronic sounds. He played a four-valve trumpet, and used such devices as the wah-wah pedal, the echoplex and other sound expanders and distorters.

Along the way Don had also put together one of the earliest Indian-oriented jazz combinations, the Hindustani Jazz Sextet, and played many outstanding gigs as featured soloist, such as a date with the New York Philharmonic at Carnegie Hall with Leonard Bernstein conducting. In the meantime Don continued to study, back at the University of California in Los Angeles. He also took on a number of teaching assignments at

UCLA. His new big band eventually did well. Among the people who heard it, and dug it was a young man named Bill Friedkin. Friedkin is one of Hollywood's most successful young film directors. He contacted Don and told him that the sound of the Ellis band and Don's writing was exactly what he wanted for the musical score of *The French Connection*.

Don had done only one previous movie score, that for an obscure English film called *Moon Zero Two*. When he got the *Moon Zero Two* assignment, he knew very little about film scoring techniques. And here is a prime example of what I said earlier about how musicians help each other:

One of Don's musician friends is vibist and leader Tommy Vig. Tommy was taking a film scoring class at the time with Earle Hagen, one of the most talented and experienced scorers in films or television. Hagen's current class had already run for a month, but he not only permitted Don to take the Course on a catch-up crash basis, but gave Don a xeroxed copy of a book he had just finished writing, but hadn't yet published, called *Scoring for Films*.

But about Earle and this excellent book more later. The point here is that, thanks to his basic training with Earle, and his background and talent, Don wrote one of the most exciting scores of the motion picture year for the Award Winning *French Connection*.

And the further point is that Don got the assignment because he had developed an exciting band of his own, and he developed the exciting band because he had studied and practiced and experimented and worked hard ever since he blew his first note. Don, incidentally, still does a great deal of teaching, conducts clinics and has written and is publishing a book of his own. It's called *The New Rhythm Book* and comes with a companion record album. The book and record are designed to help players on any instrument achieve a maximum degree of fluency in unusual meters. Don also makes a number of his arrangements available to high school and college stage bands.

Again I could run down the entire body of musical

instruments, and we would find players who have branched out into any number of complementary activities. Don Ellis's big band is, of course, still substantially jazz and education-oriented. As are the previously mentioned bands of leaders like Stan Kenton and Woody Herman.

A far broader area, of course, and an area with a far greater potential for huge financial rewards (if less satisfying esthetically) are the non-jazz, non-education oriented groups and bands. I'm talking about the Lawrence Welks and the Rolling Stones. But before we make the leap to that wild arena, let us take a look at the Conductor/Director careers.

# PART I
## SECTION THREE

### Conductor/Director

*If to do were as easy as to know what*
*were good to do, chapels had been churches*
*and poor men's cottages princes' palaces.*
William Shakespeare

119.

## 29. A LUSH AREA – FILM, TV SCORING

Truly open only to accomplished and experienced musician-arranger-composer people is a quite limited but high-paying phase of the music business. That is the area of composing and functioning as musical director for motion pictures, television, Broadway musical productions, and super-star orchestral conducting.

Unless you are willing to learn a number of music crafts thoroughly and develop your skills painstakingly with hard work and experience over a period of many years, this area is not for you. Possibly one of the most typical examples of what it takes is the talented, highly successful musician-composer-arranger-conductor mentioned in the previous chapter, Earle Hagen.

In the golden era of the big bands, the late 30's and early 40's, Earle played trombone with some of the most successful orchestras of the day: Tommy Dorsey, Benny Goodman, Ray Noble, Benny Pollack. Came World War II and Earle went into the Army. He was stationed at the Santa Ana (California) Air Force Base and played with the Orchestra there. During the almost four years he was in the Air Force, he took up the study of composition, and worked hard at it.

When the war ended he became a free lance arranger,

and a good and successful one. His work came to the attention
of the late Alfred Newman, then in charge of music at the 20th
Century Fox motion picture studios. Newman hired him as an
arranger-orchestrator, and Earle worked for seven years at the
studio. Earle got a liberal education in dramatic scoring under
Newman, and credits the latter with a great deal of his success
in the field.

In the early 1950's Earle began to score for television
as well as for pictures. Since that time he has written and directed the musical scores for more than 2000 television shows.
He is generally working on as many as four series shows per
week, and his work for *I Spy* won him an Emmy.

All through those years, and into the present Earle has
continued his studies in composition, scoring, etc. He is still
studying with George Tremblay, whom Earle considers the
most advanced teacher of scoring in the world. Earle himself,
during the television off-season, teaches classes of professional
writer-musicians, as was indicated in the Don Ellis episode.

His book, *Scoring for Films* is the definitive work in
this area. It is a big, handsome book which covers three broad
sections: The mechanics and vocabulary of film composition;
the psychology of creating music for films; and the responsibilities of the composer. In the second of these, the ideas and
theories of such top fellow musician-composers as Newman,
Lalo Schifrin, Hugo Friedhofer, Quincy Jones and Jerrald
Goldsmith are presented, along with Earle's own ideas.

Earle's book is published by E.D.J. Music, Inc. of
Hollywood and sells for $15. It is worth ten times that to any-
one ready for this advanced kind of music career.

Equally successful in film and television scoring is
another highly trained and talented musician named Henry
Mancini. And Mancini has managed to combine his outstanding
composing and arranging with a string of hit RCA albums as
one of the record business's leading instrumentalists and orchestra leaders.

The backgrounds and capabilities of just two other musicians, among the top people in this area, should serve as all

the guidance a young musician interested in film and television scoring should need. Jack Elliott and Allyn Ferguson work as a team in the field of composition/arranging/musical direction in motion pictures, television, Broadway shows, etc.

On a rare occasion when he is available, and his availability coincides with their night club or concert appearances, singers like Johnny Mathis, Steve Lawrence and Edyie Gorme and others will prevail on Allyn to work as musical director for them. I might insert here, parenthetically, that working as musical director for, and/or playing accompaniment for solo singers is another area in which some musicians work. This is generally spotty and erratic employment, and there are a limited number of worthwhile jobs. Pay is fair to excellent, however. A singer like John Gary paid his musical directors, among whom were talented pianists like John Price and John Hammond, up to $750 per week. Someone like Ferguson would get more like $2500 per week for the Lawrence-Gorme gig.)

Elliott and Ferguson also take on an occasional assignment in television commercials, utilizing the same long developed compositional/arranging/musicianly skills.

Their list of credits (separately and/or jointly): Musical director for Broadway musicals such as *Fiorello, Tenderloin, Mr. President* and *She Loves Me;* Arranger/Conductor for Andy Williams for three seasons; musical director, television specials including Judy Garland, Jack Benny, Bill Cosby, *Taking Care of Business* with Diana Ross and the Supremes, Dionne Warwick, the Osmond Brothers, *Carousel, Kiss Me Kate, Kismet;*

Television series Theme Song Composition and/or Musical Direction: *The Dick Van Dyke Show, Bracken's World, Banacek,* numerous *Movies of the Week, Wackiest Ship in the Army, Farmer's Daughter, The Flintstones, The Monkees;*

Movie scores and musical direction: *The Happiest Millionaire* and *The Family Band* (both Disney); *Where's Poppa? Support Your Local Gunfighter, Get to Know Your Rabbit, T.R. Baskin, Myra Breckenridge;*

Innumerable Arranging/Conducting Assignments in Records and Night Clubs and Concerts for Andy Williams, Jack

Jones, Johnny Mathis, Buddy Greco, Robert Goulet, Jane
Morgan, Judy Garland, Jacqueline Francois, Patti Page, Diana
Ross and the Supremes, Buddy Rich, Doris Day, Caterina
Valente, Anthony Newley, Juliet Prowse, Leslie Uggams, Peggy
Lee, Joey Heatherton, Sergio Franchi, Steve Lawrence and
Edyie Gorme, Dusty Springfield, Jimmy Webb, Abbe Lane,
Nancy Wilson and many others.

I've listed these credits in one block because in many
of their activities, particularly in recent years, these two
outstanding musician/composer/arrangers have been inseperable.

Keep in mind that to work in these lucrative, rarefied,
highly competitive areas you *do* need very substantial formal
musical training. Here's Jack's:

Masters' Degree in Composition, Hart College of
Music; Columbia University; Tanglewood; Hebrew University
School of Sacred Music; Private study with Arnold Franchetti,
Bohislav Martinu and Lucas Foss. From 1956 through 1958
Jack lived in Paris and London, working for Phillips Records
and Jacqueline Francois as composer-conductor, and con-
tinuing his studies.

Here's Allyn's educational background: Ph.D. Stanford
University, Palo Alto, Calif.; Berkshire School of Music under
Aaron Copeland; teacher at Berkshire School of Music; Foun-
tainbleu Conservatory under Natia Boulonger. Allyn also organized and developed his internationally hailed Chamber Jazz
Sextet before joining Jack and concentrating his career on Composition, Arranging and Conducting.

As I've indicated the field of film, television and Broadway show composing/arranging/musical direction is a most
lucrative and demanding one. There are few opportunities
available, and those, by and large, go only to the most talented,
most highly trained, most experienced musicians. It's a goal
well worth shooting for, but if that is your goal be prepared for
a lifetime of never-ending study and hard work.

To lead your own rock group or commercial band in
any music style you don't need quite the extensive, in-depth

study, training and experience as musician, composer, arranger, director. It is even conceivable you could do well with almost no musical skill or training. For in this area of music careers many other elements, having nothing whatsoever to do with music, come into play:

Showmanship, charisma, sex appeal, emotionalism, all these are factors. And in this area, much more so than in the areas of education and/or composition/arranging/conducting people on the business side of music are major factors: Producers, agents, managers, press agents, promotion men, record company executives, disk jockeys, tradepaper and newspaper editors and critics — any one or two or all of them may turn out to be the key element in your success or failure.

Since all these elements also apply to singers as well as musicians, many of them are discussed in the Section in this book on singers. And many other aspects are treated in the portions of the book dealing with the Producer, the Commentator/Critic and Business careers in music.

But let's take a look at the musician who wants to lead a group or band . . . from his own immediate viewpoint.

# PART I

## SECTION FOUR

Group member or Leader
Band member or Leader

# 30. ANATOMY OF 2 ROCK GROUPS

Pause for another lesson from the past. In the golden era of the big bands, the late 1930s and early 40s, the major orchestras were the Dorseys, Tommy and Jimmy, Artie Shaw, Benny Goodman, Glenn Miller and a handful of others. They were not only commercially successful, but highly respected as purveyors of exciting swing. Beyond them, holding tighter to pure jazz were Count Basie, Duke Ellington, Cab Calloway, Jimmie Lunceford, Stan Kenton and Woody Herman. And beyond them too, in the opposite direction were what were called the Mickey Mouse bands. These sold schmaltz and included Sammy Kaye, Guy Lombardo, Blue Barron, Shep Fields and his Bubbling Rhythm. These were the big nationally famed, indeed internationally heralded bands.

Regionally, in the midwest for example, a few bands struggled along. Such as Larry Funk and Lawrence Welk. Small groups in those days generally consisted of piano, bass and drums — occasional quintets with a horn or two added — and worked in what were called cocktail lounges. Even the drinkers in the lounges paid little attention to them.

I was on *The Billboard* in those days and deeply into the big band picture. If someone had asked any of us observers

of the pop music scene which of those bands were destined to
achieve the greatest long term success, we undoubtedly would
have said Tommy Dorsey or Glenn Miller, maybe Shaw or
Goodman, the King of Swing. Or even if we guessed that the
Mickey Mousers would have longer lasting popular appeal we
would have said Kaye or Lombardo. The last two anyone would
have picked would have been Funk and Lawrence Welk, and I
don't know in which order.

Yet, poor Tommy choked to death on a piece of meat;
Glenn disappeared in an Air Force plane in World War II; Jimmy
died. Artie and Benny retired from the big band business. Shep
Fields stopped blowing bubbles and became an agent. Sammy
Kaye vanished to Lord knows where. Guy Lombardo went into
speedboat racing.

And Lawrence Welk emerged as the only orchestra to
sustain a highly successful big band show on national television,
first network, then syndicated into the 70s. And was by all odds
the most successful commercial big band of them all.

Lesson from the past:

No matter what your own choice of musical style, if
you like it and have faith in it, let nothing or noone you deter!
If jazz is your thing go that way; if you dig country, straight
ahead; if anyone of the almost countless forms of rock moves
you, stay with it.

Even if you want to go so far out as to try to start a
big experimental jazz band. As mentioned in an earlier chapter,
Don Ellis did it. He put together a twenty man orchestra in
1966. But unless you're a Don Ellis, with his background,
training, dedication and connections, I surely wouldn't advise
you to try the big band route. Even Don's exciting and talented
bunch of players could only get a gig on an average of one night
a week in their earliest days. It was only by a steady series of
dates at School Jazz Festivals, and thanks to a string of attention-
arresting albums that Don was able to get the band off the
ground.

Today, of course, the situation has reversed itself completely from the big band days of the 30s and 40s. In a number
of highly significant ways:

1. Smaller groups of all kinds are in huge demand, while the demand for the larger groups is severely limited. There are many reasons for this, economic and otherwise, which we needn't go into here.

2. Where big band instrumentation was fairly constant (four or five brass; four, five or six woodwinds; piano; guitar; bass; drums; occasional percussion or vibes or accordion, etc.) today's instrumental combinations are almost unlimited. And when you add the synthesizers, wah-wahs, ring modulators and a thousand and one other electric and electronic devices to the basic instruments, the opportunities to create new sounds are truly unlimited.

3. Where the big bands of generations past had a choice of three or four basic styles (Jazz, swing, mickey mouse, etc.) musicians putting together today's groups have literally dozens of styles or combinations of styles to play in. And more develop all the time.

Here are just a few current group styles (with samplings of the groups working in each):

*Progressive Soul Rock* — Earth, Wind and Fire; Osiba;

*Country Swing/Rock* — New Riders of the Purple Sage; Flying Burrito Brothers; Asleep at the Wheel; Dan Hicks and the Hot Licks; Poco;

*Jazz/Rock* — Blood, Sweat & Tears; Chicago; Chase; Charles Mangione.

*Motown Rock* — Temptations; Supremes;

*Soft Rock* — Bread; The Carpenters; Carole King; James Taylor.

*Classical/Rock* — Emerson, Lake & Palmer;

*Bubble-Gum Rock* — Jackson Five; Osmond Brothers;

*Unisex-Bisex Rock* — Alice Cooper; the Kinks; David Bowie; Shady Lady; Queen;

*Feminine Lib Rock* — Joy of Cooking; Fanny; Birtha;

*Pop/Rock* — Kenny Rogers and the First Edition;

*Hard Rock* — Jefferson Airplane; Grand Funk Railroad; Black Sabbath;

*Latin or Mariachi Rock* — Santana;

Not to mention psychedelic, acid, and a dozen other forms developing.

Let's run down the backgrounds of each of the members in two Rock groups. The diversity in formal training, experience will once again be apparent. Let's take *Bread,* who have had a number of successful albums on Elektra, a string of guest shots on major network television shows, and do regular concert tours. In a *Record World* poll they were selected the "Best New Rock Group of the Year" (1970-1971).

The two key members are James Griffin and David Gates. I say "key" because Griffin and Gates write the great majority of the tunes the group does, and it's become almost axiomatic that the most successful young groups today have one or more members who write their own material. (I might mention here, parenthetically, that this is obviously also a great advantage to the group from a standpoint of survival and economic growth, since the writer and often the publisher earnings from these songs, goes a long way to enabling the group to sustain, build and promote itself).

Griffin is from Memphis. He plays guitar and his early training was classical. He practiced about six hours a day. Among his country friends were Dorsey Burnette and his brother John, quite active in music circles. When Griffin was about eighteen he was living in Los Angeles, already writing songs. Dorsey brought Jim to Reprise Records, where he auditioned and won his first record deal.

Gates is a Tulsa, Oklahoma boy and although he now plays guitar, his early instrument was violin. He took lessons from the concertmaster of the Tulsa Philharmonic when he was four years old. Dave's dad was band and orchestra director of the public schools in Tulsa and his mother played and taught piano. Dave formed his first rock bands to play local high school and college dates, while he was going to University of Tulsa and University of Oklahoma. He left school after his junior year, and came out to California, where he got into the music business by playing guitar at local clubs, wherever he could get a gig. He started writing arrangements, and soon was

turning out charts for people like Buck Owens, Duane Eddy,
Merle Haggard and Glenn Campbell. He wrote the chart for
Glenn Yarborough's hit record *Baby, the Rain Must Fall.* He
got into record production, and joined a group called *Pleasure
Faire,* another member of which was Jim Griffin. Jim and
Dave got along beautifully, musically and as people.

Mike Botts is from Sacramento, California. I don't
know whether the musicians' union had the Young Sounds
Program going at the time, but Mike joined the union at the
ripe old age of 12, one year after he got his first set of drums.
In his earlier years he was strongly jazz oriented. He was only
15 when he played with Wes Montgomery's group. Later, in
San Francisco, he worked with Jimmy Smith. He studied music theory, composition, orchestration, arranging and sight
reading at Sacramento City College. Mike was with a group
called The Travellers 3 when he met Dave Gates. He was already into studio work as a drummer, and had even done some
production. He put together a group of his own called *Joshua
Fox,* but the group couldn't make it. Mike went back to
studio work, until Gates finally persuaded him to join *Bread.*

The keyboard man in *Bread,* Larry Knechtel is a
self-taught musician. He's from Bell, California and plays
organ, piano, bass, guitar and harmonica. He taught himself
on an old piano his parents bought him, and while still in his
teens, played well enough to be in pretty constant demand at
churches, private parties and with various local groups. For
five years he was on the road with Duane Eddy. Phil Spector
began to use him on record sessions. He did the Byrd's *Mr.
Tambourine Man, Classical Gas* and cut sessions with Simon
& Garfunkel, the Jackson Five, John Phillips, Jimmy Webb
and many others. He was one of the busiest young studio
men in town, doing literally hundreds of sessions when Dave
Gates talked him into signing on with *Bread.*

*The First Edition,* among other honors, holds the
distinction of being the first rock group to have its own syndicated television show in prime time. Kenny Rogers is the key
man in the group (it's often called Kenny Rogers and the

First Edition) and is a singer-musician who had his first hit record *Crazy Feeling* back in 1958. He played with blind pianist Bobby Doyle and his Trio and the New Christy Minstrels. He's from Dallas, Texas.

Terry Williams is from Hollywood, California and both his mother and father were with the Tommy Dorsey band, dad on trombone, mom on vocals. Terry started playing guitar at 14, left college two days after he started. He worked for a while as a promotion man with Warner Bros. Records, and then went out with the New Christy Minstrels.

Kin Vassy does the hard rock vocals, plays piano and guitar, although he played trumpet for eight years before he took up guitar. His dad owned a radio station in Carrollton, Georgia and Kin worked as a disk jockey on the station. He learned his music primarily in church. He worked with Randy Sparks' *Back Porch Majority* before getting with the Edition.

Mickey Jones, the group's drummer is from Dallas, Texas. He worked with Trini Lopez for eight years, Johnny Rivers for three, and was a member of the Bob Dylan group called The Band, till Dylan had his motorcycle accident.

Mary Arnold replaced her room-mate, Terry Camacho, who was an original member of *The Edition*. She's from Audibon, Iowa, and majored in music at Drake University. She continued her studies at the Los Angeles Conservatory of Music, and then went out with *The Young Americans*. She also did some time with *The Kids Next Door* before she joined the Rogers' group.

The point, again, is you may be a young man or woman, from the north, south, east or west; exhaustively musically trained or self-taught, and you may work with or start your own group. There are literally tens of thousands of groups of all kinds around the country today. Some will make it; the great majority won't.

*Bread* got its initial support from a record company, Jac Holzman's Elektra. *The Edition,* because their manager, Kenny Kragen was also the manager of the Smothers Brothers' (with another young man named Ken Fritz) in those days, got their big start through exposure on the Smothers' Brothers television show. Tommy treated them almost as a personal discovery.

Before you attempt to start your own group, of course, the more experience you get working with other groups the more you'll learn about what goes into the making and development of a successful one. Maybe the best way to get a look at a number of the elements that do go into a rock group's development would be to analyze one of the most fabulously successful of them all, the Rolling Stones.

## 31. A STUDY OF THE STONES

How limited should you consider yourself to be in selecting the musical style for your group?

Back to that? Yes, but only because the Rolling Stones
are an intriguing example of how unlimited and wildly im-
probable your choice may be. The Stones were formed in 1962.
They were five working class Englishmen, and they decided
their sound was going to be the rawest kind of black, American
—Afro deep south blues. Okay?

Any sound you really are into, any music that moves
you is the way to go.

The Stones' last tour here in the United States, 53 performances in 32 cities in the summer of 1972 played to well
over three quarters of a million people and grossed over
$4,000,000. Critical raves surpassed anything seen since Presley
erupted and the Beatles were at their pre-bust up peak.

What were the Stones really selling? The same thing
Sinatra sold on the stage of the Paramount Theater three decades
earlier, when hundreds of hysterical teen age girls screamed
and sobbed and fainted in the aisles. The same thing that turned Bill Haley's *Rock Around the Clock* into a super smash
after it had lain dead for a year before it was made the theme

song of that film of youthful rebellion, *The Blackboard Jungle*.

The same thing that Presley sold when he bumped and ground his swivelly hips like a burlesque stripper, and his generation of teen age females screamed and cried in joyful, orgasmic hysteria.

Sex and vicarious danger and rebellion. That's what Sinatra and Presley and the Stones sold and sell, each to the daring permissable ultimate of his day. When Sinatra glissandoed his way through oh, such a hungry yearning burning inside of me, and caressed the mike stand he was exuding the same maximum sexuality for the sedate 40s that Presley did for the 50s and that Mick Jagger does to today's crop of young females. Presley added a then-daring gyration of his pelvic area. Jagger uses his pelvic region, his tongue, the whip, the works.

Sinatra managed through his career, to sustain a strong air of controversy, lurking wickedness and danger.

Why did he beat up Lee Mortimer, the powerful night club columnist of the New York Daily Mirror?

Did he really hang out with Mafioso?

How could he leave Nancy and the kids for that sexpot Ava Gardner?

Tom Parker, Presley's incredible manager, got maximum mileage out of the puritan protests against the young Tupelo truck driver's sexual gestures.

And Jagger and the Stones have lived a whole series of oooeeh episodes of danger and rebellion. One of their original members Brian Jones was found dead at the bottom of his swimming pool. A boy was murdered by a Hell's Angel security man at a Stones concert at the Race Track in California. The threat of drug busts hangs over the heads of the group like clouds on a stormy day. Jagger wears shirts with the word "coke" embroidered on them and nobody thinks he's pushing soft drinks. Their biggest songs are raw, sexy sagas of women ravished without sweet talk or mercy.

But do they do four million dollars worth of business on a U.S. tour just because they're naughty, seventy-two style? Of course not. It takes the highest degree  of planning and professionalism on the part of many people and organizations.

Start with a simple one:

*Make-up!*

Jagger carefully paints purple eyeshadow on his lids, uses generous applications of black eyeliner and mascara on the long lashes. Golden sparkles are meticulously applied at the corners of the eyes, sprinkled moistly over the chest, which will be bared to the navel in due course. Lipstick on the full mouth, of course, and lavish use of the more orthodox bases, powders, rouges, which are part of every performer's arsenal.

*Wardrobe:* Skin tight lilac jump suit, silver lame frock coat; pink or golden sash or belt, which later in the show, at a properly frenzied moment, becomes a natural orgiastic whip. With coat removed, black, gold and silver slave bracelets on bare arms, beads swinging from muscled neck.

Nothing new about this, of course. Liberace has worn sequined coats for years, and even throws in a candelabra. Presley and Tom Parker got great publicity mileage out of a gold lame suit, for which Nudie, the rodeo tailor, was said to have charged Tom and Elvis $10,000.

Nothing new, but one small element in building an attention-arresting, showmanly act, group or single.

Apart from writing the majority of the Stones' big songs with guitarist Keith Richard, Jagger, of course, is the non-musician of the group. But in a very real sense he is the greatest "musician" of them all.

Tommy Thompson of Life describes him:

"He is possessed, as few performers are - - - Callas, El Cordobes, Nureyev come to mind - - - with a stunning, electric shock stage capacity. Watch him prowl the space, pantherlike at first, suddenly a marionette abandoned by the string-puller, now cheerleader at an orgy, the voice harsh, torn from the throat, the lyrics banal, the music overwhelming in its amplification."

Or the view a couple of *Billboard* reviewers have of him: Nat Freedland catching a West Coast performance:

" . . . a veritable spastic Nureyev, a demonic eye-riveting

force purified with the years to an ultimate of rock showmanship." And Sam Sutherland seeing the Stones at Madison Square
Garden in New York: " . . . As for Jagger, it would be pointless
to rave: His presence, whether it is evaluated as a symbolic
cultural value or an extension of his music, is now so firmly im-
printed on our minds as to be beyond description. In short,
Jagger is, on stage, everything we want him to be, majestic
satanist and icon of supple decadence . . . "

In short, in Jagger and his performance, the musical
meaning and message of the Stones comes into blinding, sex-
oozing, wicked focus. Group planners pay heed: If you can
find a front man who conveys in his physical and performing
presence, whatever musical quality it is that your group is selling, grab him whether he plays an instrument or not, or just
counts ah-vun, ah-two, ah-three . . . vunnerful, vunnerful.

The musician Stones, Richard, Nicky Hopkins, Charlie
Watts, Mickey Taylor (who replaced the deceased Jones), Bill
Wyman (and sometimes Jimmy Price and Bobby Keys) don't
need to make-up and dress like Jagger. Keith Richard, as
normal garb, wears a gold earring on one ear, and has a
Minerva-like head of dark curls, and works his little paint
box over quite a bit before he goes on, but the frontman is
Jagger, of course, and the act's effectiveness is intensified to
the nth degree by the simple, single wise decision to back him
up with what almost all pop music critics call the best rock
band in the world.

*Billboard's* Sutherland says it for many of them, this
way: " . . . quite simply, the Rolling Stones are the most
powerful band in the world. Whether that power is a consequence of mere longevity, or a coincidence of musical and
cultural ideas, or a media fantasy, is debatable, but ultimately
impossible to determine. They're the strongest. And that
strength can pull 20,000 people (at Madison Square Garden
in New York on this occasion) together for two hours, leaving
them dazed and weary. If a sense of loneliness hangs in the
air when it's over, who's to say where that desolation
originates?"

Several items, however, in a career study, are determinable, and not debatable. In every instance of super-success the
basic musical talent, in whatever style, was and is there.
Sexuality, rebellion fine, but Sinatra and Presley were and are
vast pop singing talents, and the Stones, after working hard
and dedicatedly together for ten years are one helluva blues/
country/soul rock musical group.

So consider and try to utilize every element of showmanship, but don't neglect the basic musical quality, whatever
the style. Work, work and work to make it the best it can be.
All the other elements will contribute to bringing it out, drama-
tizing it, selling it. But they'll never substitute for it.

One other point non-debatable and fully determinable.
Studied development, planning and execution of the act and
its message by super-pros is the ultimate payoff. In the case of
the Stones I don't know whether it was their early manager,
Andy Oldham or Jagger or Richard or whoever, who dreamed
up the wicked red devil's face with lascivious, rebellious, tongue
sticking out at the world, as the group's emblem. Whoever did,
the satanic tongue says it well.

And the Stones' spokesmen, primarily Jagger and
Richard, live up to the posture of Lucifer in a very real every
day sense. Jagger told *Life's* Thompson re the murder of the
young man at the Altamont race track: " . . . some people
wanted to say Altamont was the end of an era. People like·that
are fashion writers. Perhaps it was the end of their era, the end
of their naievete. . . "

And Richard told Thompson, of Altamont: " . . . it
was just another gig, a gig where I had to split quick. There've
been far worse gigs . . . last time we played Long Beach in 1969,
a terrifying scene. We were sitting in a limousine that was literally being crushed by people sitting and jumping on the roof.
Suddenly blood spurted down the windshield and we were
holding up the roof with our hands."

Either Jagger or Stone could easily have made speeches
about their deep regret that this should have happened to one
of their fans, and vowed an unrelenting determination to see that

it never happened again. But that would hardly be the Stones'
image. Actually the planning of their last tour - - - no doubt at
fantastic expense to themselves - - - did represent as close to a
total effort to avoid violence and tragedy as is humanly possible.

And the same planning and execution by the professionals involved made the Stones' show, and makes the Stones as a
group the multi-million dollar rock success they are. A full year
before the scheduled June kick-off date for the tour a brilliant
young Cambridge graduate, a man named Peter Rudge (hired
by the Stones) quietly booked auditoriums all around the
country for dates in June and July of 1972. After the locations
were booked he let the word get out that American promoters
could enter bids to handle a Stones concert in their vicinity.
The promoters were carefully screened, not only as to financial
reliability, experience, reputation, but also security precautions
possibly unmatched in the history of American showbusiness
were made.

Rudge also worked out a most careful procedure for
selling tickets to the concerts so that the maximum number of
Stones fans could buy them at box office prices, rather than
from scalpers. In the meantime the Stones also hired a young
man, who is possibly the most brilliant stager of rock and other
attractions developed in the past decade. His name is Chip
Monck and he has done the lighting and staging for some of the
most outstanding music acts and events of recent years. These
include the *Concert for Bangla Desh,* the Monterey Pop Festival, Woodstock, John Lennon and Yoko Ono's *One to One*
Benefit and the Motown Pavillion Discotheque at Black Expo
in Chicago. Monck had also done the lighting for the Stones
previous European Tour.

The huge backdrop with Satan and his hanging tongue,
the countless lighting effects, and towers, the mirrors, all
represented the talented, untiring efforts of Chip Monck and
are yet another factor in making the Stones the group they
were.

An entire book could be written on the personnel and
the equipment which constituted the last Stones' tour. Suffice

to say here, that thirty five full time people were involved, and more than five hundred items of equipment, lights, mikes, mirrors, backdrops, flats, and on ad infinitum. Peter Rudge supervised, among his other duties, the transportation of this mass of people and materiel, via plane, train or whatever to the 32 cities on the Tour schedule.

Then, one other small detail, Jagger's idea. At every show the first twenty rows of seats were reserved. Not for important press, radio or television people; not for the state's governor or the city's mayor; not for President Nixon or even Spiro Agnew, but for the most representative of Jagger's and the Stones true fans, young people. It is to them the group works, it is from them the Stone's draw the inspiration to whip themselves and their instruments, Jagger's vocal chords and body; Richard's guitar; Hopkins' piano, the works into delivering the most frenzied, emotion-packed, yet highly disciplined rock in musical history.

All points to remember when putting together and developing your own group. Naturally you cannot do what the Stones do. In 1962 the Stones couldn't do it either. But in 1965 they broke through with their first important records, and they developed from there, step by tough step.

I have pondered the possibility of attempting to give some advice and guidance on how a group or band survives economically through its early stages. Where does it get the money to buy equipment, instruments, amplifiers, wardrobe, whatever? There is no way to answer that question.

Each musical organization, each individual member of that organization must find its or his or her own way. Many work at other jobs to support themselves and finance themselves until they get a break. Others have rich patrons who bankroll them, whether parents or relatives, affluent members of the Mafia, an agent or manager who has faith in their talent.

At a certain point of development, many get basic financing from a record company, which sees them through the roughest periods. In the final analysis, as I've said, however each must find his own way, and work and pray for the breaks.

I want to make one other point clear before going on:

I hold no special brief for the Stones or their style. I neigher recommend it or decry it. I could have used the Lawrence Welk band to make the same points. For Satan's slithery tongue substitute a backdrop of bubbles floating out of a thin stemmed glass.

I am detailing for you the elements that go into the making of a group or any entertainment body, group or single. There are, of course, others, like agents, managers, etc. but let's view them in their relationship to singers. And to a further extent in the Sections of this book dealing with the people on the commentary and business sides.

140.

PART I

SECTION FIVE

Singer

## 32. OF COMO & DARIN

Many of today's singers come out of the groups we have
been discussing:
Van Morrison, Elton John, Neil Young, Stephen Stills,
James Taylor, each of the four Beatles, of course, McCartney
(sometimes with wife Linda); Lennon (sometimes with wife
Yoko); Harrison; Starr. The late Janis Joplin started with Big
Brother and the Holding Company.
The effort to analyze the careers of many of these
young singers for purposes of professional guidance is frequently unhappily beclouded by a heavy smog of drugs, which have
become so much a part of our pop music and youth cultures.
Taylor and Joplin, just to name two, were, of course, deeply
and destructively into dope. In a later portion of this book I
will say a word about the whole drug question as it relates to
music careers. Here our purpose will be far better served if we
review the anatomy of a successful singer in examples and experiences where drugs are not part of the picture. I think this
is a valid approach because the basics are the same, drugs or no
drugs.
As an example, I don't think Elvis Presley would have
become what he became if he had not had the good fortune to

acquire Tom Parker as his manager. In like manner, I am not
sure James Taylor would ever have emerged as an important
singing star if he had not had the good fortune in London to
meet and be guided by Peter Asher, who not only served as
his record producer, but became his manager.

So let's stay with the basics.

Some ingredients:

Surely voice is no real factor. Bob Dylan's and Mick
Jagger's voices are hardly as lyrically lovely as, say, John
Gary's pure, sweet two octave baritone-almost tenor tones.
Janis never sounded like Julie Andrews. In other words, voice
is a high variable, and like the music style you choose, may
take any direction or combination of directions.

How about attitude?

In the late 40s I was director of Artists & Repertoire
for RCA Victor. The most important artist on the label at the
time was Perry Como. You have heard that Perry is Mr. Nice
Guy. Believe it, he is. He is truly one of the nicest people I
have ever known. At the time I had five producers on my
A & R staff: Hugo Winterhalter, Henri Rene, Dewey Bergman,
Steve Sholes and Charlie Grean. Each of them and I spent a
good deal of time every day of the week with talented songwriters and music publishers looking for material for the
artists on the label.

Because of Perry's importance, I instructed each of the
A & R men to hold the one, two or more of the best songs they
encountered for Perry's consideration before passing them on
to any other artists. Two or three weeks before Perry was due
to record, an accompanist and I would get with him and run
down the songs we'd accumulated. Keep in mind that these
songs were the absolute cream of the current crop. There were
usually about twenty songs in a given batch.

Perry is a careful, intelligent and deliberate man. We
would play each song, and Perry's reaction to approximately
two thirds of the twenty songs, would be:

"Hmm, that's nice. I like that. Let's hold it for a while."

The end of the review session consequently found me
with a request to hold approximately fifteen of the best pop

songs available, until Perry decided which three or four he would like to cut at the next record date. And frequently it would take Perry a month or two to make his final choice.

At the end of one of these review sessions I said, "Perry, you know that all of us recognize that you are the number one artist on the label. That's why we scrounge around and put aside all the best material we can find for you. But please consider that there are other artists on the label, and that we need strong material for them, too. So . . . "

Perry put his arm around me, and said with a little smile: "Joe, let's not worry about the other artists."

In the mid-fifties I was operating a thriving talent management-music publishing-record & show production business with my partners, Charlie Grean and Edgar Burton. We handled Eddy Arnold, Norman Leyden, (who was then musical director for the Arthur Godfrey five times a week CBS radio show, and a leading composer/arranger/conductor of the day, now a successful music educator); Betty Johnson (who had had a couple of strong records and was doing well in clubs and on television (particularly with Jack Paar); Jim Lowe (whose *Green Door* was one of the biggest hit records of the era) and a number of other people.

Ahmet Ertegun, the brilliant head of Atlantic Records brought Bobby Darin and his attorney in one day. Bobby was recording for Atlantic then, a very new young talent, and Ahmet was recommending that Bobby take us on as personal managers. We worked out a seven year contract.

Bobby, who is as you know, a multi-talented, shrewd and hard-working young man, did very well. At the end of a year or two he had a number of hit records, among which were *Splish Splash, Plain Jane* and others, all of which he wrote himself. He was getting $5000 for a guest shot on shows like The Perry Como television Show, about $2000 per week touring with Irvin Feld's Rock Shows, and had just made a most exciting album for Atlantic, entitled *BOBBY DARIN - - - That's All. That's All* was the title tune, written by a young songwriter named Bud Brandt, but the album also contained a quite spectacular arrangement by Dick Wess of a Kurt Weill song called *Mack, the Knife.*

Sometime before the album was released, however, Bobby called me from somewhere on the road.

He wanted to come back into New York for a most important meeting. He had made up his mind that he had reached the point in his career where he needed a personal manager, who would devote his full time and energies to the career of Bobby Darin. From the standpoint of my own career, I didn't think it would be wise to give up everything I had built to that point, and to cast my lot with a single artist. No matter how successful I thought that artist might become. The result was that we worked out a deal for Bobby to buy out of the remaining portion of his contract with us.

We gave him his release and he did an extremely smart thing, he took on as exclusive, full time personal manager a young man named Steve Blouner, who was an agent in the offices of General Artists Corporation, who were booking Bobby at the time. Blouner's salary was somewhere between $100 and $200 per week, so he had nothing to lose in giving up his job and working exclusively for and with Bobby. He did an excellent job for Bobby, and is today one of the more successful television and film producers in Hollywood.

These two tales point up some essentials for achieving success as a singer: - - -

In every aspect of your professional life, - - - the search for and selection of songs, a singer's life-blood - - - the time, energies, talents of those working with you be utterly, totally selfish. Perhaps that's not very nice advice, from a humanistic standpoint, but I have never encountered a successful performer in the music/record business who did not practice this kind of professional ruthlessness.

Happily other requisites for success coincide far more with humanistic considerations. The outstanding example of this, in my experience, is Eddy Arnold.

*Some nice guys may finish last, but some*
*make it bigger and last longer*
*than guys who aren't nice.*
Papa Gyor

145.

## 33.  AN ALL TIME GREAT — EDDY ARNOLD

I don't know a singer who has had a longer, more successful career than Eddy Arnold. I got to know Eddy slightly
in the early 40s when I was Editor in Chief of *Billboard*, then
developed a warm relationship with him when I became head
of Artists & Repertoire at RCA about 1948. At that time, Eddy
was already one of the biggest singing stars in the country, but
he was considered *pure* Country. He had never had a pop hit
record, nor did he work very many so-called pop night clubs or
pop shows. He hardly needed to.

My biggest problem as head of RCA A & R, when it
came to scheduling the release of a new Eddy Arnold record,
was the simple fact that at any given point Eddy already had
seven or eight records in the Country Top Ten list, and these
seven or eight records had been on the best selling lists for
many, many months. The question, eternally, was "How many
Eddy Arnold records can you have on the market all at the
same time?" There is no question that Eddy was then the number one Country singer of the day.

Some time later, around 1953 I had set up Csida-Grean
Associates, my talent management firm. Eddy called me one
day shortly after we started and told me that he and Tom Par-

ker were splitting, and he wanted to talk about my taking over
as his personal manager. When we got together he explained
what he had in mind.

"I don't want to be remembered as just a *Country*
singer," he told me. "I'd like to be remembered as a good singer,
period."

In the early 50s the flow of Country music into the pop
mainstream was barely a trickle. The prospect of trying to cross
Eddy over into the pop areas without losing his position as the
day's top country singer was a challenging and intriguing one. I
took Eddy on thankfully and with great enthusiasm.

Here are the attitudes, which contributed most (apart
from his singing and performing talents, of course) to making
Eddy Arnold one of the most successful singers in America over
the longest period of years in showbusiness. These are attitudes
every singer, every performer should strive to develop.

Our efforts to bust Eddy through into the pop areas
met with mixed success. Eddy put up his own money to finance
the production of a television film series, the first to star a singer, but we weren't able to put enough pop touches into the
series to make it effective. CBS signed Eddy to do his own network radio series, emanating from Nashville, but again we were
unable to make a pop impact with the series.

RCA went all out to help us. We recorded two of Eddy's
biggest country and western hits, *Cattle Call* and *Wagon Wheels*
with brilliant, sparkling new pop/concert style arrangements by
Hugo Winterhalter, featuring a full band with sixteen strings,
eight brass and the best rhythm section New York had to offer
at the time. It didn't quite work. The pop market wasn't ready,
and worse yet, country disk jockeys wouldn't play the record.

"I can't play a record with all them bugles," one of the
top country jockeys told me at the annual WSM Disk Jockey
convention in Nashville that year.

We managed to get major network television guest shots
like *The Ed Sullivan Show* but the result was that in the ten
year period that followed, we struggled with uneven success.
Then, some time after I had taken on the presidency of a new

record company called Recording Industries Corporation, largely through Eddy's prompting and influence, Eddy busted through on the pop side.

A highly talented Australian arranger named Bill Walker, moved to Nashville. The flow of country into the pop mainstream was beginning to become a roaring river, largely on the strength of a magic arranging touch which somehow combined country with pop to the delight of fans of both markets. Bill did Eddy a few arrangements and Eddy's records were bigger than ever, and his career skyrocketed anew. For the first time he played pure pop supper clubs like the Cocoanut Grove in Los Angeles, the major showrooms in Las Vegas. Every important television variety show used him, and his Concerts drew hordes of pop fans along with his basic country fans.

Now a major reason this happened is that throughout this period, the years when he had seven or eight of the top ten Country records on the charts, week in and week out; through the period when we were trying to find our way across into the pop realm; throughout the new hit period Eddy never changed one bit.

He never worked for a concert promoter or club owner, to whom he wasn't warm, polite, friendly and cooperative. The same went for radio and/or television producers, directors, writers, musical directors; the same for songwriters, arrangers, engineers and producers in the record studios.

He was never late for, let alone missed a rehearsal or show call. He met and was genuinely interested in, and warm and cooperative with literally hundreds of people in RCA, pro-motion men, publicity men, advertising and merchandising men, field managers, distributors and their staffs. He was never too busy, or too tired for a newspaper, tradepaper or magazine in-terview, whether the *Dubuque Gazette* or *Life Magazine*. He never made an appointment to do a disk jockey show he didn't keep.

The net result was that at the very first sign of a new breakthrough, every conceivable kind of a person and/or

148.

company involved with a performer's career jubilantly went all out. Helping Eddy hit new peaks after a twenty year career was more kicks than breaking out a new star.

But since the *don'ts* are as important as the *dos*, let me give you some examples of those.

*Every man has a right to be conceited*
*until he is successful.*
    Benjamin Disraeli

149.

## 34. DON'T DO DON'TS

Betty Johnson came from a singing family. She was born and grew up in Possum Walk Road, North Carolina. We got very lucky with her very fast when we took her on as managers, largely through the efforts of my partner Charlie Grean, who fell in love with her, and thus gave her even more attention than we generally gave our performer clients. Charlie worked very closely with Fred Ebb (who, as mentioned in the Songwriter section of this book, has since gone on to become one of the top Broadway musical comedy and drama writers of the day with *Cabaret* and other great shows to his credit). They developed a song called *I Dreamed,* then another called *The Little Blue Man* both of which became fairly big-sized hit records for Betty.

This led to a shot on the Jack Paar Tonight show, which was then at its peak. Paar, you'll recall specialized in presenting people he felt were a little unusual, Genevieve, Dodie Goodman, Charlie Weaver, et al. He found the notion of a young girl singer from, of all places, Possum Walk Road intriguing, and began to use Betty more and more frequently. Eddy Arnold used her as a regular in his television film series. She became the regular girl singer on the ABC network Don

McNeil Breakfast Club. She grew and grew.

Image-wise what I had in mind from the beginning, of
course, was the sweet, calicoed unspoiled, country girl. And
that's how it worked . . . and worked well.

Until one day we booked Betty into the Copacabana
in New York. Charlie's romance with Betty was nearing the
wedding stage, and he had lost all ability to direct her at all.
My own ability to call the shots diminished. Somewhere just
before the Copa opening she met a very talented, very chichi
man named Bart Howard. Bart wrote *Fly Me to the Moon,* one
of the best songs of its day, and still a great standard. Bart also
staged chichi style club acts.

Betty and Charlie came in one day and told me that for
the Copa they were going to do the big switch. They were going
to startle the people. A new, super Betty Johnson was going to
be born. No more calico, no more Possum Walk Road. Six
hundred dollar flowing chiffon evening gowns; Fifth Avenue
coiffeurs; a "class" society style singer was to replace the corn-
fed lass from Possum country.

To cut a long tale: Bombsville! The new Betty went
straight down. Paar wasn't interested in another girl singer in
expensive evening gowns, he'd been building a character from
Possum Walk Road. The same disk jockeys who played *I Dreamed* and *The Little Blue Man* passed up slick, sophisticated new
records.

Moral: Nine times out of ten it's better to build your
act on the solid base of what you are. Or at least what your
most saleable surface image is. Sow's ears make poor silk
purses. Girls from Possum Walk Road make poor sultry supper
club sirens. Miss Peggy Lee of North Dakota is the only exception I can think of.

But the King of the Dont's, oddly enough, is a person I
believe had a greater opportunity to become a long time super
star than anyone I've ever observed. In this book I will call him
Percy Songbird.

To begin with, I said a little earlier that voice is not
really essential to a successful singing career. But if you have a

good voice, it can be important.

A taste in voices is, of course, quite an individual matter, but in my judgment, Percy Songbird had a sweeter voice than John McCormack or John Gary, Dennis Day or Nelson Eddy. The best basic instrument, the purest, sweetest voice of any male pop singer I have ever known. While he abused himself mentally and physically, he also had developed tremendous lung power, breath control and refined most of the techniques of the singing trade.

Thanks to the extraordinary efforts of scores of people at a major record company we shall call Magnitude Records, who brought out and promoted his first albums; thanks to the efforts of his manager in planning his career; thanks to the scheming and plotting and execution of a group of agents in an agency we'll call Gigantic, (all of whom I'll cover in an exhaustive treatment of the career of Percy Songbird in the Personal Manager Section of this book) he did have one of the most meteoric rises of any singer of his era. Percy was flat broke when his manager took him on and by the end of the first year he was making more than $250,000 per year. This climbed to $500,000 per year. He had a long string of hit albums and two of his own national television shows, but here are some of the *dont's* he perpetrated:

1. As soon as he had established himself with three or four successive hit albums he began to give Magnitude's promotion men and disk jockeys a very hard time. Repeatedly he would make appointments to meet a promotion man in a given city, to make a string of disk jockey shows, and never turn up. Sometimes he claimed illness; sometimes he was too tired; sometimes he was otherwise occupied.

2. Even though he had spent the major portion of his life prior to his success singing in some of the shoddiest, most poorly equipped saloons in the world, he was a vicious and severe critic of night club and supper club sound systems and their operators. One year he was singing in the swank supper club in the Drake Hotel in Philadelphia. He became unhappy with the

sound during a performance and right on the stage, before a packed dining room, he denounced the sound and light man, and the management of the hotel. He pointed out how stupid the management was to spend thousands upon thousands of dollars in decorating the swank supper club, and then cheating all the patrons of the Room by installing a cheap sound system. Since the hotel was paying him $10,000 per week at the time to entertain their patrons they didn't appreciate his remarks.

3. On a number of important occasions, he refused to do an opening night show. One year at the Neapolitan Room in the Hilltop Hotel in San Francisco, he refused to go on for the opening night show because he was emotionally upset over an argument with his wife. His manager spent a couple of desperate hours trying to persuade him to go on. Gigantic Agency executives in Beverly Hills and New York phoned and failed. The man, who was the booker for the room threatened and pleaded to no avail. Finally the manager of the hotel called. He demanded an explantion.

"I can't go on, Percy said. "I've had a fight with my wife."

"Ve did not book your vife," screamed the manager, a very excitable German gentleman.

In Reno one New Year's eve he did the same thing. Here his salary was $15,000 per week. In both cases he went on, finally, after great turmoil and anguish on the part of everyone involved. In San Francisco he didn't go on until the entire dinner crowd had left after an announcement the show was cancelled.

4. At one period he was living in Kansas City, and a new album was scheduled. He told the record company he didn't wish to leave Kansas City, so they had their top A & R producer in Hollywood, fly to Kansas City with the tunes he'd collected for the album, to make the selection and all preparatory plans for getting the album done. The producer tried for three days to get Percy to discuss the songs and albums with him. But Percy always had something else he wished to do first. After the third day the producer flew back home to Hollywood.

5. In spite of a lifetime of experience in working before audiences, he still was frequently unprofessional and inept in handling them. One year he was getting $15,000 per week at a night club in London. At the first show, opening night there were less than a dozen people in the room. One party of six men talked all through Percy's show. He became increasingly irritated, but got through the show.

When he came down to do the second show, opening night, the same party was still there.Percy went to their table and asked them to be quiet through his second show. They told him they were discussing a business deal and weren't interested in his show. He refused to go on.

The following morning the management of the hotel told him he had violated his contract, and that consequently they were cancelling the balance of the engagement. It was for three weeks at $15,000 per week. Percy sued, but naturally was never able to collect.

When he got home after that fiasco his manager said, "Percy, when they're paying you $15,000 a week, sing! Especially if there are only a dozen people in the room."

Actually Percy knew enough, intellectually to realize that a club operator would grab any opportunity to cancel out an act to whom he had contracted to pay huge sums of money, and who then proved he couldn't draw. But Percy lacked the emotional stability, the discipline and the professionalism to ignore the rude audience and do his show.

The constant indulgence in these kinds of *dont's,* of course, resulted in a situation (quite the opposite of Eddy Arnold's picture) wherein, at the first hint of decline in Percy's popularity, promotion men and disk jockeys ignored him; bookers and promoters and club owners offered him ridiculously low money or passed on him altogether.

Percy doesn't record for Magnitude any more. He hasn't played any of the major hotels or supper clubs in years. And he has about as much chance of getting another network television show of his own as I have. Maybe less.

But he had a truly lovely God-given sound, and the most exceptional opportunity of any singer I've ever known. I hope you have a similar opportunity.

If you do, remember this basic fact: No performer ever made it by himself. You need the record company producers, and business executives and sales and advertising and merchandising and promotion men. You need the disk jockeys. You need the newspaper and tradepaper people. You need the press agents, and the sound and light men, and the club operators and the concert promoters. You need them all.

And they're all just like you and me. If they are fond of someone and if they feel a performer appreciates their efforts, they'll work to their maximum capacity and ability to help. If they feel you don't appreciate them, they'll go through whatever motions they have to, to hold their jobs, but strangely, their efforts in your behalf will not be fruitful. Percy, of course, perpetrated any number of other *Dont's,* which we'll explore in the Personal Manager/Agent Section of this book.

*I have never let my schooling*
*interfere with my education.*
Mark Twain (Samuel Clemens)

155.

## 35. TRAINING, FORMAL & OTHERWISE

I think Percy and Arnold, and Darin and Como and Ms. Johnson have served to demonstrate a range of attitudinal *do's* and *dont's*. Now a look at getting your start as a singer; and at what kind of training and coaching you should have? Basically, of course, what I've said throughout this book (and will continue to say) about getting your start, holds true here. *Get into the business.* As a singer if you can, or in any other allied occupation, if you can't break in as a singer.

Sing whenever and wherever you can. We know how many singers emerged from groups with whom they were working. But there are other ways. Aretha Franklin sang gospel in her Dad's church; Loretta Webb of Butcher Hollow, Kentucky married a man named Moonshine Lynn when she was fourteen years old. In the course of the next four years Moonshine gave Loretta four children, and a guitar and pushed her into singing and picking at every country dance they went to. Now Loretta Lynn is a millionairess country star. Eddy Arnold started with the Pee Wee King band and Sinatra sang with Tommy Dorsey and Harry James. John Gary got his break when my friend and attorney, Dick Jablow heard him sing at a party being given by Constance Hope, then a press agent in the Classical Music division of RCA Victor, and wife of our family optometrist, Dr. Milton Berliner. *Small world!*

So sing!

And what about training? Very few of the pop singers with whom I have worked over the years ever had formal musical training. A number of them studied with vocal coaches, but most frequently to learn to sing without damaging their larynxes, vocal cords, or to learn proper usage of supraglottic air spaces and breath control, and other mechanics and techniques of singing.

The U.S. budget deficit could probably be made up, if all the money singers failed to earn because their throats were not up to performing on given shows were accumulated. Gary, for example, blew literally tens of thousands of dollars over the seven years we worked together by being unable to do shows due to throat problems. At random I could name dozens of other major singers who have fallen out of shows, time and again over the years: Como, Darin, Mathis, Bennett, Vicki Carr, Patti Page, almost every professional pop singer, at one time or another.

Two of the most effective and helpful people I know for singers, who want to learn as much as possible about the the physiological aspects as well as the mechanics and techniques of singing, are a West Coast music educator, the late William Vennard, A.B. B.Mus., M.Mus., Chairman of the Voice Department of the School of Music at the University of Southern California; and Dr. Friedrich S. Brodnitz, who is associated with Mount Sinai Hospital, the Pack Medical Group, Hunter College and The City University of New York all in New York City.

Both have written valuable books, which would be useful to singers who are serious enough about their careers to want to understand as much as possible about the physiological aspects of the mechanics and techniques of their trade. Bill Vennard's book is called *Singing, the Mechanism and the Technique,* published by Schirmer.

Dr. Brodnitz's book is called *Vocal Rehabilitation.* It is

157.

highly technical, and actually prepared for the use of graduates in Medicine by the American Academy of Ophthalmology and Otolaryngology. It's available, I would guess, through the Academy in New York.

I was once managing a girl singer named Susan Barrett, and in the middle of the most important engagement of her career to that date, at the Persian Room of the Plaza Hotel in New York, Susan developed severe laryngitis. Dr. Brodnitz worked some kind of magic on her, which enabled her to go right through the engagement without missing a single performance, and without any harmful effects to her throat.

Other than singing at every opportunity, and getting into the business in whatever most effective way you can, I think some of the best current training grounds for singers are right in our high schools and colleges. Vocalists singing with stage bands or other groups in secondary schools and colleges, and particularly those singing with the Swing and Show Choirs being developed in more and more high schools, are getting the closest thing to professional experience available anywhere.

This is particularly true of those schools, whose stage bands and or swing choirs participate in the many Festivals held in all parts of the country. *Downbeat* publishes a very comprehensive list of schools which participate in these Festivals each year.

The extent to which the Festival situation has developed may be seen in the fact that the 12th Annual Reno Festival, held at the University of Nevada in Reno, under the Chairmanship of Dr. John Carrico of the Department of Music will have well over 200 bands and close to 100 swing and show choir groups participating this year.

An idea of how the Swing and Show Choir Festival trend is developing may be garnered from a look at the growth of the first Swing Choir Festival. This is the Northwest Swing Choir Festival, inaugurated at Mt. Hood Community College in Gresham, Oregon in 1968. That Festival drew 17 Choirs. The 1972 Festival, the name of which has been changed to Northwest Vocal Jazz Festival, will have more than 80 Choirs participating. Hal Malcolm, founder of the Gresham event, has had inquiries from 31 other States, about how he puts his Festival together. It is a spreading movement, and one which will be increasingly helpful to young singers.

Young contemporary music educators like Doug Anderson of McMinnville Senior High School in McMinnville, Oregon, are tremendously helpful to young pop singers. Doug's own group The McMinnville High School Twilighters has won first place in the Division AA of the Northwest Vocal Jazz Festival three years in a row, and you may be sure those young people in his groups, who care to pursue commercial singing careers are getting better than a fair start.

Even on a smaller, much more localized level the band and singer festivals are proliferating. Roger Rickson, one of the most able and progressive young music educators in the country conducts an annual Festival and Mini-Jazz Workshop at his school, Corona Senior High School, in Corona, California. The following 12 high school stage bands and vocalists participated in his 1972 event: Norco, Ramona, Hemet, Corona, Hemet Jr. High, Savanna, Bonita, Venice, Ramona Intermediate, Eisenhower and Chino. Professional musicians and newspaper people are frequently Clinicians and Adjudicators at these festivals, and thus the singers and players have an opportunity to come to the attention of pros who are in a position to help them get started. The Carpenters are just one example of young singer/musicians who came out of this background.

Whatever formal training - - - schools, private teachers, friendly pros - - - you decide to take, be sure they are really qualified to help you. A bad vocal teacher can do a commercial pop vocalist more harm than no teacher at all. A teacher who doesn't know what he's doing may ruin your voice. Check any teacher you consider studying with as thoroughly as you can.

When all is said and done, there is still one most effective way to learn and develop as a commercial singer. It is fundamentally the same process I have recommended for songwriters, musicians and creative people in any entertainment field. Any creative area of human endeavor is necessarily imitative to a large degree. We improve our own creative abilities by a close study of the techniques and practices and experiences of those we admire most in the area we've chosen.

If you're a male and want to be a country singer study Eddy Arnold, Charlie Pride, Johnny Cash, Marty Robbins, any one of a dozen others. If you're female look at Loretta Lynn, Donna Fargo, Susan Raye, Tammy Wynette. But you don't really need me to name your favorite singers, the ones you'd most like to emulate.

Listen to them, and watch them on tv, in clubs, concerts, wherever you can . . . and *study* them, carefully, conscientiously, analytically. As I've said about writers or players, you'll tend, initially, to be imitative, but if you have the talent, a style of your own will evolve.

The point is that that kind of study can be more effective than any other form of training you can get.

You will discover, however, the closer you get to being ready to embark on a professional career, that you need all kinds of help from all kinds of people, to enable you to have a real shot at making it. Virtually all of these people and their functions are covered in depth in the appropriate Sections of this book, but here let's review them from the special viewpoint of the would-be singing star.

## 36. DIRECTIONS & OTHER ESSENTIALS

A singer, like any other musical attraction, has two broad avenues in which to attempt to develop a career. The first might be called the "live and audio-visual" area, which would, of course, include concerts, clubs, television, motion pictures, etc. And the second might be called the "record-radio or audio" area. In the past decade, or more, it has been repeatedly demonstrated that the second area is the quickest, shortest route to success, even though television, motion pictures and concerts might ultimately prove the most profitable. In other words a hit record is the simplest, most direct route for a singer to make the kind of impact necessary to opening up all the other doors of exposure.

Wherever possible, however, a singer should pursue his or her career along *both* of the avenues described. The single most important truth I learned about show business careers in the forty years I've been involved is that no performer, no manager ever knows for sure, whence the break will come. Examples of this will enfold in the Personal Manager and other Sections of this book. But accept here the statement that a singer must try to move ahead in *every* phase of his career simultaneously in order to create a maximum opportunity to break through.

This, of course, is much easier said than done. To develop in the live and audio-visual areas, clubs, concerts, television, etc. the singer needs, among many essentials, the following:

1. A good act;
2. Conceivably some kind of wardrobe. (This is expecially true, obviously, in the case of female singers.);
3. Good arrangements;
4. Photographs;
5. Biographical, background and other press material.

To develop in the audio-record-radio areas, a singer needs the arrangements discussed above and at least such other essentials as:

1. Some musicians to make a demo record;
2. A studio or other facilities;

All of these essentials cost money. In the next Chapter I am presenting pertinent, non-confidential sections of the Cash Receipts and Disbursements statement for a one-month period, November through December for a girl singer. I have deliberately selected from my files, the records of a girl I've mentioned earlier, Susan Barrett, who was very talented, who worked very hard for many years, and met with some measure of success, but never really made it as a star. (To give you the picture of a singer considerably less successful, or considerably more successful would not serve the purpose as well.)

Some of the people needed to perform the functions outlined above are:

1. Act builders. These, of course, are people who know something, not only about music, but about staging, lighting, wardrobe, and many or all the other elements that go into creating and developing a professional act. While it is true that many singers (and groups, for that matter) have developed without the services of an act builder in the earliest stages of their careers, there is no question that the services of a good, competent act builder are highly desirable.

2. A good clothes designer. *(See Susan Barrett Statement).*

3. Several good arrangers and/or a musical director, who writes arrangements.

4. Photographers and press agents.

Of course, once a singer has reached the point where he or she has been contracted by an established, properly organized and staffed entertainment company, whether it be record company, television station or network, or a motion picture company, these organizations supply personnel for many of these essential functions, such as press agents, photographers, advertising and promotion people, etc.

Discouragingly enough, however, in the earlier stages of a singer's career, when all these services are urgently needed, the singer has no company relations to supply them. And it falls on the performer to somehow employ these people himself. In this situation again, each singer's case will vary. If you have an independent income, or your family and/or friends are wealthy and willing to back you there's little problem, other than finding the right people to do the jobs.

If you don't have that kind of financing, you obviously have to look elsewhere. Many singers, in the early stages of their careers, have contracted to give service people a percentage of their earnings for a specified period of years in exchange for their services. Sinatra did this with a very able press agent named George Evans, who made a major contribution to Sinatra's career in the earliest stages. Other singers have signed away 10% or 15% to arrangers, musical directors, clothes designers, sound engineers and all kinds of other people in order to acquire essential assistance in the early stages of their careers. Some singers are financed by managers.

It goes without saying that a manager or potential backer of any other kind must have a great deal of faith in the performer's talent and potential. It must also be pointed out that, again ironically, at the point where a singer needs a good manager and/or agent most - - - in the early stages - - - the majority of good managers and almost all agents will refuse to have anything to do with the singer. The simple reason for this is that the investment in time, money, energy that goes into try-

ing to build a performer's career is substantial, and the chances
for success unpredictable.

After you have made a certain amount of progress on
your own, after you have achieved a certain amount of recog-
nition and are earning a certain amount of money you will find
it easier to acquire a good manager. Here, even more than in
the case of any prospective vocal coaches, you should exercise
the greatest of care, and make the most thorough kind of investigation before signing a contract for any appreciable length
of time with any manager. Managers range all the way from
thieves and incompetents to capable honest men.

The great majority of the best managers, in my opinion,
are members of an organization called the Conference of Personal Managers. There is a Conference of Personal Managers West
in Los Angeles, and a Conference of Personal Managers East in
New York.

Of course there are some personal managers who are
capable and honest, who are not members of the CPM. Many
of the trade publications mentioned earlier in this book publish comprehensive lists of personal managers in several of their
Special Editions each year.

Wherever, whenever you make a deal with a personal
manager, make it carefully, get all the best advice you can get,
from family, attorney, friends, school counsellors, whoever. I
believe a good personal manager may easily be the single most
important factor in a performer's career. But a bad or a dis-
honest one can wreck it.

Once you have found a good manager, he should be the
key if not the total determining element in setting you up with
all the other essential help. He should select one or more booking agencies. Some people do not understand the essential differences between personal managers and booking agents. Indeed
some professionals in show business believe an act does not need
both, that he should have only an agent or a manager, serving
both functions. I totally disagree with this. I know there are important specific functions which a manager serves, which an

agent cannot properly serve. And vice versa. Those functions are covered in detail in the Personal Manager-Agent Sections of this book.

Accept my statement for now, that there are differences, and that a manager should line up the one or more agencies, which will be most effective for you. He should also be a major factor, if not necessarily the determining factor, in who your press agent should be; who your musical director and/or arrangers should be; to whom you should go for whatever staging help you require, etc.

And it goes without saying that he should be the major factor in setting your career course, and working with you, to see that you stay on it. I am sure that there are some singers who have developed successful careers without the help and guidance of a good personal manager. Not many. There are many, many more who have developed with the guidance of good personal managers.

You may reach a point in your career where you do not need a personal manager any longer. Many singers do, or at least believe they have reached such a point. That's another story. To get your career rolling, my urgent recommendation is that you get a good personal manager as soon as you can.

The Susan Barrett statement which follows, will give you some of the financial reasons why.

# 37. THE HIGH COST OF BEING A SINGER

Here are specially selected and non-confidential items from singer Susan Barrett's Cash Receipts and Disbursements statement for the period of November 1 through December 1, 1967. I have written an explanation or commentary at appropriate points in the Statement. I think this gives a rather vivid picture of some of the expenses involved in building a career as a singer.

## RECEIPTS

| | Gross Income | GAC Commission | Proj. Taxes | Road Exp. | Net |
|---|---|---|---|---|---|
| Dean Martin Show | $1000.00 | $100.00 | $304.30 | | $595.70 |
| Joey Bishop Show | 291.50 | 26.50 | 77.55 | | 187.45 |
| Cocoanut Grove Ambassador Hotel | 7500.00 | 750.00 | | 943.79 | 5806.21 |
| Private Party, Club Date (Ambassador) | 600.00 | | | | 600.00 |
| Joey Bishop Show | 291.50 | 26.50 | 77.55 | | 197.45 |

TOTAL NET RECEIPTS

$7376.81

166.

## COMMENTARY & EXPLANATION

GAC is the Ganeral Artists Corporation, now CMA (Creative Management Corp.) the booking agency which booked Susan. Their commission is 10% of the gross amount Susan's paid. The "Proj. Tax" column indicated monies the accounting firm set aside for Susan so that she would not be in trouble with the Internal Revenue Service at the end of the year. You'd be surprised how many singers wind up in such trouble, for lack of foresight like this.

The Road Expenses item embraces a multitude of sub-items. They were high in connection with the Cocoanut Grove date because Susan readied herself for the date by working with various people involved, in New York City, where she was simultaneously making preparations to do her first RCA Victor album.

The big difference between what she was paid for her guest appearance on the Dean Martin television show and the two Joey Bishop shows is explained simply, of course, by the fact that the Bishop show, like other late night network talk shows, paid scale to all performers on the show. The Martin show paid whatever agent or manager could persuade Greg Garrison, the producer the attraction was worth. $1000 for a girl at Susan's stage at that point was not bad.

## DISBURSEMENTS

Michael Ross (on account) . . . . . . . $800.00
Romain Johnson (bal. in full) . . . . . 150.00
Marty Gold (bal. in full) . . . . . . . . . 245.00
Jack Elliott . . . . . . . . . . . . . . . . . . . 400.00
Sidney Feller . . . . . . . . . . . . . . . . . . 352.00
Dick McQuarry . . . . . . . . . . . . . . . . 15.00
Joseph Estren . . . . . . . . . . . . . . . . . 207.08
Bernie Ilson, Inc. . . . . . . . . . . . . . . . 400.00

## COMMENTARY & EXPLANATION

The $800 payment on account to Michael Ross was part of the $3500 Susan paid Ross to write, build and stage her act. She had paid him $200 previously and still owed him $2500.

The $150 to Romain Johnson, one of the more talented set designers working in television, was part of a $350 payment Susan made to Romain for designing and building a special bench she used in an autoharp sequence in the act. Paid in a previous statement was $500 to Bob Mackey, one of the most talented clothes designers in show business for creating a special gown for Susan.

The payments to Marty Gold, Jack Elliott and Sid Feller were for music arrangements, which averaged out at about $250 per arrangement. These three gentlemen, plus the others Susan used, were, of course, among the best in the business.

The $312 to McQuarry and Joe Estren was merely part of the bill for copying the arrangements.

The $400 payment to Bernie Ilson was part payment on the services of Bernie and his organization in Publicity.

At the end of this period, the following were Susan's Unpaid Bills, which we had arranged to pay off on a deferred basis, with each of the people and organizations involved:

*General Artists Corporation*
*(deferred commissions)* .................. *$210.00*
*Mickey Ross (balance)* ................... *2700.00*
*Bernie Ilson, Inc. (balance)* .............. *700.00*
*Gerald Miller & Co.*
*(Accounting services,*
*5 months @ $200 per mo.)* .............. *1000.00*
*Joseph Csida Enterprises*
*(Deferred management commissions)* ...... *5660.61*

These are, as I've said, just a few selected and non-confidential items which go into the making of a singer. It's been done for less. It frequently costs much more. But any singer trying to build a career will need help. Help in people and organizations. Help in financing. Try to get your own help intelligently, carefully, with competent people you can trust. And then work with them, intelligently and whole-heartedly. The degree to which you do this will determine to a large measure how successful a career as a singer you'll be able to build.

# PART I

## SECTION SIX

### Arranger

*I am a great believer in luck, and I
find the harder I work the more
I have of it.*
Stephen Leacock

## 38. BACKGROUNDS & REPUTATIONS

When a song and a performing medium, whether solo
singer, instrumentalist, rock group or big band find each other,
another essential talent comes into play. I'm speaking, of course,
of the arranger. (Even if head arrangements are utilized, the
process of arranging goes on - - - to bring out the best in the
tune and the artist, and to blend the two into the most appealing and successful possible whole.)

I have known many talented arrangers:  Allyn Ferguson
and Jack Elliott, whom I mentioned earlier, Jack Smalley, Joe
Reisman, Ralph Burns, Marty Paitch, Marty Gold, the list is
long - - - but I have never known a more talented arranger than
my partner in First Place Music, Dick Grove. And since Dick is
not only a gifted arranger, but has made it a substantial part of
his life to write about, and teach arranging, it was obvious that
he should do the Arranger section of this book. So

*Here's Dick Grove:*

The backgrounds of successful arrangers are similar in
one vital, if obvious respect:  They begin their musical experiences by playing one, and frequently several instruments, and
thus gain practical knowledge and impressions by playing with
bands or groups, and at first subconsciously, finally consciously

studying arrangements written by others. This, of course, is not to say that many, if not most, successful arrangers do not also avail themselves of formal musical education and/or private study. The most consistent fact is that virtually all of them lived and played music through a formative stage of their careers, and in so doing received an understanding and familiarity with basic concepts and styles of one kind or another of music.

Of course some of the most important and successful contemporary arrangers became famous instrumentalists in their own right before embarking on their writing careers. A few who come to mind readily are Billy May, Oliver Nelson, Shorty Rogers, Bill Holman, Thad Jones, Zoot Sims, Lennie Niehaus, Neal Hefti, J.J. Johnson and Quincy Jones.

Many fine arrangers got their major opportunities and built their reputations with one or another of the famous big bands: Ralph Burns with Woody Herman; young Alan Broadbent, more recently with Herman; Neal Hefti and Sammy Nestico with Count Basie; Russ Garcia, Bill Russo, Lennie Niehaus, Bill Holman with Stan Kenton. A number of leaders themselves, of course, combine their own writing with conducting their bands. Among these would be Stan, Duke Ellington and Don Ellis.

Still other arrangers won their stripes while working regularly with top singers: Nelson Riddle with Frank Sinatra; Peter Matz with Barbra Streisand; Ralph Carmichael with Nat Cole; Dave Grusin with Andy Williams.

Today an increasing number of writers are doing arrangements of their own compositions successfully. Two notable examples, Burt Bacharach and Jim Webb.

These particular examples, however, pick up arranging careers at a point where the writers I've mentioned have won national reputations, at least within the music business. Many fine arrangers, I hasten to point out, have achieved considerable success by association with a number of different bands, television shows, motion pictures and/or records.

Each arranger, before his important "break", of course, had to learn the technique of arranging, and each had to experiment in his own way with whatever tools and means were at his disposal. Those who received a formal college education learned many of the basic and academic aspects in their courses. However, until the somewhat recent educational development which finds an increasing number of schools including contemporary arranging and orchestration in their curricula, even the traditional formal music education background fell short of providing an aspiring writer with a realistic grasp of the whole subject of arranging. It is now possible in many leading modern music departments and schools to acquire all the basic knowledge and approaches needed. Among the most outstanding of these are the Berkelee School of Music in Boston, Mass.; North Texas State College, Indiana University.

Most important to developing an arranging career, in my opinion, are these elements:

1. A total committment;
2. Continuing experience in writing one arrangement after another; writing; writing; and more writing!
3. An innate talent, on which to build.

*The man of virtue makes the
difficulty to be overcome his first
business, and success only a
subsequent consideration.*
Confucius

## 39. EARLY EXPERIENCES

As with most other music/record careers, arrangers
come out of a multitude of diversified backgrounds. As my
partner and friend, Joe Csida has done, with his own career and
careers in other areas, I'll cite my own case for whatever
practical guidance it may give:

I began as a pianist. Growing up in a small town in Indiana in the 40s, I had little or no opportunity to study with
experienced teachers. However I was intrigued with writing,
even at the stage where I didn't know what I was writing. I just
wrote it down in the only way I knew, which was for piano.
These periods of writing, poorly productive as they were, were
my happiest times, during a generally painful period of attempting to develop facility at the keyboard. At one stage I didn't
even realize that a major part of my difficulty was a complete
lack of knowledge of basic harmony and theory.

After three or four years of studying strictly on my
own, I was introduced to the Joseph Schillinger System of
Composition, which finally was something specific, detailed
and, to a degree, comprehensive. I worked with the Schillinger
books on my own, and for the first time, began to absorb a
terminology and a concept, which was, at least, tangible. I

literally drank up this newfound knowledge in my small town musical desert. It was the only way I had to go. The system, of course, did not concern itself specifically with practical arranging techniques, but concentrated on compositional approaches. I remember attempting one arrangement for the band I was then playing with. The chart was a complete disaster. I couldn't figure out *why* it failed, nor could anyone else in the band. The experience was so discouraging that I immediately stopped all my writing.

Even a while later, when I was co-leading my own band I didn't attempt to do any charts. I did, however, continue a very intensive study of composition. It wasn't until several years after this frustrating and unhappy experience that I became aware that my failure was due to a simple, almost screamingly obvious fact: My lack of any kind of true basic understanding of the ranges and characteristics of the instruments. This, lack, of course, made it virtually impossible for me to write a chart which was musically correct.

When I was eighteen I enrolled at the Lamont School of Music at the University of Denver in Denver, Colorado, with a Composition major and a Piano minor. I had no trouble absorbing the formal approach, and I gained valuable additional information to supplement my own very limited knowledge at that time. I continued to study the Schillinger System on my own.

At the end of my second year at the school, however, I found my Composition teacher's attitude so utterly rigid and uncompromising that I decided to drop out, and concentrate once again on my playing. Shortly after leaving school, I met Earle Brown, who is today rather well-known in avant-garde, John Gage style musical circles. I studied with Earle for some time. It was Earle who really provided me with what was the first real, clear explanations of arranging techniques. However, Earle was an authorized Schillinger teacher at that time, so the information he imparted was conveyed in the language of the System.

During this period I formed a Jazz Workshop Orchestra,

comprised of a number of good musicians in the Denver area, and those stationed at the Air Force base in Denver. This was probably the most important step I'd taken in my development as an arranger up to this time, since it enabled me to *hear* what I was writing. I realize now that I was writing a very stilted, mechanical kind of music, largely due to the heavy Schillinger influence in my background up to that time. Schillinger is a mathematical, formula approach to music, which I soon found incompatible with my own jazz concept.

At this time I also began writing for a quintet, with which I worked for several years. This helped me as an arranger a great deal, since I was interpreting standard tunes, and truly beginning to understand the role of the practical, working arranger. I began to become acutely conscious of stylistic concepts, the importance of melodic values, and I developed a perspective of the desirability of frequent usage of the more common, practical voicings and sounds. Too often we tend to lose sight of using these sounds in the purer, more uncompromising jazz approach to writing.

Shortly after my Denver experiences I moved to Los Angeles. For a time I worked with Alvino Rey's small group, and wrote a great deal for that group. The experience I had acquired, writing for my own group, was invaluable to me in the work I did for the Rey group.

## 40. OF TEACHING & WRITING

A year after I'd arrived in Los Angeles a development took place in my own career, which was a major factor in helping me acquire an ability to impart information about arranging, composition, harmony, theory and other aspects of music to young people. I joined the faculty of the Westlake College of Modern Music on a full time basis. The funding and general nature of this very contemporary music school was such that all of us on the faculty had to write our own text books, if we were to be able to teach effectively.

I sat back and re-evaluated everything I had learned about all the areas of music up to that time. I put together Courses, and had the opportunity, on a totally practical basis, to discover which approaches in teaching worked and which didn't. By having to explain and teach, I found that I was taking a new look at my own approaches and concepts, unlike any I had ever taken before. These years enabled me, I think, to come up with a thoroughly modern, and completely understandable point of view about writing.

During these four years at Westlake I was also exposed for the first time to almost everything that was happening in contemporary writing. I also had the opportunity, for the first time, to meet the most active and successful professionals on the West Coast. And maybe most important of all, for the first time I listened and listened and listened to well written music with a completely analytical ear. While I had always leaned toward writing as an ultimate career, these were the years which finally brought me to a total commitment.

I began to write arrangements on assignment for all kinds of situations. To this day, I have the good fortune to combine professional writing for telelvision, motion pictures, records, concerts, night club acts, et al with writing educational books such as my works on Arranging, Harmony and Theory, and particularly big band charts for college and high school stage bands. As Joe's book goes to press I am writing for network shows like Bobby Darin's, Julie Andrews, many specials, etc., and continuing to write jazz charts, which are being used by an increasing number of schools. I'm also in the middle of composing and arranging all of the tunes for a new record album starring Roy Burns with my Big Band.

Formal training, as I've said, is increasingly and ever more effectively available to young arrangers these days, and so is private study. (I have a handful of good, young students myself). Many excellent books are also available. In my own work I found the following most useful: *Orchestral Techniques* (Jacob), Oxford University Press; *Composition with 12 Notes* (Rufer), The MacMillan Company; *A Concentrated Course in Traditional Harmony* (Hindemith), Associated Music Publishers, Inc.; *The Theory and Practice of Tone Relations* (Goetschius), G. Schirmer. I also studied countless miniature scores of many classical composers.

Among the most commonly used non-classical books are Russ Garcia's *The Professional Arranger;* Henry Mancini's *Sounds and Scores;* Gordon Delamont's *Modern Arranging Technique;* David Baker's *Arranging & Composing for the Small Ensemble;* Jimmy Joyce's *A Guide to Writing Vocal Arrangements;* Jack Smalley's *A Simplified Guide to Writing & Arrangeing for Small Groups & Swing & Show Choirs;* Ralph Mutchler's *A Guide to Arranging & Scoring for Marching & Pep Bands;*

Van Alexander's *First Chart*.

Any number of books on Improvisation and Harmony and Theory, of course, might also be useful to the young writer. David Baker has written some excellent works in these areas.

I myself, as you may know, have written rather complete modern works on Improvisation, Harmony & Theory and Arranging. My Improvisation work is published in three volumes called *The Encyclopedia of Basic Harmony and Theory as Applied to Improvisation on All Instruments*. And my arranging book is called *Arranging Concepts*.

In these works I have endeavored to summarize all of my own years of experience and study. The books contain all of my own knowledge and impressions of what I believe to be the proper foundational information and an overall concept that any writer/arranger would benefit from in the development and refinement of his own work. Some detail of the contents of my books, and others published by First Place Music will be found in the last pages of this book.

Perhaps here a brief summation of the areas in which arrangers may find work and develop their careers might be in order.

1. Motion pictures - - -

Orchestrating the composer's sketch; arranging source music; arranging vocal backgrounds; arranging production numbers.

2. Records - - -

Arranging and orchestrating for all styles of recorded music; demos for songwriters; etc.

3. Television - - -

Arranging and orchestrating vocal backgrounds; dance production numbers; background music for dramatic and/or comedy shows and/or individual sketches; original themes or orchestrating composer's sketches for foregoing.

4. Transcriptions - - -

Orchestrating and arranging for wired music services such as Muzak.

5. Live Shows - - -

Composing, orchestrating, arranging vocal backgrounds, band music, etc. for Industrial Shows, Travelling companies such as Ice shows, etc.

6. Bands & Groups - - -

Arranging for beginning or established bands and/or groups.

7. Publication - - -

Composing, orchestrating or arranging for professional firms and/or schools:

Sheet music (piano & guitar arrangements;) vocal arrangements; band or group arrangements; instruction and/or method books, etc.

Breaking in as an arranger is about the same as breaking into any other phase of the music/record business. As Joe has advised in earlier chapters, the important point is to get in. Check the tradepapers for opportunities. Join the musicians' union as soon as you can. Hang around.

If you can get with a band or group, begin to write for it. Write for a singer, in or outside the group. Submit some of your better charts to publishers. Donate charts to schools, churches, charity productions. But *get in*. Start writing, keep writing. Write, write and write some more.

If you have the same urge to write that I've always had, you'll find your career as an arranger one of the most satisfying in all of the creative arts.

# PART I

## SECTION SEVEN

### Producer

*Show me a good loser, and I'll show
you a loser.*
　　Woody Hayes


## 41. A PRODUCER – MULTI-SPLENDORED THING

　　I reflected at great length on the question of whether the Section of this book dealing with Producers in the Music/ Record business more properly belongs in Part Two - - - *Creative Careers,* or Part Four - - - *Business Careers.* Actually it belongs in both, for a successful producer may be the most creative person involved in a given project, or without the slightest creative ability.

　　And the degree of creative ability and/or business ability required to be a successful producer in music varies hugely, to begin with, depending on what kind of producer we're talking about. A producer of musical comedy or drama? A producer of musical motion pictures? A producer of music-variety network and/or syndicated and/or local television shows? A record producer?

　　Here's what Hilliard Elkins (producer of the musical drama *The Rothschilds* and the musical show *Oh, Calcutta,* (among other theatrical and film works) said in a book about him called *The Producer:* (Incidentally we will omit detailed discussion of motion picture musical production, because we would merely be duplicating points made in reference to the theatre music production."

" . . . There are as many ways to produce as there are producers. Truly. I admire David Merrick's way of doing it. It's of no value to me. It's of no interest to me, except in depressed periods. As there are no qualifications for a producer, I don't think that I really want to set any up. I'm a meddling producer. I usually start with the idea, then assemble the units - - - the elements - - - and make it happen. I try to assemble the elements I really believe will be best; but compromise is your full time partner because you get what's available, you get what you attract, you get what you can afford, and, all too often, you get what you deserve.

" . . . I have a couple of qualities. One is tenacity. The other is a fortuitous lack of foresight, because with any degree of foresight one would either go into another business - - - or go into another business. I am proud of what I do most of the time. I have another quality, which is mine alone - - - my taste."

Merrick, of course, is one of the most successful producers in the history of the musical theatre, but his talents are substantially as a promoter and a Barnum-like publicist. To begin with he almost never undertakes to produce an original work. He takes a property which has been eminently successful in another medium, and puts together a team of top people to convert it into a musical.

Just a few examples: *Hello, Dolly* based on the hit stage play, *The Matchmaker; Sugar,* developed from the successful motion picture, *Some Like It Hot,* with Marilyn Monroe, Jack Lemmon and Tony Curtis; *Breakfast at Tiffany's,* based on the best selling Truman Capote novel.

A few years ago Merrick made a deal with George Marek, then head of the RCA Victor record division, whereby RCA agreed to put up a substantial amount of the financing for any show Merrick wanted to do, in exchange for the original cast album rights to the show.

And with show after show Merrick comes up with

promotional and publicity ideas which sell tickets. One approach he has consistently used with great success is to attack and deride the theater's leading critics. He set up a well-publicized feud with the *New York Times'* Clive Barnes, for example.

All this, of course, is creative in its own way, and vastly successful commercially.

A totally different kind of Broadway musical producer, and one who exercises an enormous creative talent - - - greater than any other producer I know - - - is Harold Prince. He is even more successful commercially than David Merrick, and achieves his success by producing fresh, daring, innovative ideas in the theatre, and developing and encouraging fresh talent. Among his long, almost uninterrupted string of artistic and commercial successes are *Cabaret, Fiddler on the Roof, Company, Follies* and a dozen others, going back to *Damn Yankees.*

Hal, and his first partner, the late Bobby Griffith, both studied drama at school, then worked their way up in the theatre, under old master director/writer/producer George Abbott, starting as stage managers for Abbott. Merrick's background is in the legal and business areas. Both, obviously are enormously successful.

But musical theatre production is something you will have to work your way towards over a period of years of hard experience. And the same goes for musical motion picture production. It's a tough, tough world, as careers go.

A long experienced producer, Zev Buffman, recently closed a new musical show, *Mary C. Brown and the Hollywood Sign* (book, lyrics and music by Dory Previn) after a few weeks of previews at the Shubert Theatre in New York. Over a quarter million dollars of the backers' money, (some of it Buffman's) went down the drain. But then, the eminently successful, aforementioned Merrick, closed *Breakfast at Tiffany's* the day of its last preview in New York, with a loss of over three quarters of a million dollars to the backers.

So on your way to the heady career of Broadway or motion picture producer, proceed with caution. Remember, it's tough - - - and it's limited, as to how many people may operate in this stratospheric atmosphere.

Almost as limited, but requiring totally different background, education and qualifications is the lush area of producing musical and/or music-variety shows in television. Here again, possibly even to a greater degree than exists in connection with theatre and film musicals, the basic requirements are varied to such an endless degree that it is pointless to attempt to present any of them in detail or in depth.

One of the more successful television producing teams, for example, is Saul Ilson and Ernest Chambers. The first music-variety show they produced was John Gary's CBS network television show. They have since produced music-variety network television specials for Julie Andrews and Carol Burnett; Doris Day; Sinatra; Pearl Bailey, the music-variety series called *The Bobby Darin Amusement Company* on the NBC network and many others. Saul got his training in Canadian television in the days when everyone involved did a little of everything, (writing, directing, staging, choreographing, costume and set design and sweeping up). But Saul is primarily a writer, and so is Ernie. They were key writers on the Danny Kaye network show, when Perry Lafferty, West Coast programming v.p. of CBS gave them the opportunity to produce the Gary show.

Fundamentally what enables people like Ilson and Chambers, Hal Prince, Merrick, Buffman and all other producers in theatre, motion pictures, television to operate successfully is an ability to recognize the outstanding talents operating in all the involved areas and persuade those people to give their all. A good producer, as Hilly Elkins pointed out, "assembles the units - - - the elements - - - and makes it happen."

I have devoted this Chapter to musical film, theatre and television production because they are obviously valid, and from many standpoints, highly desirable music careers. The opportunities are, equally obviously, limited in number.

It is possible that a career of live Concert or Show Promoter (Producer) might legitimately be included here in the

Producer section. Indeed some Promoters are as talented in their own areas as the Hal Princes, David Merricks, Hilly Elkins', Saul Ilsons, Ernie Chambers, et al. Certainly promoters like Norman Granz, (who has successfully promoted major music concerts all over the world), and George Wein, (whose recent Newport in New York Jazz Festival was one of the great musical productions of all times) are truly fine producers.

Certainly younger promoters like Bill Graham, (whose Fillmores West and East, now closed, played a major part in the development of many outstanding rock attractions); Jerry Weintraub (who with the blessing of Tom Parker promoted the recent Elvis Presley tour and promotes others, along with many other activities) are producers in a full sense.

Yet the essence of being able to promote concerts successfully lies in a maximum awareness of the drawing power of music acts at any given point in time - - - and beyond that having contacts with the managers and booking agents who okay dates for those acts.

Indeed many of the most successful promoters (Granz, Weintraub, Tom Parker himself, and others like Sid Bernstein) are or were agents or managers themselves.

Beyond that the requirements are to be willing to gamble; to know how to get the best possible deal on booking an auditorium; to know how to direct publicity, promotion, advertising, etc.; to know how to get maximum cooperation in these areas from other people involved, notably the record companies.

The area of Production open to young people to a far greater degree is, of course, the career of Record Producer. Let's get into that production area in more depth.

*To believe your own thought, to believe
what is true for you in your private heart
is true for all men - - - that is genius.*
Ralph Waldo Emerson

## 42. A GENTLE MAN

In the Country Music Hall of Fame in Nashville there is
a plaque which reads:

STEPHEN H. SHOLES
February 12, 1911 - April 22, 1968
RECORD COMPANY EXECUTIVE AND GIANT INFLUENCE
TOWARD MAKING COUNTRY MUSIC AN INTEGRAL PART
OF CULTURAL AMERICA. WITH GREAT FORESIGHT
HE ESTABLISHED THE FIRST PERMANENT RESIDENCE
OF A MAJOR RECORDING COMPANY IN NASHVILLE,
DISCOVERED MANY RECORD STARS INCLUDING EDDY ARNOLD,
CHET ATKINS, JIM REEVES. SERVED AS CHAIRMAN
OF CMA BOARD. GRADUATE RUTGERS UNIVERSITY.
HONORARY CITIZEN OF NASHVILLE - - - AND A GENTLE MAN.

There are two other things about Steve I'd like to get
into the record:

1. He, and he alone, was responsible for Elvis Presley
being with RCA Victor. When Elvis's first hit records on the
Sun label in Memphis erupted, every record company in the
business tried to buy him from Sam Phillips, the astute and
well-liked head of Sun and the studios in which Elvis recorded
*Good Rockin' Tonight, Baby, Let's Play House* and some of his
other early hits. Among the aggressive, resourceful artist and

repertoire directors chasing Elvis was Mitch Miller at Columbia Records.

Elvis had a year to run on his contract with Phillips. Steve talked his nervous RCA bosses into giving Phillips $35,000 in cash for the contract, for which they acquired all rights to all his released and unreleased sides. RCA also gave Elvis a bonus of $5000 for signing.

And then, at the critical record period of Elvis's career Steve was the A & R producer of Elvis's records. The big question was whether RCA would be able to produce the same kind of raunchy, exciting gospel sound Phillips had produced in Memphis. It was Steve who put the Jordanaires, the best gospel-country vocal group in the business on Elvis's first sessions in Nashville. I can tell you from first hand experience how talented and effective they were, because when I produced the Eddy Arnold TV Film Series we used them as regulars on the show. They not only made the best rockabilly back-up sounds a singer could want, but they made frequent and valuable contributions to sessions with their ideas for "head" arrangements. ("Head" arrangements, of course, are musical arrangements worked out in the studio spontaneously by the producer/conductor/singer/musician or any combination thereof, as opposed to arrangements carefully planned and written in advance of the session by a pro arranger.)

And not only did Steve have Gordon Stoker, Neal Matthews, Hoyt Hawkins and Hugh Jarrett (the Jordanaires) on Elvis's sessions, he had the best studio musicians in Nashville on the dates. Among these was Chet Atkins, whom Steve had signed as an RCA instrumental artist in his own right some time earlier.

As the Hall of Fame plaque says Steve was a Record Company Executive when he died of a heart attack while driving to a record session (in Nashville, strangely enough, even though he spent ninety percent of his time in New York, and his home in New Jersey). He was a company vice president, but throughout his working life the job he liked best was sitting in that studio booth, an engineer by his side, producing. He played saxophone, and right after graduation from Rutgers joined RCA as a clerk in the record department. He was with RCA all his adult life. Even when he was in the army in World War II he produced records (the extended disks called transcriptions) for the Armed Forces Radio Service.

He was on the A & R staff at RCA in 1948, when I became head of the Artist and Repertoire department. He was in charge of the Country and Western department, although he was a capable producer of any kind of record, rhythm and blues, pop, folk or whatever.

He had all the qualifications of a good record producer, and these are as valid today as when Steve was around:

He realized that "the song is the thing." He searched tirelessly, day in and day out, looking for strong material for his artists. Although he was, again in the words of the plaque, a gentle man, he pulled no punches and played no favorites when it came to selecting material.

In the period when I was Steve's boss, Wesley Rose and his dad, the late Fred Rose, highly able and talented Nashville music publishers came to see me to protest that Steve was recording too many Hill & Range songs (a rival publishing company run by Jean and Julian Aberbach) and too few of theirs. They implied that Steve was favoring the Aberbachs for reasons other than the excellence of the material they were submitting. I investigated the situation thoroughly, and told the Roses in due time that they were dead wrong. Steve Sholes selected songs strictly on one basis - - - was it or wasn't it the strongest piece of material he could find for a given artist?

This policy will get you into considerable trouble as a producer. Writers, publishers, sometimes the artists themselves will disagree with you, and resent your turning down a given song, particularly in some situations in which the song is the artist's own, or the artist or someone close to him has a piece of the song. But the best producers make it a religion to find and record the strongest material with an artist, without fear or favor.

Of course if you're Peter Asher and you're producing James Taylor you don't have too much trouble finding good songs, and you don't fight too much with Taylor about his doing them; or if you're Bob Johnson and you're producing Bob Dylan; or Lou Adler, producing Carole King.

But not all producers have such talented songwriter/ artists to record. Steve Sholes also worked tirelessly to familiarize himself thoroughly with all the elements, which are involved in producing a good record. He not only knew every good musician in New York, in Nashville, and later in Hollywood, when he headed RCA's new West Coast operations - - - he knew every good arranger, and he was constantly searching for new arranging, musician talents.

Similarly he involved himself tirelessly in studying the technical facilities with which he worked. He spearheaded the construction of the RCA studios, both in Nashville and Hollywood.

It is impossible to say to what degree, for example, the echo chamber in the Nashville studio in which Steve recorded Presley's first RCA sides, contributed to the success of *Heartbreak Hotel* and other sides. But the chamber was there, ingeniously contrived out of the stairway in the rear of this studio, which RCA then shared with a local church and Steve used it to telling effect.

Steve also handled his artists (singers or musicians) with great natural warmth, consideration and insight. He never embarrassed them if they sang or played a wrong note. He never refused any reasonable request they might make. He took a keen interest in all phases of their careers - - - far beyond records and the call of duty. He devoted his nights to attending their night club openings or closings, their concerts, their critical television guest shots. Although he was not eager to do so, he also concerned himself, to whatever degree was requested of him, with their personal lives.

He was unfailingly polite, considerate and fair with the

188.

audio engineers on his sessions, in the studio or mixing rooms
and consequently got total 100% cooperation from them.

He concerned himself, and spent countless hours with
those aspects of the fate of records of his artists, which were
not his responsibility. He cajoled, pleaded and nagged his
colleagues in the publicity department, the advertising department, the sales and merchandising department to extend
themselves in behalf of the records he produced.

He spent untold days and nights with disk jockeys,
trade newspaper reporters and editors, anyone and everyone,
who might help the record of an artist he produced sell one
more copy, get one more play, move the artist one more step
ahead.

Steve produced the great majority of all the records
Eddy Arnold ever made, and they say Eddy has sold something
over 60,000,000 records so far. He produced the greatest percentage of records Elvis Presley ever made, and Elvis's sales are
in the hundreds of millions, surpassed possibly - - - and only
possibly - - - by the Beatles.

Steve produced literally scores of hundreds of records
by all kinds of artists, and literally hundreds of hit records.
Among these were the bulk of the thirty albums presently on
the market by Chet Atkins, one of the biggest selling recorded
instrumentalists of all time. Steve signed Chet by mail in 1950.

And of course Chet, in turn, became a record producer,
(having learned a good share of the trade at Steve's knee) and
head of RCA's Nashville operations. Chet, in turn, has produced
literally hundreds of hit records by scores of important artists,
and is as much responsible for what is frequently called the
Nashville Sound as anyone in the music business.

I've seen Chet produce, and worked with him on and
off, over the years, and he has all the same qualifications for
being a record producer Steve had. These are the qualifications
you should develop. Many elements of record production have
changed since Steve started making records, and we'll get into
those in the next chapter, but the qualifications I've outlined are
basic and eternal.

*I'll say this for adversity:  People seem*
*to be able to stand it, and that's more*
*than I can say for prosperity.*
Frank McKinney Hubbard

## 43.  INDEPENDENT $$$$$

In the days when Steve Sholes and I worked at RCA, the
late 40s, independent record producers were almost unheard of.
At RCA, as I've mentioned in an earlier Chapter, we had Steve,
Hugo Winterhalter, Charlie Grean (today better known as Charles
Randolph Grean), Henri Rene and Dewey Bergman. All good
seasoned, well-trained experienced professional musicians and/or
arrangers and/or conductors and/or composers.

Columbia had the same kind of structure with a man
named Manie Sacks, heading A & R, and people like Percy Faith
on his staff. Decca had Milt Gabler, Harry Meyerson and other
highly qualified people. Capitol had Dave Cavanaugh, Lee
Gillette, Ken Nelson and Voyle Gilmore.

Publishers and/or writers submitted songs, A & R men
listened to them, picked the ones they liked, pitched them to
the appropriate artists, who either rejected or recorded them.
Publishers and writers were making demonstration records of
some songs (demos), but not too many of those.

For the most part competent, professional arrangers
were given the assignment, usually by the A & R man, sometimes by the artist, to do arrangements of the songs selected for

recording, and that was it. (As was indicated in the previous chapter many country and western records and rhythm and blues records were created via head arrangements.)

I'm quite sure that when I set up Csida-Grean Associates, Trinity Music (BMI) and Towne Music (ASCAP) in 1953 as a modest talent management, record and show producing and music publishing complex, it represented one of the pioneer independent record producing operations. And I can give you a couple of examples of what happened (with us and some other independent producers, of course), which explains the phenomenal growth of the independent production movement.

In the mid 50s we had a team of songwriters, Bob Davie and Marvin Moore under contract to Trinity Music. We also numbered among our clients, as managers a personable, talented young man named Jim Lowe. Davie and Moore wrote a song called *Green Door.* Charlie Grean produced it with Jim Lowe. We took the masters to six record companies, who turned it down before we took it to Randy Wood, head of a young, aggressive, fast-growing new record company called Dot Records.

We made a deal with Randy to release *Green Door* by Jim Lowe with *The Little Man from Chinatown,* (the story of which I've told in the Songwriter section of this book) on the other side. The deal was that we were to receive a 7% producer-artist royalty on the retail selling price of 90% of all records sold - - - the 10% deduction is standard and provides for records returned - - -.

(The normal, standard artist record royalty is 5%, but independent producers can negotiate for whatever royalty the excellence of their product may demand. Some producers have gotten 10% or 15% royalty deals. And the producer, in most cases, has his own deal with the artist involved.)

As the publishers of the two songs on the record, Trinity naturally received a 2¢ copyright royalty for each record sold, for each of the two songs, or 4¢ per record.

We gave Jim 4% of the 7% producer/artist royalty and we kept 3%. Marvin Moore and Bob Davie, as the writers of the two songs, received half of the 4¢ per record we were paid as publishers. The record sold more than 3,000,000 copies world wide, so that you can see that independent record production was an attractive and profitable music business occupation.

Of course the record also made a very temporary singing star out of Jim Lowe (and he went on to a long and most successful career as a disk jockey, about which more in the Disk Jockey and the Agent/Manager Sections of this book). The substantial amount of money Jim and Marvin and Bob and our production and publishing companies made is only a small fraction of what independent producers like Richard Perry, who produces Carly Simon, Barbra Streisand, and others; Bones Howe, who produces the Fifth Dimension; Lou Adler, with Mama Cass, Carole King; Jimmy Bowen with Glenn Campbell and a dozen others have made.

We'll take a look at the backgrounds and experiences of some of the current independent producers a little later. But, as I say, it's easy to see the reasons for the proliferation of the independent producer.

A bright and hardworking music/record man named Larry Uttal, as a matter of fact, built one of the most successful of the new record companies, Bell Records by adopting the concept that Bell Records would have no staff A & R producers at all. Bell bought or leased masters from a series of independent producers, and supplied strong distribution, promotion, publicity and sales operations.

Many of the independent producers in recent days have been setting up their own record labels, and are having major companies like Warner Bros./Atlantic, Columbia/Epic, RCA, MCA, Capitol and others press the records, promote, sell them and handle all the business details.

Against this trend we have the most fascinating recent development which sees one of the most progressive and successful record companies of all, Warner Bros. going back to a fully staffed, company-controlled artist and repertoire department.

Whichever way the trend goes, fully-staffed, company controlled A & R producers or independent, a record producer these days earns every dime he makes. For the business of producing successful records has become vastly more complex on many levels, for many reasons than it ever was. Before we go into a review and analysis of some of these reasons let's have a look at the backgrounds and experiences of some highly successful current producers.

*Mediocre minds usually dismiss anything*
*which reaches beyond their understanding.*
Francis Duc De La Rochefoucald

193.

## 44. WEXLER & PERRY

About, 1953, the time I was putting together my pro-
ducing-talent management-publishing operation, Jerry Wexler,
a man I mentioned earlier in this book, and will mention again
in other Sections, was learning to become a record producer.
Jerry is the most complete, well-rounded music/record man I
know. As I mentioned I hired Jerry as a reporter in the Music
Department on *Billboard,* and he was the best music reporter
the paper ever had. He had worked briefly for BMI prior to
joining *Billboard.* In those days he seemed to be leaning toward a writing career.

He had had a fine short story about Edgar Allen Poe
published in the prestigious O'Brien Short Story Collection just
before he joined *Billboard,* and his writing talent was evident
even in the trade stories and features he turned in every week.
He left *Billboard* after three or four years and worked for the
big music publishing firm, Robbins-Feist-Miller. After a brief
fling at the song plugging, advertising and promotion end of the
publishing business, he went to work for his good friends Ahmet

and Nesuhi Ertegun, who had started a small rhythm and blues and jazz record company called Atlantic, and soon became a partner.

Ahmet and Nesuhi, sons of a one-time Turkish Ambassador to the United States are two of the most fascinating, cultured and able people I've ever met. Both were into record production, and Ahmet, particularly, had learned to work effectively as a producer with black talent.

Ahmet took Jerry into the studio with him when they recorded people like Ray Charles, Chuck Willis and many others, and Jerry was a most apt pupil. Over the years since, Jerry has produced gigantic hit records with all kinds of talent, notably in recent days with Aretha Franklin, who had previously languished at Columbia for a number of years.

Jerry is a non-musician, but knows songs, knows sounds, particularly knows rhythm or time. He also has the capacity to recognize the musical talent, writers, musicians, whoever are required to deliver the sound that will sell. He is also tireless in searching out, across the country, and abroad to an extent, the places and people who are making today's most popular and saleable sounds. Like almost all producers in the 50s, Jerry used the top studio musicians in New York, and the most in-demand arrangers, people like Ray Ellis or Howard Biggs.

When these records, for whatever reason, began to lose their appeal, when sales figures dropped, Jerry shifted his recording activities to New Orleans, to Memphis, to Muscle Shoals, wherever fresh, vital sounds were emanating. Like Steve Sholes in the country field, Jerry Wexler, particularly in the rhythm and blues field, has left his mark. And like Steve, Jerry has become a record company administrator, executive vice president of one of the largest and most successful record/music organizations in the world since Warner Bros. acquired Atlantic (and incidentally, added several more million dollars to the bank accounts of Jerry and the Erteguns). And like Steve, Jerry still enjoys the producing phase of his job more than any of the many other areas of responsibility in which he works.

Jerry industriously pursues all the seemingly

extra-curricular activities in connection with his records and his artists, which I detailed Steve as pursuing: Involvement in their careers, their personal lives, promotion, publicity, advertising, sales, the works.

We'll have a look at some of Jerry's work in these areas in the Business and other Sections of this book. In the meantime let's check still another producer, one of the young independents. I've selected Richard Perry primarily because he seems to have produced successfully in a much wider area of musical styles than most young producers today.

Among the first records he made was a Tiny Tim album for Warner Bros. in 1965. I don't know what style you would call that, but it was a successful record. In the same period he also produced in several styles I can identify: Theodore Bikel (folk); Fats Domino (rhythm and blues); Ella Fitzgerald (jazz). He's also worked with such widely diverse talents as Johnny Mathis, and Bobby Hatfield, formerly of the Righteous Brothers.

He's thoroughly competent in the rock field as his big hit single and album with Laura Nyro, *Stoney End* and his recent fine work with Carly Simon clearly demonstrated. And yet he accomplished the tricky and delicate feat of taking a top, sophisticated, pop superstar and producing an album with her, which sold to the multi-million dollar primary rock market. That was *Barbra Joan Streisand* by the girl singer of the same name. The boldness of his pop/rock mix approach is further evidenced by the fact that on the Streisand album he used an all-girl rock group called *Fanny*, whom he produces independently for Warner Bros.

Perry's background is vastly different from either Sholes's or Wexler's. He is one of the highly trained and capable musician-producers. He played violin, drums and oboe at Michigan, from which University he graduated in the early 60s. (Incidentally, one of the most successful of all producers of the previous generation, Mitch Miller was also an oboe player, recognized as one of the best in the field - - - even while Mitch was head of A & R for a rival record company, Mercury Records, we frequently used him as an oboe player on dates at RCA).

Perry, too, follows the eternal basic rules:  Find the right song; build a warm, productive rapport with the artist; all the prerequisites I've already outlined.

We could dissect the backgrounds of a hundred more producers from the colorful young rock and roll pioneer Phil Spector, through George Martin, who produced many Beatles records, through top company producers like Joe Reisman at RCA, through English producers like Mickie Most or Gordon Mills, Motown producers like Norman Whitfield, Fifth Dimension's Bones Howe, endlessly, in any and every musical style and we would generally find the same ingredients mentioned in the cases of Sholes, Wexler and Perry.

What we haven't reviewed yet are the vast changes of the past twenty years, which have made record production today far more difficult, complex, a far greater challenge than it ever was. And the qualifications those changes call for in today's producer.

*Whoso belongs only to his own age, and reverences only its gilt Popinjays or soot-smeared Mumbojumbos, must needs die with it.*
Thomas Carlyle

## 45. ALL IS A-CHANGIN'

Start with the basic changes:

We've already discussed, in several sections, Songwriters, Musicians, Singers, etc., the growth in popularity of a substantial number of musical styles and combinations of styles, which had miniscule acceptance, if they existed at all, twenty years ago. In the 50s, for the most part a producer working with an arranger or an artist had approximately thirty, forty or fifty musical instruments from which he could create his colors, his dynamics, his saleable sounds.

Brass included the B♭ trumpet, the flugelhorn, the French horn, the tenor, valve and bass trombones, the E♭ and BB♭ tubas. And the venturesome creator shaded some of these with Harmon, straight or cup mutes, hats, buckets or plungers.

Saxophones and woodwinds offered B♭ soprano, tenor and bass horns, E♭ alto or baritone; piccolo; C, alto G or bass flutes; B♭ clarinet or B♭ bass or contra bass clarinet; oboes, bassoon and English horns.

The rhythm sections sometimes used electric piano or novachord along with piano, bass and guitar, and the drummer occasionally got percussive assists from timpani, bells, marimba, xylophone or vibes.

Some used the string family, violins, viola, cello, et al.

Producers and their engineers played with echo chambers, tape reverb and other distortive treatments. But, generally speaking, life in the recording studio was simple.

Place the mikes, section by section; isolate the vocalist; get a balance and away we go.

Today's producer has all those beautiful sounds to play with, along with Moog and other synthesizers, which in the creative hands of people like Gerson Kingsley's First Moog Quartet, the Mike Quatro Jam Band, Keith Emerson, Dick Hyman and a rapidly increasing horde of other musicians and arrangers are resulting in colors, dynamics, harmonies, tones - - - records with new dimensions.

There are, of course, amplifiers of every shape, size and description for almost every orthodox musical instrument known. There are, for a handful of examples:

Guitars with bi-amps and four 12" speakers with high horn, fuzz, wah-wah, reverb and vibrato;

Cross referenced speakers for electric pianos with rheostat control for "chorus" to "celeste" to "vibraharp" and everything in between;

Fender's "Bassman" with 100 bi-amps, 2 channel master volume control, 100 W-RMS power, four 12" speakers in tuned cabinets with wheels.

And in the studios there are an almost countless number of technological improvements being introduced at a dizzying rate. Varied-purpose, new microphones, equalizers, mixers, limiters, reverb devices seem to be developed almost daily. Overdubbing and utilization of all sixteen tracks is commonplace. Quadrasonic is here, and video cassettes are coming. Some record producers like Frank Zappa and Lou Adler are already deep into visual as well as audio production.

It's enough to boggle the young producer's mind, not to mention his ear, but by the same token it's the most fascinating challenge in the history of the music/record business. I believe that the standard pop, jazz instrumentation which has served us through modern times will survive, with a continuing, possibly increasing amount of experimentation, variation and change. But I also believe that some of the newer electronic and electric instruments and accessories will lead to exciting, dramatic and beautiful sounds we've never heard before. And the producers who produce them will prosper.

Now how to best prepare yourself to be one of those producers?

*Knowledge is the great sun in*
*the firmament. Life and power*
*are scattered with all its beams.*
Daniel Webster

## 46. SKILLS & THEIR ACQUISITION


While there will always be successful producers who are
not musicians, like Jerry Wexler, there is little doubt that it becomes increasingly desirable for a producer to be a musician,
and as versatile and well-trained a musician as possible. For once
a would-be or budding producer discovers that he has that ear
for picking the songs and sounds the public will buy, he needs
some technical qualifications for achieving them.

Musicianship may not be the least of these. A second
highly desirable area of expertise for a producer these days is
audio-engineering. As a matter of fact, Tom Dowd, who produced the Allman Brothers and other top acts, had a long
background as an engineer at Atlantic Records, and played an
important part in many of the hit records produced by Jerry
Wexler and the Erteguns. Any one familiar with record production, is aware that a good engineer can be a vital factor in
getting a sometimes elusive sound or effect.

It is quite obvious that with the thorough understanding of the characteristics and capabilities of musical instruments, and with the understanding of what the increasingly
sophisticated studio equipment can do, a producer will be able

to employ the tools with which he is working to a maximum degree.

It also goes without saying, of course, that if a would be producer is an excellent musician and engineer, but does not know a potential hit song and/or arrangement when he hears it - - - and does not know how to "inspire" his players and vocalists to get that sound, he will not be a very successful producer.

As our review of producers has shown: Songwriters, musicians, engineers, tradepaper writers have all become successful producers. What would seem to be needed is a "school" where any person, with any of these other skills, or without any of them at all, might go to study and train specifically for the career of producing records.

There are not many such schools, but a start has been made. Each of the five local Chapters of the National Academy of Recording Arts and Sciences, (as mentioned in earlier sections of this book and to be mentioned again later) are running one week Seminars each season, with top professionals in every phase of the record business, lecturing on their individual areas of activity. Among the top people in New York, who participated in the last Seminar were Billy Taylor and Manny Albam; producer-engineer Phil Ramone, engineer Brooks Arthur; producers Johnny Pate and Elliott Horne.

In Chicago producers Smokey Robinson, and Jerry Butler conducted classes. In Nashville Danny Davis, Brad McKuen, Shelby Singleton and other producers with a long string of hits to their credit told how they did it. In Atlanta people like Bill Lowery, Tommy Roe, Phil Walden and Wade Pepper all shared their experiences with students.

And in Los Angeles producer Hal Davis, engineer Larry Devine, arranger Ernie Freeman and many others talked about the stuff of which record hits are made.

Also in Hollywood in each of the past two years a seven-week Seminar for professionals has been held at the Sherwood Oaks Experimental College. Among the guest

speakers last May were Phil Spector, Bones Howe and Jerry
Fuller, three of the most successful and experienced producers in the field.

Naturally it's questionable how much you can learn
from a seven-week, let alone a one-week Seminar of record
producing. It is the kind of knowledge you must seek to
acquire from every possible source. If you're a musician you
must try to learn as much about your own area, *plus* as much
as you can learn about all the other elements which go into
producing records. If you're an engineer, likewise.

And you must learn as much as you can about all these
elements through whatever sources are available to you. Again,
as stressed in previous sections on other careers, there are
countless books, almost as many courses, some in schools,
some private on every phase of musicianship, engineering, any
and every skill or craft, which is a part of record production.
Far too many books and courses to list. But you should seek
them out, study the best ones. It's a continuing, on-going
learning process.

And again, most important of all, start actually producing records yourself. As soon as you can, on any level you
can. For in a career like record production, even more so than
in more specific, less all-embracing careers like writing, playing
or engineering per se, experience is what will make you an outstanding producer. Doing it. Over and over. Learning by your
own failures and successes.

Again the tradepapers referred to earlier in this book will
give you the names of the recording studios in your own city; or
you may, or course, even look them up in the Classified telephone
directory. Check the studios for the quality of their engineering
help, their experience in making contemporary records, if any,
their costs, etc. These naturally vary a good deal.

Record producing is truly one of the big jackpot careers
in the music/record business. A tough and demanding one, but
worth it - - - if you enjoy it, and can do it successfully.

A new tradepaper, *Recording Engineer/Producer,* 6430
Sunset Blvd., Hollywood, California 90028 is a valuable new
source of information.

# PART II

## THE COMMENTARY
## CAREERS

Trade & Consumer
Newspaper & Magazine
Editor
Reporter
Critic
Disk Jockey

# PART II

## SECTION ONE

### Editor
### Reporter
### Critic

*It is much easier to be critical*
*than to be correct.*
Benjamin Disraeli

203.

# 47. THE PRESS, VETERANS & YOUNGSTERS

In the earlier chapters of this book I stressed the importance of the tradepapers to anyone seeking a music/record career. Careers on these tradepapers, and on consumer papers covering music - - - editors, reporters, critics/reviewers - - - are, of course, interesting pursuits in themselves. A number of people combine such careers with other activities and many have moved on from careers as newspaper people to other areas of the business.

As stated, my own career began on *Billboard*, and spun off into a number of other areas. We have seen where Jerry Wexler moved from an early start as a *Billboard* music reporter. A quick review of the backgrounds, training and activities of some of the veterans in this phase of the business once again demonstrates how wide open the field may be to persons of many different beginnings.

Paul Ackerman, another man I mentioned earlier, who is music editor and executive editor of *Billboard*, started on the publication in 1934, a few months after I did. Paul had an extensive formal education, having received his B.A. at William and Mary College, and at Columbia University in New York.

Oddly enough, when Paul started on *Billboard* he had no musical background whatsoever. As a matter of fact he worked in
many departments of the paper including Burlesque, Vaudeville
and Radio before he got into the music department at all.

Once in the music field, however, he applied himself to
such a degree (listening to records, reviewing bands and singers,
talking with and learning from people in the field on every level,
that today he is considered one of the most knowledgeable
music commentators in country and western, rhythm and blues
and other areas of the business. He also edited *This Business of
Music,* a book which I also mentioned earlier. In 1963, Paul
won the Jesse H. Neal Achievement Award for outstanding
journalism.

Two other veteran commentators, one, an Ivy Leager,
the other a very versatile Englishman, were musicians. The first,
George Simon started on a jazz magazine called *Metronome* in
1935. George was a Harvard graduate and had his own band at
that distinguished school. He played drums. George was with
*Metronome* for some twenty years, the last sixteen as Editor
in Chief. Down through the years he has not only continued
his writing (he is the author of *The Big Bands* and *Simon Says,*
two excellent books on the big band era) but has participated
in a number of other important activities, including writing and
producing radio and television shows and records.

George, until recently, was also the Executive Director
or the National Academy of Recording Arts and Sciences, and
is one of the six members on the Board of the Newport Jazz
Festival.

The Englishman to whom I refer is probably the most
prolific writer/critic on music/records (with special emphasis
on jazz) the industry has ever known. I speak of Leonard
Feather.

About the time Simon and I were getting started,
Feather came to New York from London. He had studied piano
in London with Leslie Taylor. In New York he continued his
study of piano and harmony with Lennie Tristano, and took

clarinet lessons with Jimmy Hamilton. He became considerably more active, however, as a writer/critic. He wrote articles for such magazines as the *Saturday Review, Esquire, Look* and dozens of other magazines. He was also the New York correspondent for the British paper, the *Melody Maker,* as well as jazz papers in France and Germany.

He also wrote songs, and has more than 300 compositions to his credit, many of them recorded by people like Duke Ellington, Count Basie, Dinah Washington and Sarah Vaughn.

In 1949 he published his first book, *Inside Bebop,* title later changed to *Inside Jazz.* In 1957 he wrote his first comprehensive Jazz history, called *The Book of Jazz.* He also is the author of the awesome Encyclopedia of Jazz, which contains the biographies of over 2000 jazz people and 200 photos.

While turning out this vast volume of printed material, Leonard also produced dozens of radio and television shows and concerts. Today he is the jazz critic for the *Los Angeles Times,* still writes dozens of other pieces and still runs the popular Blind Fold Test record review feature for *Downbeat.* (I think he's been doing that feature for some twenty years). And he still produces a weekly television show for KNBC in Los Angeles.

Another veteran music writer, Nat Hentoff, not only continues to write regularly on music/records for publications like *Playboy,* where he does the commentary for their annual jazz poll, and *Cosmopolitan,* for which he does the regular monthly record review column, but is one of the most highly respected writers in many important social areas. He is on the staff of the *New Yorker Magazine,* does a regular column in the *Village Voice.* He has written both fiction and non-fiction books on many aspects of civil rights, education, politics etc. for both adults and children. Nat, too, has had occasional flings in radio, television and record production. He also teaches at New York University's Graduate School of Education.

And some of the most influential people in the

publication field got their training in the music industry itself. Probably the two most notable examples of this are Hal Cook and Chuck Suber. Hal is publisher of *Billboard*. His background was in the record business itself, and a substantial one it was. At one point, during the company's most successful years, Hal was Sales Manager for Capitol Records. He also was sales manager for Columbia Records and played a key sales and merchandising role in the earliest days of Warner Bros. Records.

Chuck Suber, who is publisher of *Downbeat,* and does a very influential regular column called *The First Chorus* had a sound schooling as an executive with General Artists Corporation, one of the industry's leading booking agencies.

Today's crop of writer/critics seem to be following in the footsteps of the veterans insofar as versatility is concerned. John Carpenter and Don Heckman are two examples. Carpenter was at one time manager of *The Great Society,* one of the early sixties San Francisco rock groups (Grace Slick was with them before she joined *Jefferson Airplane).* Then he did a column and wrote reviews for the Los Angeles *Free Press* and *Rolling Stone.* He'd also worked as a disk jockey-commentator of Pacifica radio station KPFK in San Francisco and KRLA in Los Angeles. He's still active as a free-lancer and renaissance rock music/record man.

Heckman produced many highly successful rock records, became music critic for the *New York Times* and recently became head of the contemporary-music Artist and Repertoire Department of RCA Victor records.

Like the styles in music itself, the styles of today's writers seem to have changed somewhat too. Far more than any of the editor/writer/critics of the 40s, 50s and 60s ever did, today's commentators seem to personalize their commentary, and get deep into the social aspects of given situations.

Here are a couple of examples from two of the younger writers on *Record World.* Mitchell Fink, in a feature review of The Moody Blues, British rock group, says:

"What position do you take when, as a professional in

the music business, you are faced with writing about a group who you not only hold in awe for *their* professionalism but who have provided the background music and perhaps the inspiration for a most important love affair. You certainly can't sit and write objectively about five guys who sang about Tuesday afternoons while you were living them.

"Riding the music business merry-go-round, a music freak gets very lucky. Dancing in front of Jagger, asking your own questions of respected and long admired people, smoking joints in your living room with musicians you really dig, could, I suppose jade a bit, taking the magic and perhaps mystery out of some of what you see. Maybe it puts it all in perspective, maybe it reteaches that we're all human. But shaking Mike Pinder's hand (Pinder, of course, is one of the Moody Blues) backstage after a Madison Square Garden concert, I could only grin like a bat boy meeting Mickey Mantle . . . "

That kind of enthusiasm is refreshing and probably is one of the things that makes a good *today* music reporter/critic.

And here's *Record World's* Mike Cuscuna's lead off to a recent Jazz column:

"The results of this election should not make us despair. Nixon's landslide is simply the result of his appealing to the basest emotions and fears of a confused people. And he will usurp more power, violate more peoples' rights, make friends with more fascist countries and try to install himself as emperor as a result of all his psychoses. But his time will be up in four years. Even now, his party is hardly as strong as he is.

"That re-election should drive people back into the streets. Humanitarianism and social progress are not dead. Those of us in the music business should once again become vocal. Yet we have not raised our voices loud enough when the FCC indulged in political censorship with its intimidating tactics. Charlie Parker, among others died for Nixon's sins and Faubus's and Joe McCarthy's. Anyone who professes to love artistic music, especially blues, rock and black music cannot stand by silently. We must use our voices and our power at outrage. We cannot let the cruelty and bigotry of capitalism continue to destroy people in so many ways. If John Coltrane or Fred McDowell or Jimi Hendrix has given you just one minute of pleasure, do something in their memory to help further the welfare and self-respect of all the people . . . "

I don't quite follow a good deal of that, but I think you see what I mean about the kind of involvement today's trade-writers display. Cuscuna, incidentally was also a disk jockey and a record producer, among other diverse music activities.

Some of the best young writers get so diverse, as a matter of fact that they work effectively in fields quite removed from music/records. Nat Freedland of the West Coast office of *Billboard*, for example, recently wrote a book on all phases of the Occult, which got some of the most fabulous rave reviews in the *New York Times* and the *Los Angeles Times* book review sections I have ever seen. Or is the occult that far removed from the music/record business?

At any rate - - - the point is that trade and consumer editor/reporter/critic careers are among the more fascinating in the music/record business. And again almost any combination of education, training, experience will prepare you for a crack at it. You have Simon of Harvard, Ackerman of Columbia and me. I graduated from De Witt Clinton High School and took a newspaper correspondence course, the Newspaper Institute of America. On the other hand I have read and continue to read every conceivable book on writing, which I think might help. I've also managed to acquire a considerable amount of practical experience and knowledge about the music business, and so can you.

I have found this area I call the Commentary area one of the most fascinating of all music/record careers. As a reporter/critic/editor on an important trade or consumer newspaper or magazine you can be influential in advancing the careers of writers, artists, producers or any number of other creative practitioners in the business.

You and another group of Commentators, the disk jockeys, another interesting music/record career.

# PART II

## SECTION TWO

### Disk Jockey

*People who know little are*
*usually great talkers;*
*while men who know much*
*say little.*
Jean Jacques Rousseau

209.

## 48. THE DEEJAYS & TOP 40

One of the good reporter/critic/editors on *Billboard*
was my wife, June. After putting in a number of years in the
Music Department she wound up as Radio/TV editor of the
publication, and to this day, annually writes the Radio and
Television sections of the *World Book Encyclopedia.* (This
year, 1972, she has also written a Special Feature article on
the Women's Liberation Movement for the 1972-1973 edition
of the *World Book Encyclopedia.*

June went to Los Angeles City College in California,
set up her own publicity office with another young woman
named Auriel McFie, now Auriel Douglas. The McFie/Bundy
office handled singers, record companies and other music
business accounts, but after a valiant struggle the girls decided
to quit. June went out on the road as an Advance woman and
publicist for the Spike Jones' band, while still in her twenties.
Then she came to work as a reporter in the Music Department
of *Billboard.*

For a number of years, among her other duties, June
wrote a weekly *Billboard* feature called *Vox Jox.* This was, and
continues today, a column concerning the activities of the most
influential of all groups in the Commentary areas of the music/

record business, the disk jockeys. Claude Hall (about whom more later) now writes this column for *Billboard.*

Martin Block with his *Make Believe Ballroom* in New York and Al Jarvis in Hollywood were two of the grand-daddies of the powerhouse airmen.

June did the column in the heyday of such program directors and superjocks as Bill Stewart (who, working for Todd Storz was largely responsible for the top 40 format and the first disk jockey conventions in Kansas City and Miami). In New York there were Alan Freed, Murray the K Kaufman, William B. Williams, Art Ford, Scott Muni; in Philadelphia, Dick Clark emerged as a powerhouse TV jockey and is today a top musical producer; in Buffalo there was the late and legendary George *Hound Dog* Lorenz; in Chicago Howard Miller; in Cleveland Bill Randle and Joe Finan; in Los Angeles Peter Potter; in Boston Bob Clayton and Joe Smith; in San Francisco Tom Donahue and Jack Carney, and others far, far too numerous to mention.

The influence of these jockeys on record sales (and consequently the ultimate success of songs and artists) was staggering. In my own experience, for example, Alan Freed, almost singlehandedly, was responsible for making Santo and Johnny's *Sleep Walk* the number one record in the country; Bob Clayton, Bill Randle and Howard Miller were major factors in breaking out Jim Lowe's *Green Door* and making it one of the biggest selling records of all time; Howard Miller was largely responsible for Betty Johnson's success; and Jack Carney in San Francisco, again virtually single-handedly (and in a heavily rock-oriented market), broke out John Gary as a hit record artist.

Since jockeys have had such a profound influence on the careers of so many other music/record people, and still do, it might be interesting to take a brief look at the history and evolution of radio and its disk jockeys, since the end of World War II, about 1945. In that year there were about 1000 radio stations in the United States. Less than five years later, about 49 - 50, there were over 2500 stations.

And it was about that time that a young man in

Omaha, Nebraska, the late Todd Storz, took a very old network radio idea, *The Hit Parade,* adapted it to local radio, and changed the face of radio and, to a large extent, the record and music businesses forever. For the so-called Top 40 format (playing the more or less carefully surveyed forty best selling and most popular records of the day) was really nothing more than hit parade around the clock

Storz kicked it off at KOWH, Omaha, and introduced it at WTIX, New Orleans with phenomenal success. About the same time, another brilliant young broadcaster, Gordon Mc Clendon introduced a top 40 format at KLIF in Dallas, Texas. Stations all around the country followed in introducing the new format.

As more and more radio stations began to build an overwhelming percentage of their programing around records a strange development took place in the record industry. There were really only three record manufacturing companies of any substance in the field even as late as the late 40s and early 50s. They were RCA, Columbia and Decca. There were, of course, a number of struggling so-called independents, most of them specializing in limited-audience music (rhythm and blues, jazz, etc.) A small, newer company, trying to make it as a pop operation, was Capitol.

The Decca brass decided that radio stations should pay for the right to play their records. They recruited a substantial number of the top bandleaders of the day to their cause. They hired lawyers and formed an organization dedicated to collecting from radio stations for the right to play records.

Columbia's and RCA's management continued to service radio stations, but primarily with a subscription service, whereby a station which wanted all the records in each release was required to pay a nominal subscription price. Somebody at Capitol got the brilliant idea of going completely overboard in servicing every influential radio station in the land with free records, happily, enthusiastically and without charge. They also supplied the stations with gratis supplementary services like biographies of the artists, so that disk jockeys could talk about them in introducing the records.

The result of this situation, which seems so incredible today, was that almost overnight Capitol became one of the industry's important record companies.

Csida-Grean Associates was about to form a partnership with Todd Storz to start a record label just about the time the payola investigations erupted. We had actually cut a half dozen quite exciting sides by new artists, when we decided to shelve the project because - - - while our own plans for the new record company were completely legitimate in every sense - - - we both felt it was a poor time for a company which owned a string of important radio stations to own 50% of a music publishing/ record company organization.

Payola matters got no better. In the late 50s, 58 - 59, a United States House Legislative Oversight Committee found that more than $250,000 had been paid by record distributors to disk jockeys in about 20 cities for plugging their records. A number of jockeys were indicted and convicted on bribery charges. This, and other discoveries of hanky-panky led to passage of the law which imposes a fine, up to $10,000 on any person and/or company engaging in record performance bribery.

All through this period, then, station managers and owners like Storz (up to the time of his untimely, early death), McClendon, Harold Krelstein of the Plough chain, (headquartered in Memphis) the Storer group, Westinghouse and others developed strict formats within which all program directors, music librarians and disk jockey personnel were required to work.

This did little to decrease the importance of disk jockeys to record and music people. Although there are few jockeys today with the vast influence and power of the Freeds, the Randles, the Millers, et al there are still hundreds of jockeys around the country in major, secondary and tertiary markets who are extremely important to record companies, songwriters, musicians and singers.

We will go into the manner in which record companies attempt to work with jockeys and radio stations in considerable depth in the Business Section of this book, specifically the Chapters dealing with record promotion men.

Here let us simply be aware that the number of radio stations has grown from the 2500 in 1950 to more than 7200 today. The greatest percentage of this increased number of stations, of course, is in the FM (as opposed to the AM) station category. A solid proportion of these FM stations play rock and so-called underground music.

Let us also be aware that the impression some people have that almost all radio stations really play nothing other than Top 40 records is quite incorrect. With 7200 stations around the country, there are more program formats than ever before. Some of the most powerful stations in the country, WGN, Chicago, WSB, Atlanta and many others still play solid middle of the road music and feature regular newscasts. Many stations are all news. Many are all-talk (phone chats with listeners, etc.) operations. Many are country music, some classical, an almost endless variety of and combination of formats.

But the disk jockey is still a highly important person on the music/record scene. Again let's review the backgrounds and experiences of some of them.

*I like Wagner's music better than anybody's; it
is so loud one can talk the whole time without
other people hearing what one says.*
Oscar Wilde

## 49. STYLES – JIM LOWE & THE WOLFMAN

My own favorite disk jockey (and one of my favorite
people) is Jim Lowe. I mentioned earlier that we managed Jim,
that his record of *Green Door* on the Dot label sold over
3,000,000 copies, and that Jim had a very temporary career as
a singer. Up till the time Jim recorded *Green Door,* he had spent
most of his professional life as a disk jockey. Originally in Springfield, Missouri, where he was born. Jim's dad was a doctor and
one of the most popular men in town. Jim's brother Arch also
turned out to be a doctor, but when Jim graduated as a political
science major from the University of Missouri, he decided to
make it in the music business.

After learning the disk jockey trade in Springfield, Jim
moved on to Chicago and got with a station there. He also began writing songs, and soon wrote one of the biggest hits of its
day, *Gambler's Guitar.* Jim hadn't begun recording himself at
that time, and Rusty Draper recorded *Gambler's Guitar.* We began to work with Jim when he came to New York, and very
shortly sold him to WNEW as one of their key disk jockeys.

Jim continued to write, and we started to record him.
Then came *Green Door.* The record was so big that we began to

get requests for Jim to sing in clubs, and on network television shows. Jim and we decided the offers were so lucrative he would take a shot at becoming a performer. We got him an act builder, who turned out to be so bad that after we saw what he had done to Jim after his first week, we dropped him. We had taken a break-in night club date at the Village Barn in New York, but unfortunately hadn't really left enough time for Jim to learn to be a performer. He sang all right, and he could fake his way along at the piano, but on the stage he had all the grace and style of an overgrown, poorly coordinated puppy.

After the first show, opening night at the Barn, the owner, Meyer Horowitz asked me what he would have to do to get out of his one week contract for Jim's services. We worked out a pleasant and kindly settlement. Jim was game and worked hard, and both he and we tried for a few months to shape him into a performer. He even played a few more break-in type of engagements, and did the Walter Winchell network television show and other shows. But after a while, smash hit record or no, Jim and we agreed that live, stand-up performing was simply not Jim's thing. As warm and easy, as confident and appealing as was and is Jim's voice on the air or on a record, just so awkward and lumbering was his style on a stage.

He concentrated on his career as disk jockey with great success. After a five year run on WNEW, with approximately one week in between he switched to WCBS, where Allen Ludden was then the program director, and had a five year run with Allen on that CBS station. After the CBS run, again with a short break in between, we sold Jim to WNBC, where he remained for another five years.

For almost twenty years Jim has been one of the highest paid, most successful disk jockeys in the radio business. Today he adds to his air work, voice-over commercials for many of the leading accounts in television. Jim's style is relaxed, cool, friendly, intimate. Sponsors and agencies flock to him because he makes their message sound believable.

His voice and his style, *plus* his very intimate knowledge

of and love for everything about the music business, be it pop, jazz, folk or whatever made Jim's career the success it has been.

Another friend of mine, a jockey with quite a different style, was building himself a reputation about the same time Jim was starting his career. That was George Lorenz, who died recently. George worked on WKBW in Buffalo and called himself the Hound Dog. He featured the barking of dogs, wolves howling and other frantic noises on his show. One of George's more successful current descendants is Bob Smith, better known as Wolfman Jack.

The Wolfman's background and training is considerably different from Jim Lowe's. Smith was born in Brooklyn and his parents died when he was quite young. He got a job as a janitor-handy man in a small radio station in Brooklyn, and soon they permitted him to go on the air to read an occasional commercial or two.

He decided he wanted to be a jockey, and began studying all the most popular personalities of the day. It was the day of the screamers. Alan Freed and Murray the K, mentioned earlier, were playing the kind of music Smith liked best, and pitching it with a frantic, exciting style he thought he could handle. Then he heard Hound Dog, and as he shifted from one small station around the country to another (Trenton, New Jersey; Richmond, Virginia; Shreveport, Louisiana), he worked his way toward becoming the Wolfman.

Incidentally the standard training and career development procedure for the great majority of disk jockeys is moving from town to city, station to station, hopefully a more important station in a bigger market with each move, and finding and refining a style along the way.

Bob Smith wound up making his fortune and a considerable fame as Wolfman Jack on a Mexican radio station, XERF, with studios and transmitters in Ciudad Acuno, across the river from Del Rio, Texas. The station had one of the most powerful transmitters in the industry, 250,000 watts, which sent the Wolfman's howls and hit rhythm and blues records clear through the south, the west, the southwest, and even into the midwest. He learned a great deal of his style from the healers, evangelists and preachers, who pitched their holy wares on the Mexican station. Today the Wolfman works out of an elaborately equipped studio in his expensive home in Beverly Hills, California.

Between Jim Lowe's relaxed, warm, soft sell style and the Wolfman's growls there are, of course, a multitude of approaches a would-be disk jockey may take. Right here in Los Angeles, for example, we have Dick Whittinghill on KMPC, specializing in mildly naughty jokes, a great sense of comedy timing and a good, straight kind of delivery. Whittinghill is probably the dean of the town's disk jockeys at the present time.

Dick Haynes on KLAC keeps his audience chuckling between country and western records with quickie, one-liner gags. Bob Morgan on KHJ plays to the rock fans with a fast brand of outspoken, often brash kind of comic commentary. Chances are, if you're interested in a career as a disk jockey, that you already have one or two favorites, and if they are your favorites, they're probably working in the style in which you'd like to work.

Basic ingredients for success seem to be a genuine interest in, and a sound knowledge of the music you're going to feature. And a conscious effort to develop an air personality and a style to appeal to the people who dig that kind of music.

There are some ways of getting formal training for a broadcasting career. Let's review a few.

*Let such teach others who themselves excel,*
*and censure freely who have written well.*
Alexander Pope

## 50. LEARNING & JOB-HUNTING

Happily the career of disk jockey is one for which excellent and specific formal training is available. I refer, of course, to the radio stations in many colleges across the country. Not only is working on a college radio station a most effective way to learn, but such activity will naturally lead to at least two other avenues through which invaluable opportunities for acquiring knowledge and experience become available.

One is the regional collegiate radio conference. More and more schools are setting up these conferences, where every phase of the problems of college radio are discussed. Two recent examples of such conferences were the one sponsored by Loyola University of Chicago in that city in November, and one hosted by Stevens Institute of Technology in Hoboken, New Jersey in October of 1972. The Stevens station, WCPR, presented Workshops on programming, news and engineering. Registration fee for students was $4 in advance, and $5 at the door.

The Loyola meetings also included sessions on programming, news, sales, business and management. John Landecker, disk jockey on WLS, for example talked about the problems a disk jockey faces in trying to create a personality or identity of his own within the limitations of a station's strict format. Landecker also discussed radio personality careers in general. For example, he cautioned his young listeners that they would be shortsighted to concentrate their experiences in music in the rock field, rather than broaden their tastes. The broader a jockey's range of interests, he said, the better his chances for a long and successful career.

A second helpful offshoot of activity in college radio and attendance at the regional conferences described is the opportunity to meet professional music and record people, who may very well be your entree into the field. Record companies in recent years have set up departments, whose sole responsibility is the servicing of college radio stations and their personnel. Many of the representatives of these companies are attending the regional conferences these days.

Atlantic Records is a good example of how earnestly commercial record companies are attempting to help college radio people. A young man named Gunter Hauer is Atlantic's director of college promotions. He is compiling a directory of college students interested in getting into commercial radio. Early in 1973 the Directory will be sent to the entire list of commercial radio stations, both AM and FM, regularly serviced by Atlantic. Students are asked to send postcards outlining their radio experience and indicating the section of the country in which they would like to work. I don't know how frequently Atlantic intends to revise and/or up-date this directory, but their address is Atlantic Records, 1841 Broadway, New York, N.Y. 10023.

If you require information about radio activity in colleges, you might write to the Intercollegiate Broadcasting System, Box 592, Vails Gate, New York 12584.

The link between student broadcasters and the professional music/record business is further strengthened by the fact that each of the three music/record tradepapers today publishes College or Campus departments. The editors of these are: *Billboard,* Sam Sutherland in New York, *Cash Box,* Irv Lichtman

220.

in New York; *Record World*, Gary Cohen in New York. Addresses are given in an earlier Chapter, The Trade Press.

There are also several radio/record industry professional conferences, which are considerably more advanced and more expensive than the school meetings. One is conducted annually by Bill Gavin of San Francisco. Gavin is the editor/publisher of a highly respected *Record Report*, and his conference is in its seventh year. Held November 30 through December 2 in 1972 at the Hotel St. Francis in San Francisco, the conference covered such subjects as radio advertising by record companies; special problems of various current radio formats; growing listener attraction to FM stereo and technological improvements in radio's sound.

*The Billboard*, under the directorship of its Radio/TV editor, Claude Hall, whom I mentioned earlier, has an even more extensive Radio Seminar each year. It covers not only programming, but other aspects of radio such as promotion, sales, etc. Full details may be secured by writing Claude at *Billboard*.

I mentioned earlier that we would discuss Claude Hall at greater length. He is one more example of an apparent change in style from the days when I was editor in chief of *Billboard* and June was writing *Vox Jox*. Claude uses an editorial approach in the column, which somewhat resembles that of a small, hometown newspaper. He chats with his readers, scolds and editorializes in an authentic back porch manner. Here are a couple of examples from a few of Claude's recent columns:

" . . . As usual the radio industry had a lot of turnovers last week and some of these were not exactly appetizing. For example, Jim Edwards, KGAL-AM in Lebanon, Oregon reports that he got fired while in the hospital. That's a pretty shabby way of treating a human being. At the moment I certainly can't recommend anyone going to work for KGAL-AM . . . " (I hope Claude checked that item out with the management of the station, but that's not the point here.)

A Claude social note: " . . . a big dinner party will be held Nov. 2 in honor of George Wilson, who's leaving Milwaukee in body if not in spirit after many, many years as national program director of Bartell Broadcasting . . . I think the attendance will be limited to only about two or three thousand of George's closest friends, but if you would like to attend, you can call Howard Bedno at (312) 664-6054."

But most important of all to people seeking to get into the disk jockey business is the fact that Claude's column represents one of the most effective employment services extant. And it's free. Here are a few of the items *Vox Jox* has carried recently:

"WSEB-AM-FM, Sebring, Fla. is looking for two or three air personalities and David M. Goulet says he'll be interested in hearing from guys who want to get started in radio. Talk to Gene Gray between 6 a.m. and 2 p.m. and David, 5-11 p.m. at (813) 385-5152 . . . Jay Shankle is looking for work as music director or program director; 10 years of experience. (817) 322-7337 . . . Joe Finan, general manager of KTLK-AM in Denver, is taking over a training project for the radio chain that entails helping convicts get into radio; thus the station last week was seeking a new manager . . . Ted Marvelle has left WSGW-AM, Saginaw, Mich., and is looking for either an air personality or newsman position. You can call him at (517) 685-3865."

Bob Hamilton, who does the *Communication Music* column for *Record World* and also has a service in Los Angeles called *The Radio Report,* is another employment opportunity center for disk jockies and other radio personnel. In a recent column in *Record World,* Bob said: " . . . *The Radio Report* office in Los Angeles has (by evolvement) become the center for information on where the jobs are in radio programming. This includes not only program directors, but disk jockey jobs and other facets of the industry covered as well. We welcome this because we realize (by experience) that there's really no place else to go when you really need a gig."

Broadcasting Magazine has a Classified Advertising

column, which is frequently used by station management and/ or jockeys. Here are some typical ads from a recent issue:

ANNOUNCEMENTS

**Modern country** jock major midwest market, C&W has excellent day shift opening for good experienced jock. Send tape and resume to Box E-294, BROADCASTING.

**Major midwest** market C&W has an excellent dayshift opening for good experienced jock. Send tape, resume to Box E-328, BROADCASTING.

**Oldie format,** mature delivery announcer, first phone preferred. Send non-returnable tape, picture, resume, to Box E-351, BROADCASTING.

**Established** upstate New York station needs contemporary MOR announcer. Talent and energy more important than experience. Extra money for first phone. Box E-361, BROAD- CASTING.

**Announcer** with mature voice for middle music network station in Texas gulf coast city. Box F-36, BROADCASTING.

**Immediate opening** for experienced drive time announcer. Contact John Reardon, KBIZ, Ottumwa, Iowa 52501. 515-682-4535.

**Experienced announcer** . . . good voice/production. MOR, plus TV. Resume, tape, snapshot and salary requirements first letter. KODE, Box 46, Joplin, Missouri 64801.

**Mature sounding** voice on contemporary format. #1 in major Indiana market. Send air check, resume to WJPS, Evansville, Indiana. Must be first ticket. Equal Opportunity Employer.

**Top 40 DJ** with large market experience. First phone desired but not required. Not MOR–top 40; not scream top 40 but a warm moving blend in between. Call Tom Bell, 703-534-9625.

In the third ad above, the *Oldie format* one, note the reference to "first phone preferred." This indicates the station prefers a jockey with engineering credentials and training. On smaller stations, particularly, jockeys are often required to "run their own board" or handle the technical details which are handled by an engineer in larger operations. We will not go into technical training aspects here.

There seem to be more direct ways of breaking in as a disk jockey than in some other music/record careers, but again remember, if you can't break in as a jockey, get in any way you can. The Wolfman swept up the station in Brooklyn. Once you get in, there are also a number of organizations you might find it profitable and interesting to join. Among these are:

American Federation of Television & Radio Artists (AFTRA), 1350 Avenue of the Americas, New York, N.Y. 10019. (This is actually the performer union and you must join it to work regularly in Radio or TV.)

National Association of Television and Radio Announcers (NATRA), 1408 So. Michigan Ave., Chicago, Ill. 60605. (This is an organization of talented black radio people).

National Association of Progressive Radio Announcers, Inc., Box 2021, Los Angeles, Calif. 90051. (This is a new organization, intended for the announcers and jockeys on the country's progressive radio stations; organized by disk jockey Jim Ladd of KLOS-FM, Los Angeles.)

A handful of disk jockeys have, of course, become television personalities. Among them are Dick Clark, Lloyd Thaxton, the Real Don Steele and a relatively small number of others, generally on local or on syndicated shows.

The commentary careers, then, are interesting, satisfying careers in themselves, and frequently lead to music/record careers in other areas. It depends on where your interests lie, how you apply yourself, how hard you're willing to work.

And there's one other type of communications medium which deserves a passing mention for whatever potential it may have of becoming an important Commentary device of the future: The mixed media record and print publication. There's one in New York called *Current Audio,* which carries records (music and interviews), along with the printed pages of the magazine. If this type of publication prospers and develops, it will be an interesting new area for Commentary careers.

# PART III

## THE BUSINESS
## CAREERS

Music Publisher
Personal Manager
Agent
Administrative
Sales & Marketing
Advertising, Promotion, Publicity
in
Record Manufacturing Companies
Record Distributing Organizations
Independent Operations

Attorney & Accountant

# PART III

## SECTION ONE

### Music Publisher

*The world is moving so fast these days*
*that the man who says it can't be done*
*is generally interrupted by someone doing it.*
Elbert Hubbard

## 51. SOME PUBLISHING GIANTS

A good deal of what I have to tell you about the Music
Publishing business, and careers therein, is contained in the
earlier sections of this book, the introductory chapters, dealing
with history and background and particularly in the songwriter
chapters. I don't think it's necessary to belabor the question
of the profitability of the publishing business. In those earlier
chapters I cited just two cases of friends of mine, Lou Levy and
Tommy Valando, who started music publishing companies
from scratch and sold them for millions of dollars.

My own experience was more modest. I started Trinity
Music, Inc., a BMI firm (with Georgie and Eddie Joy) without
a single copyright about 1953, and sold it about eight or nine
years later to Bobby Darin for $350,000. Bobby, in turn, sold
it a few years later to a conglomerate called Commonwealth
United for a million dollars, but since Commonwealth ran into
trouble shortly after they bought the firm, I don't know how
Bobby really made out.

The publishing business is, indeed, a lucrative and exciting one, rich with opportunity and challenge. It is difficult
to discuss specific careers within the publishing business per se

because the functions of key people vary from company to company, and overlap a good deal. For example in one company a so-called professional manager may concentrate his energies on romancing songwriters and acquiring songs; in another on producing records or supervising production of records of the firm's songs; in still another, on promoting the songs via disk jockeys and other sources; in yet a fourth on chasing down record company staff and independent producers, and singers, groups and their managers to secure records of the company's songs.

I know professional managers and members of the professional staffs in many publishing firms, who perform any one or any combination or all of the above functions. There are also other careers in publishing firms, which are quite necessary to successful operation, which are fundamentally legal and/or accounting functions. Since the handling and development of copyrights on a world wide basis requires great skill, technical knowledge and training in both these key areas, they are obviously important music careers, but will be discussed as part of the Attorney and Accountant Chapters of this book.

Here let us concentrate on the basic careers in publishing, no matter how difficult to pigeon-hole and define. Again an analysis and review of some of the most successful companies and people in the publishing field will serve us best. Begin with a simple definition of the essential nature of a publishing company:

To create and/or acquire copyrights and develop them to their fullest potential all around the world.

And the manner of the acquisition and development of copyrights depends on what kind of a music publishing enterprise you're involved in. For example if you're Famous Music Publishing, which company also was acquired by a conglomerate named Gulf & Western, and which also owns Paramount Pictures and Paramount Records, you create and develop copyrights to a large degree by having competent writers write songs and scores for your pictures. For example, for their super-smash *The Godfather,* they developed three songs out of the score, written by Nino Rota and L. Kusik.

One was the instrumental *Love Theme,* on which they secured records by Nino Rota on Paramount; Ferrante & Teicher on United Artists; Roger Williams on Kapp; Paul Mauriat on MGM; Percy Faith on Columbia; Hugo Montenegro on RCA; Brass Ring on Project 3; Hugo Winterhalter on Musicor and Gene Barge on Paramount.

They had lyrics written to the theme, and called the song *Speak Softly Love.* On this they secured records by Andy Williams on Columbia; Al Martino on Capitol; Ray Conniff on Columbia; La Lupe on Tico; Johnny Mathis on Columbia and Vikki Carr on Columbia.

The score also contained a waltz, which they named *The Godfather Waltz,* and this was recorded by The Assembled Multitude on Atlantic; Hugo Montenegro on RCA; Percy Faith on Columbia; Nino Rota on Paramount; Enoch Light on Project 3 and Brass Ring on Project 3.

There was also an Original Soundtrack album, released on Paramount Records, and a souvenier songbook, which was published and distributed by Charles Hansen Music and Books, the largest in the music business.

Previously they had published *Love Story* from the phenomenally successful picture of the same name, and it is an open question whether the earnings from the song *Love Story* from all sources, records, sheet music, folios, performances, et al matched the gross earnings (let alone the net) of the motion picture.

In the immediate future, Famous will be publishing songs and/or scores from motion pictures like *The Little Prince* by Alan Jay Lerner and Frederick Loewe; *Charlotte's Web,* score by Robert and Richard Sherman; *Badge 373* (a sequel to *The French Connection)* and *The Friends of Eddie Coyle.* You may be sure that there will be a substantial number of new copyrights developed via records and other sources from these films.

The Famous Music Publishing Companies Chief Operating Officer (that's his title - - - conglomerates tend to those kinds of titles) is an old friend of mine named Marvin Cane. Marvin is a pure and total music publishing man. He had a long, successful background with a number of important publishers, among them Howie Richmond's and Allie Brackman's The Richmond Organization. On Marvin's staff, among others in the Professional Department, is a man named Julie Chester. Julie, too, is an old hand at the music publishing business. I don't know how many of the records I've listed on *The Godfather* were secured by Marvin or how many by Julie, but I would bet the majority of the records were lined up by either one or both.

They have made it their business to keep a strong and friendly relationship with scores of record producers (both company staff and independent), and an even larger number of recording artists, arrangers, managers, agents and any number of other practitioners around the music/record business who might have a voice in the decision on what song should be recorded.

It goes without saying that they have an equally strong relationship with countless writers of both music and lyrics, and they are also extremely active in promoting their copyrights with disk jockeys, trade and newspaper people and others.

Julie's background is much similar to Marvin's. He worked for years for Bobby Mellin, whom I mentioned earlier as a successful publisher.

Another example of a music publishing empire, far larger than Famous-Paramount, which is part of a motion picture producing, record company family is Warner Bros. group. This collection of publishing catalogs is the largest in the world (with the possible exception of the Chappel companies, about which more later.) The Warner Bros. firms collect millions of dollars annually from ASCAP in performance monies on the standard songs in their catalogs.

I've mentioned the late Herman Starr, who played a large part in bringing the Warner catalogs to their eminence and an equally large part in determining the destiny of the music business and many people in it. Today the president of the Warner-Elektra-Atlantic (they've all been absorbed into an operation owned by yet another conglomerate, Kinney) is a long-haired, mustachioed, very contemporary young man named Ed Silvers.

His professional manager is an equally long-haired mustachioed young man named Artie Wayne. They have taken this venerable old music giant into the contemporary music publishing scene with vigor and abandon.

Silvers contends with today's realities (which find many top writer-artists insisting on ownership of their own publishing companies) by making various kinds of deals with important artists. If the Warner group cannot be the exclusive publishers of the songs, they'll make a deal to co-publish with the artist/ writer or producer. If they can't make a deal to co-publish, they'll work out an arrangement to promote and administer the copyright; or they'll make a deal for the print rights.

With their tight connections with top contemporary writers, Silvers, Wayne and a half dozen or more other professional people in the organization have great success in getting records by company-staff and independent producers and artists on all labels. Silvers told *Billboard's* Nat Freedland late in 1971 that the huge amount of record activity that he and his staff had generated for new copyrights and resurrection of old standards, plus the volume generated on the increasing sales of song books and folios had increased the Warner music operation's income from these sources alone (not including performance money) by more than $1,000,000 in the preceding fiscal year.

Among top contemporary artists with whom Warners has such deals are Laura Nyro, Crosby, Stills, Nash and Young and Elton John. They have made an extensive drive through the Warner-Elektra-Atlantic Distributing Corporation to place song folio books on racks in the busiest retail record outlets. The

230.

WEA Distributing operation is headed by Joel Friedman, who worked in the Los Angeles office of *The Billboard* during my time on the paper.

(Joel has developed into one of the most knowledgeable and effective sales and marketing executives in the record industry, about which more in those sections of this book.)

Another highly successful motion picture-affiliated music publishing operation is Columbia-Screen Gems. Among its top writers are Carole King, Michele LeGrand and Marilyn and Alan Bergman, whose many hits include *Brian's Song*. The professional manager for Screen Gems-Columbia is Irwin Schuster, who got his basic training in ten years at Trinity Music. Irwin possesses all the qualifications I attributed earlier to Marvin Cane and Julie Chester.

Another *Billboard* alumnus, Norm Weiser, currently is vice president and general manager of the monster Chappel publishing empire. Chappel is not affiliated with a motion picture or a record company, but has long-standing relationships with the top people in the musical theater including Richard Rodgers, and holds or has an interest in the copyrights of such departed theatre greats as Cole Porter, Oscar Hammerstein and scores of others.

Weiser, in addition to working a number of years on *Billboard*, also put in a couple of years as publisher of *Downbeat*, and head of the *Twentieth Century Fox* record operation. Weiser has moved Chappel into the contemporary scene by setting up Songwriters' Workshops. The first of these was set up in Chicago about 1969 with highly successful songwriter/ record producer Jerry Butler in charge. Butler has developed and worked with writers like Rod Stewart, James Brown, Daryl Hall and John Oats of the Whole Oats, an Atlantic Records rock group.

Weiser has also staffed the Chappel operation with seasoned ex-song pluggers, called professional men. His director of professional activities is Buddy Robbins, one of the sons of the late Jack Robbins, co-founder of the giant music combine,

Robbins-Feist-Miller. And a Chappel vice president these days is George Lee, who also worked for many years for Bobby Mellin, and the Warner Bros. music and record operations.

These are a few of the multi-million dollar, multi-catalog music publishing combines in the industry. It's apparent that the people who run them and staff them are, once again, people with varied but extensive backgrounds in a number of music/record areas.

The best training for the key jobs in the music publishing business is working any number of other phases in the industry. This shows up in the cases of somewhat smaller publishing operations, which have slightly different problems from the giants with film/record relatives.

## 52. EXPERIENCE & ONE SCHOOL

Most record companies have their own affiliated music
publishing operations. Motown, for example, has made millions
through the copyrights it controls in its ASCAP and BMI firms.
And MCA, Columbia, RCA, Capitol, all have their own publishing wings.

Producers of major network television shows frequently
set up their own music publishing operations. Norman Lear and
Bud Yorkin, for instance, who have three shows in the top ten
in recent days (*All in the Family; Maude;* and *Sanford & Son)*
just set up an ASCAP and BMI publishing operations. Their
performance earnings from the themes on these shows, alone,
will be substantial, and they have developed and will continue
to develop many other sources. Atlantic Records recently released a second *All in the Family* album, after the first one sold
several hundred thousand copies.

Broadcasting chains these days - - - unlike the Todd
Storz era - - - are not loathe to get into the record/music publishing business. John Kluge's Metromedia is a fine example of
a leading station group, which purchased a publishing operation
(the Valando firms I mentioned earlier) and started a thriving

record company to go along with it. The Metromedia publishing firms these days are run by Gerry Teifer.

I first met Gerry about twenty years ago, when he was a busy and successful songwriter. We recorded several of his songs with Eddy Arnold. Gerry also performed on records, frequently as a whistler, (at which art he is highly accomplished) and also produced a number of successful records. More recently he was head of the RCA music publishing firms, Dunbar Music and Sunbury Music.

Gerry is another prime example of the diversified and substantial background which is essential to operating a music publishing company. Independent publishers, those smaller firms who do not have entertainment-complex connections like the ones I've described come primarily from the ranks of ex-song pluggers or professional men.

In the era of the big bands, and the days when Sinatra, Como were aborning, I spent many an evening at the Glen Island Casino, the Cafe Rouge of the Pennsylvania Hotel, the Astor Roof and other spots which played the bands in the company of two highly capable and most entertaining song pluggers. Both worked for Shapiro-Bernstein, one of the more successful and larger ASCAP firms of the day. They were George Pincus and Al Gallico.

George is a Jewish gentleman with a fast comic wit, and Al an earthy Italian. Before Al went with Shapiro-Bernstein he worked as a songplugger for Lou Levy, whom I've mentioned earlier. Both George and Al today run their own extremely successful independent publishing companies. George has bolstered his operations by taking on personal management of an occasional rock group, whose members also write; and Al's destiny and irresistible enthusiasm have taken him primarily into the country music areas. His music firms are among the most successful in that area of the music business. While they don't quite match the veteran Wesley Rose catalogs or the Jim Denny-founded Cedarwood or Aberbach catalogs they are vastly successful and growing.

Music publishing, in short, is a career you work your way into with almost any combination of formal business training and/or music/record business experience. As I've noted many young writers and artists immediately set up their own publishing firms. If you are determined to do this, it's important that you hire the best available, most honest (and that's important) experienced help in any of the aspects of the business in which you lack experience.

The book I mentioned earlier, *The Business of Music* will give you an excellent, comprehensive rundown on the areas you must be concerned with. Here are some:

The Nature of Copyright in the United States; Songwriter Contracts and Statements; Performing Rights Organizations; Foreign Publishing; Mechanical Rights; Arrangements and Abridgements of Music; Co-Ownership and Joint Administration of Copyrights; Writer as His Own Publisher; Demonstration Records; Infringement of Copyrights; Show Music; Music and Movies; Buying and Selling Copyrights; Commercial Jingles; International Copyright Protection.

Again, as with all other careers, if you want to work into music publishing it's important to get into the business. Start as a delivery boy, if necessary but get in. A job as a professional man (songplugger) 1972 style is good training. And, as has been shown, so are any number of other related careers in both music and records.

If you want to control your own copyrights, but aren't quite ready, you may also make any one of the kinds of deals for co-publication with any number of reliable, established publishers I mentioned earlier. If you take that route, the important thing to do is be careful - - - check out the company and its people thoroughly, and get the best professional advice you can, when it comes to contracts and agreements. And read the small print!

The best training for getting into the music publishing business is working in the industry, as I've indicated, but I must stress that there is one University in the country, which can go a long way toward preparing you for a career in the music publishing business.

This is the University of Miami in Coral Gables, Florida. Professor Alfred Reed and William Lee, Dean of the University's School of Music have put together a four year course of study leading to a new degree, BMMM (Bachelor of Music in Music Merchandising.) The program embraces courses in the publishing, distribution and retailing of sheet music, provisions and workings of the Copyright Law and virtually every area of the music industry.

Since it is a Course which is potentially as valuable to people who want to get into any other area of the Business side of the music/record industry as well as in the publishing end, I am devoting an entire chapter to the Course at the end of the business section of this book.

Details of the Course may be secured by writing: Alfred Reed, Professor of Music and Director, Music Merchandising Program, University of Miami, School of Music, P.O. Box 8165, Coral Gables, Florida.

# PART III

## SECTION TWO

Agent
Personal Manager

## 53. AGENTS & MANAGERS — ALL SHAPES & SIZES

Even at the risk of becoming dully repetitious I must say, again and again, about almost all the business careers in music/records, that persons with an infinite variety of backgroungs, training (formal or informal) and experience may achieve considerable success. This is as true of the careers of Agent and Personal Manager as of any other music/record business pursuit.

I have known agents like Shep Fields, who was a ranking bandleader of his day, and Buddy Howe, President of Creative Management Associates, who was a hoofer. Dozens of agents started as mail boys and secretaries, particularly in the William Morris Agency, the world's largest. Among these was David Geffen, one of this era's more successful young personal managers.

There are and have been agents who were lawyers, accountants, promoters, waiters, Borscht circuit entertainment directors, chefs and tailors. And the same variations apply to personal managers. I knew a manager, who was a minor member of the Mafia, whose primary business was loan-sharking. When one of his acts got out of line, he straightened him out quickly.

"Kid," he would say, "I don't want they should find you in a cellar."

I know a manager who was a union official and went to jail for absconding with the union treasury. He's out, long since, and doing very well.

One of my good friends, Dick Linke, is one of the most successful personal managers I have ever known. He manages and/or has managed in the past such major entertainers as Andy Griffith (with whom he's still partners), Jim Nabors, Ken Berry, Bobby Vinton, Tommy Leonetti and many others. Dick was a promotion man for Capitol Records, and was sent on the road with a young entertainer named Andy Griffith, to promote his first record, *What It Was, Was Football.* That experience led to Dick becoming Andy's personal manager. Dick was also producer of three highly successful network television series, *Mayberry, RFD; the Jim Nabors Show;* and the *Andy Griffith Show,* as well as of many specials.

Right up with the most successful personal managers in the music/record business is a young Welshman named Gordon Mills. He took a rock singer from Wales named Thomas Jones Woodward and made him into Tom Jones; another singer from the English provinces named Arnold George Dorsey and transformed him into Englebert Humperdinck, and most recently created Gilbert O'Sullivan out of an Irish lad named Raymond O'Sullivan.

Mills was born in India. He was raised in Wales. In London he formed a vocal group called the Viscounts, after having played harmonica with the Morton Fraser Harmonica Gang, a kind of English version of the Borah Minnevitch Harmonica rascals. Besides being a most astute business man, Mills has a background as songwriter and producer.

Allen Klein, once manager of The Rolling Stones, and still manager of three of the four Beatles (all but Paul McCartney) was an accountant. And I've mentioned Lee Eastman, who with his son John, has been involved with management of acts like Grand Funk Railroad, and Paul McCartney. Lee, as I've said, is an attorney.

I became a personal manager after long years as trade-paper reporter/reviewer/editor and major record company artists and repertoire director. We all take pride in our work and talents, and I consider myself to be as good a personal manager as anyone I've ever known, with one possible exception. That exception was originally a carnival concessionaire and showman. I speak, of course, of the inimitable Tom Parker, or Colonel as he and everyone else calls him these days. I think so highly of Tom's talents that I'll devote a brief chapter to some of his exploits and techniques.

In this Chapter I think I've made the point that Agents and Managers can come out of an infinite variety and combination of backgrounds. I would also like to make the point that, in my opinion, there is a great difference between the true functions of Agents and Managers. I stress this because there are many people in the music/record business who do not agree with this concept, who believe that a person can and, indeed, should function in the dual capacity of Agent/Manager; that they are interchangeable and inseparable.

Most agencies (and the agents therein) represent long lists of acts, in the case of the larger ones, William Morris Agency, CMA, International Famous Artists, Associated Booking Corporation, literally hundreds. The agents in each department, television, films, night clubs, concerts, records, etc. cannot possibly concentrate on any one, two or three acts.

Being as human as the rest of us the agents take the path of least resistance. They sell the acts that are easiest to sell, the ones with the big hit records, the ones with major acceptance for whatever reasons. These acts are not only the easiest to sell, but they command the highest prices. Any but these currently hot acts, consequently, are likely to get far less than effective maximum attention and effort from the agent.

It is clear to me, too, that an agent, by any objective final analysis, must work as much for the buyer of the attraction, as for the act. Agents will protest this, and insist they

work as hard to get the top dollar for each act as the manager
himself would work. Not so. It can't be. The agent has to sell
that buyer acts, week in and week out, year in and year out if
his own career as an agent is to prosper, and if the agency is to
survive. He can't afford to "push" a network programming
executive, or a night club operator, or a concert promoter too
far.

I can cite two quick examples of this in my own experience with the William Morris Agency, one of the very best,
by the way. Early in John Gary's development I got a call from
the booker for a midwest night club. I told her that John's
price was $2000 per week (he'd never received more than
$1000 per week till then), but that she would have to book him
through the William Morris Agency. The following day I got a
call from one of their ablest young agents.

"Hey," he said, "I can get John two weeks at Sutmiller's
for $1500 per week."

"Try for $2000," I suggested, and of course we got it.

I had a similar experience a little later, when the agency
called me with the first offer for John at a Lake Tahoe club,
Harvey's. The offer was for $5000 per week, and the agent sug-
gested we grab it, since it was twice as much as we'd received
for any pervious date. I told the agent I wanted $10,000 per
week, and again we got it.

This is not to suggest in any way that I, or any manager,
for that matter am smarter than a good agent. It is merely to
say that an agent cannot possibly be inclined to push a day-in,
day-out good customer, who buys a couple of hundred thousand
dollars worth of acts per year, in the same way that a manager
can.

On the other hand the agency, in my opinion, is vital
to a performer's career, because no personal manager, or no
effective personal management organization can possibly cover
all the potentially important buyers and areas in which a performer's career may develop. No manager has the contacts and
knowledge to cover every key area. In order to be in a position

to take advantage of every possible opportunity to advance a performer's career that performer must be pushed on records; in live appearances in concerts and night clubs, fairs, theatres; in television; in motion pictures; in legitimate theatre.

Only a well-staffed agency with capable personnel in all these areas in all key buying centers, New York, Los Angeles, Chicago, London, Paris and many other cities can keep aware of the opportunities. No single personal manager, no matter what his connections, his experience or his willingness to work eighteen hours a day can duplicate this coverage.

It is the manager's job to see that that agency personnel around the world is aware of his specific artist, and puts forth the effort on behalf of his artist, rather than on any of the hundreds of other artists the agency represents.

It is also the manager's job to study and analyze the potential of his artist and to map out the strategy for his career, and then work toward activating every conceivable possible force toward executing that strategy and to develop that career to its maximum.

I think that in reviewing the experiences of my friend, Jeremy Johnson, in managing Percy Songbird (whom I mentioned briefly as the King of the Don'ts in the Singer Section of this book) I can put together a virtual text book of Personal Managers/Agents and their problems, standard and extreme.

But before we get into this text book case history, let me tell you about a few managerial gimmicks utilized by Tom Parker in building a couple of far more successful careers than Percy's.

*When you have got an elephant by the*
*hind legs and he is trying to run away,*
*it's best to let him.*
Abraham Lincoln

## 54. TOM PARKER, SUPER MANAGER

To understand Tom Parker's unique approach to the
personal manager trade it is useful to know a little of his background. His family, his mother, father and uncle were carnival
showmen. Tom is proud of the fact (and has every right to be)
that he achieved prominence in his chosen profession despite
never having gone beyond fifth grade in school). His mother
and father died when he was very young, and Tom went to
work for his uncle.

At one WSM country music disk jockey convention in
Nashville in the early 50s, Tom had a covered wagon, towed by
the most appealing set of miniature ponies you ever saw, parad-
ing around Nashville, advertising Tom, his Jamboree Attractions
and other activities. I found out he came by his interest in, and
love of the little horses legitimately. The show he toured with
when he joined his uncle was The Great Parker Pony Circus.
On his farm to this day, Tom still raises ponies, or did the last
time I saw him.

When he reached the ripe, old age of seventeen he felt
it was high time he became an entrepreneur in his own right.
He put together a pony and monkey act, made a deal with a

couple of soft drink companies to present the show in their behalf (admission charge: bottle caps only, please). The pop
people paid Tom $3 per day to tour this troupe.

In the later stages of his carnival career he joined one of
the largest touring shows in carnival history, the Royal American Shows. Among his other activities with Royal American,
he ran the pie-car, carnie name for dining car, and a mitt camp,
carnie talk for fortune telling via palm reading.

It is not known whether any of the mitt readings reveal-
ed that he would one day become personal manager for one of
the great song stars of his day, Eddy Arnold, nor that he would
mastermind the career of one of showbusiness's superstars,
Elvis Presley. When I met Tom he was managing Eddy, and when
I went to work for RCA we became good friends. *Billboard* was
the carnival man's bible in my early years there, and I knew
many carnival people, and this probably had something to do
with the rapport between Tom and me.

At any rate I loved his style. One evening RCA was
giving a cocktail party in Eddy's honor. A very swank New York
style party it was. Indicative of Eddy's stature in the company,
and thanks to a little muscling by Parker, General David Sarnoff,
Chairman of the Board of the Radio Corporation of America
and Frank Folsom RCA president were both at the party. Eddy,
at the time, was sponsored on radio by the Purina company,
of famed Checkerboard Square. Tom arrived at the party with
a couple of dozen funny straw hats with red and white checkerboard bands on them, advertising Eddy and his Purina show.
The first two people Tom fitted with the hats were the General
and Mr. Folsom. They were a little stunned, but Tom Parker is
no man to be thwarted in his conviction that noone is too
prestigious or dignified to push a Parker star. And there is no
occasion, no time of day or night, when Tom is not working for
his artist. I recall the WSM disk jockey convention in Nashville
the year Elvis went into the Army and was shipped off to Germany. Tom was at every seminar, at every social function
through the entire three day convention, pitching Elvis photo-

graphs in black and white and full color, handing out Elvis buttons. The young man was abroad and likely to be for a long time, but Tom kept the Presley pot boiling, so that the young singer's army service didn't hurt his career at all.

There are any number of stories about Tom's encounters with the city slickers of the television and film business, at the early eruption stage of Elvis's career. This one occured after Elvis's six spectacular guest shots on the Tommy and Jimmy Dorsey television show, produced by Jackie Gleason. Jackie's working producer, Jack Philbin was steered on to Elvis, and figured his hip-swivelling performance might give the show a much needed shot in the ratings. It did! And Elvis's first RCA records were hitting high on the national best selling charts.

A Hollywood film producer called Tom.

"Colonel," he said, "I'm very high on your boy. I'm going to make him a big movie star. Now, here's what I want to do. I'll give you $25,000 - - - "

Tom interrupted.

"That's good for me," he said, "now what are you going to give the boy?!!

I don't know the exact figure, but when Tom did make his first motion picture deal it was an incredibly lush one for a young singer with no acting experience.

The central gimmick Tom used to get an extraordinary contract was that he agreed to keep Presley off television for the duration of the film contract. Thus, he argued, Presley would be the only top singer of the day, who could not be seen, except in a movie theatre. Every other leading pop song star was being seen regularly on network television, if not in their own series, then in frequent guest shots. This element of the contract, as all the rest of it, was a well kept secret.

Consequently advertising agencies and sponsors kept calling Tom, trying to work out a deal for television. Tom got a call from the head of the television department of a major Madison Avenue advertising agency one day, some time after the film deal had been signed.

"Colonel," the man said, "we'd like to use Elvis as a guest star on - - - "

"Forget it," Tom interrupted. "You can't afford him."

The man indignantly explained that not only was his agency one of the biggest in the world, but the sponsor was a vastly rich one.

"Well," said Tom, "that's different. Our guest shot price is $100,000."

In the middle 50s nobody was getting $100,000 per guest shot. I'm not so sure anyone is getting it today.

"I'll have to think about it," the man said.

"Do that," suggested Tom, "and please don't waste your time or mine by calling me with an offer for anything less. And I mean, don't offer me $99,999."

The lunch tables at "21" and Cherio's and Toots Shor's buzzed for weeks about Presley's outrageous guest shot demands. Then the man called Parker again.

"Colonel," he said, "you've got it. One hundred thousand dollars."

"Now wait a minute," Tom said. "Whoa, whoa, not so fast! Who's the sponsor?"

"Colonel, if the sponsor is able to pay you a hundred thousand dollars for a guest appearance, he has to be a responsible and important American advertiser, does he not?"

"Who," insisted Tom, "is the sponsor?"

The man named a ranking, very prosperous brassiere manufacturer.

"I was afraid of that," Tom said. "You don't think I'm going to have this boy go on national television advertising brassieres, do you?"

As this is being written Parker has made plans to have Elvis do a telecast via the Globcom Satellite, which is expected to reach over one billion people in approximately forty countries around the world. The show will be a one-hour concert originating in Honolulu. It will be called *Aloha from Hawaii,* and RCA will release an album of it simultaneously in every one of those countries. RCA president Rocco Laginestra has announced that the company has advance orders for over a million albums.

A long way from soda pop bottle caps, and driving trucks in Memphis, Tennessee.

They tell a story about Tom Parker painting a bunch of sparrows yellow and selling them for canaries. I don't know if that's true, but I do know that the first time Elvis played a concert at the huge Pan Pacific Auditorium in Los Angeles, Tom went down to case the joint. He discovered that the $2 seats were a far, far distance from the stage. He sent one of his assistants to an Army & Navy Surplus store to buy about 500 pairs of binoculars for something like a dollar each. Hawkers sold them at the Concert in the cheap seats for $2 each.

From the standpoint of your own career as a potential personal manager these brief tales about my own favorite personal manager simply indicate that imagination and hustle are two essential ingredients.

Having a performer with the charisma, magnetism, talent and intelligence of a Presley helps, too.

I wonder what Tom would have done with Percy Songbird.

## 55. AN AGENCY FOR SONGBIRD

So here comes the text book case history of Percy
Songbird. His personal manager, as I've said was a man
named Jeremy Johnson. Johnson was an experienced, capable
manager, a professional who had launched and/or developed
the careers of a number of other successful entertainers. Songbird, as I said in the singer section, had a sweet and lovely
voice, purer than John McCormack, richer than Nelson Eddy,
truer than John Gary, more lyrical than Dennis Day.

There were several obvious handicaps to be overcome
in taking on the task of building the career of Songbird. To
begin with it was an age of youth and rock, and Percy was in
his mid-thirties and sang beautiful ballads. Also he was what
may accurately be described as a singing bum, i.e., he had been
singing professionally since he was six years old, in his native
Georgia.

Being a careful business man, eager not to waste his
time with projects which could conceivably explode for reasons
beyond his control, Jeremy questioned Percy about his personal
life and background at great length. Percy told him that in his
youth, from time to time, he'd been a mite mischievous.

For example, he'd been tossed out of the Navy with a bad conduct discharge, but only because he was a headstrong high-spirit-
ed child of eighteen with a temper. He had long since matured,
of course. As a matter of fact he'd left a wife and three children
in Baton Rouge, while he came on up to New York to have one
last fling at making it as a singer. On balance it didn't sound too
horrendous. And Jeremy got one big, immediate break. He took
Percy to the top man in the Artist and Repertoire department
of one of the big record companies, Magnitude Records, and
this man went completely overboard for Songbird.

Not only did he sign Songbird and recruit (with the aid
of Johnson, with whom he worked very closely) the finest production, arranging and supportive talent for his first album, but
fired up all the other key departments of the big record company about this potential new star. The advertising, promotion,
publicity, sales, merchandising people could hardly wait for
Percy Songbird's first album, *Songbird on the Wing,* to be
released.

They devised one of the strongest campaigns to launch
the album, ever put together in the record business to that date.
The cost of the campaign would run about a quarter million
dollars. Johnson, who maintained good relationships with key
people on the trade press (as a manager should), planted the
story of Magnitude's great plans to build a new star named Percy
Songbird. It was a very legitimate, significant story with many
excellent trade angles, and the press gave it a big play.

I have mentioned earlier that there is indeed a difference
in the agent/manager function, and that it behooves a good
manager to select the right agency for his attractions, and to
somehow keep the attention and efforts of the working agents
on his acts, rather than the several hundred other acts every
large Agency books.

The tradepaper stories put Jeremy Johnson in a position
which enabled him to sign Percy Songbird to one of the most
important agencies in show business, under the most favorable
circumstances.

The agency was Gigantic Artists' Group, GAG. GAG was as big an agency as IFA (International Famous), CMA (Creative Artists Management), in fact almost as big as WM (the William Morris Agency). All of these began to call Johnson as soon as the tradepress stories appeared. Their reasoning was as sound as it was obvious. If a major record company is willing to spend $250,000 to promote an unknown artist, and the artist is managed by an established personal manager, that artist is likely to turn out to be a profitable property.

Johnson decided to sign Percy Songbird to GAG, but he laid down a couple of extraordinary conditions:

He insisted that, contractually, GAG commit Chauncy Steinmerz to take a direct, continuing personal interest in the career of Songbird and serve as the GAG internal liason with the heads of each of the agency's departments and the agents in those departments. Steinmerz worked in precisely that capacity in the Agency, but only for three other acts handled by the Agency, all of them established stars.

As a good manager, Johnson also arranged a very special introduction of Percy Songbird to the Agency and all its personnel. As is the case with all big entertainment agencies made up of numerous departments, with hundreds of individual agents in those departments in offices in key cities around the world, GAG held full staff meetings in each of their offices every Monday morning at 10 a.m. At these meetings each of the department heads, Steinmerz and other executives laid out the strategies the agency would pursue in the upsoming week to move along the careers of all of their most important clients.

Plans were made to get a starring role in a film for this one; his own television show for that; a concert tour laid out for a third. Individual agents were given specific assignments. The acts discussed in these meetings got the lion's share of the attention of the hustling, hardworking men of GAG. Detailed reports of the minutes of the meetings were exchanged between offices in New York, Hollywood, Chicago, London, Paris, etc. An automatic, vivid "High Priority" was stamped on the mind of every agent in the company alongside the name of every act mentioned in those weekly minutes.

The GAG New York office meetings were held in a huge Conference Room. The executives, heads of the television, motion picture, night club, legitimate theatre, concert and all other departments and all of their staffs assembled around a conference table, roughly the size of a hockey rink. Adjoining the Conference room was a Projection/Playback room, from which films and records were piped into the Conference room, as occasion demanded.

Occasion demanded one Monday morning as the meeting got under way, and the sweet, lilting voice of Percy Songbird, backed by thirty six of the finest studio musicians in New York (including sixteen strings) soared and swirled around the vast GAG conference room. It was a song from Percy's first album, *Songbird on the Wing*. It was better than hitting a mule on the head with a two by four. As the last exciting notes died the door of the Projection Room opened, and Steinmerz led the potential new star to be represented by GAG, and his manager, Jeremy Johnson into the Conference Room.

After appropriate introductions Johnson talked to this group of thirty or forty men, in whose hands now rested a good part of the destiny of Percy Songbird. He explained, in carefully rehearsed detail, the almost staggering dimensions of the promotional plans Magnitude Records had for making Songbird one of the biggest stars of his era.

He also told the group precisely what his own management strategy for developing Songbird's career beyond the record business was, and how Johnson and Magnitude Records felt each of the departments of GAG could best advance this career drive.

*On the Wing* was to be released the following day. Songbird was to start on an eighteen city promotional tour, paid for by Magnitude. On the second stop of that tour Songbird's career would have died, but for another sound managerial move by Jeremy Johnson.

*So live that you wouldn't be ashamed to sell*
*the family parrot to the town gossip.*
Will Rogers

251.

## 56. DISASTER STRIKES

Johnson was basking in the afterglow of a phone call he had received from Philadelphia where the Songbird tour to promote *Songbird on the Wing* kicked off. The Magnitude records headquarters' publicity man, travelling with Songbird on the entire tour, had called to say that the reaction to Percy and his album was phenomenal. Every disk jockey in the area, every newspaperman on the entertainment desks of the local dailies had turned out for the cocktail party Magnitude gave at the town's swankiest hotel.

They were all enchanted with the album, even more so with Percy's live performance (his musical director led a trio, which would play in every city on the tour - - - Magnitude picked up the tab for these musicians, too). And Percy's shy, modest personality had won over not only the press and the broadcasters, but also the local distributor's executives and promotion people.

"We've got a big one," the publicity man told Jeremy Johnson.

All this caused a subsequent phone call to Johnson on the following day from the publicity man's boss at Magnitude's New York headquarters to come as even more of a shock than it would have been ordinarily.

Somebody had told somebody some stories about Percy Songbird's past. That somebody had told somebody at Magnitude Records and eventually the stories reached the sensitive ears of the heads of the company. One story was that Percy had been arrested in a small town in Mississippi for breaking and entering a liquor store. Another was that he had been arrested in Cleveland for corrupting the morals of a minor. The head of publicity told Johnson that Magnitude was calling off the tour and cancelling Songbird's contract, which of course, contained a morals clause, which permitted them to do this.

Johnson protested vehemently. He insisted on an immediate meeting with the Magnitude brass to discuss the situation calmly. The meeting took place within the hour. The Magnitude brass would not reveal the source of their stories. They simply took the position that the company had too fine a reputation to run the risk of exposing themselves to charges of attempting to popularize an unsavory character. (It should be mentioned that this was in an era before record companies openly promoted artists and records who were (or sang about) transvestites, homosexuals, drug addicts and other deviates from the establishment norm.)

The decision was that Johnson and two key executives of Magnitude would immediately fly to Pittsburgh, where Percy was next preparing to charm the influential locals, stage a Songbird illness, rush Percy back to New York, and keep him there until a thorough investigation of the Mississippi and Ohio charges could be made.

If the Magnitude brass had not held Johnson in high and respectful esteem based on prior dealings, he never would have been able to arrange for this reprieve in the plan to drop Songbird.

In Pittsburgh Percy admitted that he had borrowed several bottles of liquor from a local store in Mississippi, but only because he and a group of friends were having a party and had run out of refreshments and money. In Cleveland there had been a little thing with a rather young girl, he said, but it had occurred at the instigation of the girl's mother, who it seemed was an adoring Percy Songbird fan.

"This is the story of my life," Percy wailed. "Every time I get a break something like this comes up."

Nevertheless he gave an Academy Award performance of a man being ill for the Doctor who was summoned by the Magnitude Records' artists' relations man, who had flown to Pittsburgh with Johnson. Or maybe it wasn't so convincing a portrayal. The doctor gave him some shots for his fake illness and the following morning, when the time for the flight back to New York drew near, Percy did indeed become quite ill. On his knees, his head over the toilet bowl, he pleaded with Jeremy Johnson:

"Oooooohhh, can't we make a later plane."

Johnson said no.

*All progress is based upon a universal,*
*innate desire on the part of every organism*
*to live beyond its income.*
Samuel Butler

## 57. FROM $300 to $15,000 PER WEEK

Percy Songbird spent two restless, anxious weeks laying
low in New York, while the Magnitude investigation went on.
Johnson wasn't exactly relaxed either. But he occupied himself
by touting the *Songbird on the Wing* album to his friends on the
trade press, calling disk jockeys around the country and urging
them to join the movement to discover this exciting new star,
and other such activities. Normally these would be performed
in a singer's behalf by publicity and promotion people, but
conscientious managers take on these duties at the stage where
the artist cannot afford to pay for them. I might add here that
Johnson was also deferring collection of all commissions, and laying out monies of his own toward essentials for Songbird's career.
(Also frequently done by personal managers.)

Among these essentials was building an act for Percy.
At the end of the fortnight word came to Johnson that Magnitude was ready to send Songbird back on the road. The
incidents which had been reported to them had actually taken
place, but in both situations Percy had been exonerated, at
least to a degree to satisfy the record company. It is possible
that the early favorable sales reports and reviews of the album
may have had a small bearing on the decision.

At any rate the tour continued to a triumphant conclusion. *Songbird on the Wing* was one of the more successful albums by a new artist in some time. Percy behaved well, working his shy, modest young man routine for all it was worth. And as soon as he got back to New York Johnson had him begin work with Luigi Castlemarre, one of the more capable act builders of the day.

In spite of the fact that he had been singing professionally for some twenty years, Percy was strictly a left-handed singer. That is to say, his concept of moving about a stage effectively was to hold the microphone in his right hand, and make what he considered to be appropriate dramatic gestures with his left. He never changed the mike from right to left, nor made any other kind of gesture or move.

Castlemarre worked so hard and long to correct this rather minor and other more serious flaws in Songbird's performing style that on several occasions Percy threatened to slug him. But it paid off. Percy went quickly from a salary of $300 per week in a Canadian night club into which Gigantic had booked him for his maiden engagement to his first five figure per week gig, $15,000 for six days out of seven in a club in Reno.

On the way Jeremy Johnson personally planned, wrote and executed publicity, advertising and promotion campaigns for Songbird. Some in collaboration with the record company; some with the clubs involved; some as independent enterprises. For example Johnson prevailed upon GAG to turn over to him complete lists of the names and addresses of every producer of motion pictures and major television shows, and he sent each of these producers a copy of each of Percy's hit record albums as they were released. With the album he sent along a personal letter, in which he extolled Percy's tremendous appeal, as evidenced by the increasingly important engagements he was playing in the nation's leading supper clubs, guest appearances on major network television shows, etc.

And it began to pay off. Percy's income was running at

$500,000 per year mark, and Johnson actually began to collect
some of the $30,000 in commissions he had deferred for the
first several years of Songbird's career. The next big objective
in the Songbird career was to try to get him his own television
network show. Few singers, even long established stars, had
their own network show, but Johnson and the key people in
the television department of GAG felt they had a chance. By
this time Songbird had had ten hit albums in a row, and had
won rave notices as a night club and concert performer, and the
promotion behind him had been increasingly effective.

Yes, indeed there was a chance. However a book which
attempts to reveal the problems and pitfalls involved in a personal manager's or an agent's career would be less than honest
if it completely ignored some of the personal aspects of some
performer's lives. In this respect, too, the saga of Percy Songbird and his manager, Jeremy Johnson is classic, and a text
book case history of its kind.

*A cynic is a man who knows the price of*
*everything, and the value of nothing.*
Oscar Wilde

257.

## 58. SOME PERSONAL PROBLEMS & A TV SHOW

I mentioned earlier that when Percy Songbird came to New York for a last fling at making a career as a singer he had left a wife and three children in Baton Rouge. Not desertion. The wife had worked and earned most of the family's living ever since she and Percy married. She was merely making her own contribution to Percy's career by supporting them all until he could become a star. When he was almost a star Percy divorced the lady from Baton Rouge.

"I'm never going to get married again," he told Johnson, "It just doesn't work out for a performer."

Three months later he married a lady from Tempe, Arizona.

In the meantime ghosts from Percy's past materialized and joined the spirits from Jackson, Mississippi and Cleveland, Ohio to plague, not so much Percy, as Jeremy Johnson. A Frenchwoman, a couturier, now living in New York, produced a managerial contract wherein Percy Songbird had agreed to pay her 25% of all of his earnings for ten years. She was about ten years older than Percy, and she claimed that she had spent literally thousands of dollars buying Percy clothes and hosting expensive parties to which she invited influential friends, who could help Percy.

258.

Percy pooh poohed the whole episode on the grounds
that he had given her excellent service as a companion, but her
attorneys bugged and threatened Jeremy Johnson for a considerable time before he was able to persuade them they were
fighting a cause they could not win.

Hardly had the Frenchwoman written Percy off as a
hopeless investment, when another former manager turned up.
This was a Southern gentleman, who owned a small chain of
theatres. He too produced a managerial contract, wherein
Percy agreed to pay him 25% of his earnings for ten years. (Johnson's management commission, incidentally, was 15%, which is
the precise management commission on which I worked with
Eddy Arnold, Bobby Darin, Jim Lowe, Betty Johnson, John
Gary, Santo and Johnny and all the other entertainers for
whom I toiled). He, too, claimed to have supported Percy for
a number of years, and to have purchased wardrobe, sound
equipment, musical instruments and other items for the advancement of Songbird's career.

This episode, too, hardly disturbed Percy. He felt he was
now earning enough money to pay managers, accountants and
attorneys to take care of such minor matters. He had a concept
of finance which talented people sometimes display, which is
nevertheless difficult for personal managers like Jeremy Johnson
to grasp. While Percy felt he was earning enough to pay people
who applied their technical skills to keeping him out of jail, he
also used those same monies to indulge himself in various hobbies.

Johnson discovered shortly after Percy's first five figure
engagement at the club in Reno, that Percy had lost not only
the $30,000 represented by his salary for two weeks, but had
additionally written IOUs for an additional $30,000 to loan in-
stitutions, which use very severe collection methods. In order to
prevent the loan people from perpetrating their collection methods on Songbird, Johnson and Percy's lawyers and accountants
found themselves falling seriously behind on alimony and child
support payments to the ex-wife in Baton Rouge. This lady
naturally hired aggressive and able lawyers to collect this money,

which was so justly due her, and Johnson and his attorneys had one more expensive time-consuming, energy-draining contest on their hands.

I will not belabor the point that all of these functions which a personal manager and/or agent must frequently perform in behalf of a naughty artist, not only take time and skill, but require one other highly essential talent: The ability to somehow make a Percy Songbird continue to appear to his adoring fans (in Percy's case the majority of them were sweet, wholesome middle-aged and older ladies) the shy, modest, pure person they believe him to be, rather than the monstrous character he really is. I do not know what books you read, courses you study to learn this quite vital skill.

Ask Jeremy Johnson. He protected Percy Songbird through all these escapades and others too dull and numerous to mention, so that in spite of this juvenile and psychotic be-havior on the part of the singer, the GAG TV department agents nevertheless did get Percy his own network television show.

One summer, replacing a long-time Western adventure favorite on the World Wide Network, *The Percy Songbird Show* made its debut.

*Many a man in love with a dimple makes*
*the mistake of marrying the whole girl.*
Stephen Leacock

## 59. A PIGEON & HIS MONEY

,

By this time the new wife from Tempe and Percy had
three children of their own. It was as stormy a marriage as had
been the one to the woman in Baton Rouge. It is something of
a Songbird specialty, stormy marriages. It's pertinence here is
that a good personal manager like Jeremy Johnson finds it impossible not to get involved, no matter how hard he tries.

And Johnson tried. When he wasn't busy working with
the Magnitude Record people to continue to promote Songbird's albums, he was working with the Concert Department
people at GAG, lining up increasingly remunerative and important Percy Songbird Concerts in auditoriums and theatres
around the country. When he wasn't dissecting the night club
and supper club structure of the world to find profitable but
safe places for Songbird to play, he was trying to eradicate
the ghosts, which kept materializing from the Songbird past.
(Perhaps agents and managers should be doubly wary of
singers who have been active for twenty years prior to their
own association. Some people can get into a good deal of mis-
chief in twenty years.)

All of these chores of Johnson's had become increasingly difficult. As mentioned in the singer section, the more successful Songbird became the more inconsiderately did he treat the Magnitude Record people who had worked so hard to advance his career. Johnson had an increasingly difficult time trying to persuade them to keep working in Songbird's behalf any more than they had to to keep their jobs.

And Johnson had discovered that the answer to preventing Percy from losing all his and everybody else's money at dice and roulette tables was not as simple as not booking him into supper clubs in Reno, Tahoe, Las Vegas, Puerto Rico or other placing where gambling is legal and readily available.

To avoid this catastrophe in the gambling areas, during one very lucrative engagement Percy played in Las Vegas, Johnson went so far as to write the manager of every gambling spot in the area that he was not to extend credit to Songbird for more than $200; that if he did, he was doing so at his own risk; that Songbird's business managers would not honor loans beyond that amount. It didn't work at all. Songbird simply borrowed from various loan sharks.

But there was even a problem in the areas where gambling was not legal. In these areas word had, as it will, gotten around in professional gambling circles that a very new plump pigeon, named Percy Songbird had come upon the scene. The gambling fraternity kept its chapters informed as to Songbird's bookings.

Almost invariably after the opening show in a given city, a pleasant gentleman would visit Songbird in his dressing room, introduce himself as a friend of a mutual friend and invite Percy to join in a friendly poker game any day or night of his choice.

Invariably Percy would accept such invitations. Invariably he would lose. And lose large amounts of money. On one occasion in a major Western city, not a legalized gambling area, Songbird accused his poker playing friends of having won all his money by cheating him. They hit him over the head with the butt of a gun. He wound up in a hospital, from which he called Jeremy Johnson and told the manager a long, lying story about having been waylaid by thugs and robbed on the way home from the club. The club owner was a friend of Johnson's, so one call from Johnson to the club owner exposed the unhappy truth of the situation.

"Jerry," said the club owner, "He's lucky they didn't kill him."

The parade of wraiths of former managers had slowed down but at one point ten different people from Hollywood descended on Johnson with claims that they had put up $1000 each toward a motion picture Songbird was going to produce, starring Songbird. The picture had never been made; their ten thousand dollars and Songbird had disappeared. But now that he was a big star with his own television show, making $20,000 per week in night clubs (Percy generally said $50,000 in interviews with more gullible small town newspapermen), they wanted their money back

And when Percy was not entertaining or gambling he was busily falling in love with various females in the cities he played. Too often they were ten or twelve years old, and their mothers tended to be irritated when they learned that Percy had promised their children undying devotion, but left town without so much as a goodbye. Sometimes even the older females, approximately of the ages of the ones Percy married, would protest to Johnson that they had been treated unfairly and make threats which occasionally required defending.

And speaking of marrying, in due time Percy found the relationship with the lady from Tempe so stormy that he divorced her.

"Jeremy", he said to Johnson, "I know I said this last time, but this time I mean it. I swear I'm never going to get married again."

A week later he married a widow from Dodge City. A month later they had their first child.

Johnson plodded on, squaring beefs, pushing the budding career of this idol of more middle-aged and older ladies than anyone since Liberace. He made frequent pleas to Percy that he should try to be a nicer, more stable person, but to little avail.

*Against stupidity the very Gods*
*themselves contend in vain.*
Johann Von Schiller

## 60. CAREER DIVERSIFICATION – SOMETIMES IT WORKS, SOMETIMES NOT

*The Percy Songbird Show* on the WWB network ran its thirteen week summer course. Percy's active personal life was beginning to take its toll. He went through all rehearsals clear through showtime, all during the run of the show, sipping at a mug filled with coffee and bourbon. He popped uppers.

Johnson told me later that he felt one of the reasons Percy didn't do better on the show was that the nervous tension which possessed him began to come across on the tube, that the relaxed quality so essential to the star of a show of this kind was simply not there. Percy was unaware, as the show progressed, that there was any chance that it would not run forever. Each week as he watched the graceful abstract swallow swooping over the tv tube, spelling out in dazzling multi-colored letters, *The Percy Songbird Show* he became more convinced that he had arrived as a super star. He began to treat his guest stars, some of the most talented and important entertainers in show business, the same way he treated the Magnitude Records' promotion men. His popularity with his peers did not grow.

It is not the business of a personal manager or an agent, however, to be deterred by temporary setbacks like the failure of a television network to pick up his singer's show for the fall season. *Reevaluate the situation; plan the next step; tote that bale.*

Johnson figured that Percy's career as a straight singer, as a singer tv-star was beginning to show signs of wear. What obviously was needed was to try to diversify, expand the career in new directions. As a matter of fact he had already launched a couple of efforts toward this end. Percy was a handsome young man, with good features, if slightly prissy of mouth, and had a charming, shy, small-boy manner which had considerable romantic appeal.

One rather obvious direction which these attributes (along with his sweet, pure voice) suggested was that of romantic songstar in the tradition of Nelson Eddy or Alan Jones. Johnson had lined up a reading for Percy with the producer of a major new dramatic tv series. The part was the male lead of the show. Percy was out on the road, when the arrangements for the reading were made. He had met a young lady, who was in the chorus line of the club in which he was playing, and had decided to bring her home to California with him. His then-wife found out about it and had a young man serve Percy with divorce papers as he stepped off the plane with the chorus girl. He was so upset he refused to come with Johnson to the reading. Somebody else, naturally, got the part.

Johnson, nevertheless, kept trying. That's what a manager does. He kept trying, along with the people in the legitimate theatre and motion picture and television departments of GAG, to find romantic dramatic roles for Percy - - - and then, he had the inspiration to end all inspirations:

Percy was young, pretty, articulate. The television talk shows were increasingly effective and influential. The only singer-hosted talk shows Johnson knew were Mike Douglas, John Gary and Della Reese. The Gary and Reese shows only ran some 26 weeks, but Douglas was making a million dollars a year on his syndicated talk show.

Sure enough, Johnson, with the substantial help of

some of GAG's brightest agents, got Percy another national
television show. This one syndicated, and this one with Percy
not only singing, but interviewing guests a la Johnny Carson,
Mike Douglas, Merv Griffin. Johnson did not know how good
an interviewer Percy would be. He knew that Percy was one
of the most egocentric people he had ever met. He knew that
Percy had no interest in anyone or anything in the world, except as it related to Percy Songbird. He knew that Percy found
it virtually impossible not to be the total center of attraction
every possible waking moment of his life. Particularly if a
camera was on him.

Aware of all this Johnson gave Percy a long and earnest
lecture before the talk show series began.

"The essence of successful interviewing," he told Songbird, "is to be - - - or at least appear to be - - - totally absorbed
by and interested in what your guest is saying. To be so aware
of what your guest is saying that if he is wandering off into
something dull, interrupt with a new question or comment to
get him onto something entertaining or exciting. And most of
all, keep yourself out of the interviews!"

Johnson preached that credo to Songbird as an experienced manager, anticipating the pitfalls, should. He preached
it and preached it until Percy said:

"My god, Jerry, you think I'm stupid or something! I
know what you're talking about. Don't worry."

On the first show one of the guests was Dr. Christian
Barnard, the heart transplant specialist. After Percy greeted
him and asked him what he was doing, and Dr. Barnard said
he had just written a new book, concerned with heart trans-
plants, Percy did twenty two uninterrupted minutes on the
medical and moral issues involved in transferring a heart
from one person to another. Fortunately the shows were taped
for later showing, and the director was able to edit out almost
all of Songbird's assinine remarks before the show was telecast.

Johnson knew right then that the new Percy Songbird
nationally syndicated show was not going to make it. He

nevertheless, as a good manager should, struggled with Percy and the show's bankrollers, and the director and every one else involved to keep it running. He even wrote Percy's cue cards, but all to no avail. After 39 episodes the syndicate production people hollered uncle.

All the while, of course, Johnson was probing and pushing toward the phase of Songbird's career which would make him one of the big dramatic, romantic stars of the day. Again with the tireless cooperation of the people in the GAG legitimate theatre department, Percy had his chance.

A summer stock theatre tour was lined up for Percy. He would play the lead in *The Vagabond King*. Percy found stardom in this romantic, dramatic setting before live audiences even headier than being a television superstar. Within the first two weeks of the tour he managed to inaugurate a mad, passionate affair with the company's leading lady. Percy not only made no effort to keep this fiery new love match a secret from the other members of the cast, he even managed to see to it that his then-wife in New York heard about it. This was one element which served to keep that marriage at the state of storminess, which Percy found so necessary to his well-being.

Nevertheless Percy turned out to be a highly capable, exciting natural actor. His performances drew rave reviews, and Johnson told me that at many of the shows he attended, Percy's acting moved segments of the audience to tears. The result again, however, was that Percy imagined himself an unshakeable superstar. Before the tour was over, he had gotten into a fist fight with one of the other actors, a younger and stronger man, whom Percy nevertheless defeated by kicking him in the groin. He also hit an elderly stagehand in one of the theatres, making it necessary for Johnson to square the matter with the stage hands' union.

The head of the touring company, Philip Rank, visited the show on one stop, and introduced himself to Percy, whom he hadn't previously met.

"I'm Rank," he said.

The leading lady was present, and Percy couldn't resist displaying his devastating wit.

"You certainly are," he told Philip Rank.

Rank later told Johnson that he felt Percy badly needed the services of a shrink. Johnson did not disagree. But by that time Percy had reached a point where he was many thousands of dollars behind in alimony and child support payments to the wife from Baton Rouge and the one from Tempe; owed the Federal and State governments well over a hundred thousand dollars in income taxes; owed additional hundreds of thousands of dollars to people who had been trusting and greedy enough to sell him small planes, large wardrobes, deluxe homes, mobile and stationery and scores of other items and services. In a desperate and continuing effort to help Percy work his way out of this mountainous mess, Johnson had once again begun to defer his 15% commission. The deferments reached $20,000, and Johnson reached the end of his patience and faith.

He suggested to Percy that Percy manage himself and use the 15% to pay off some of his debts. Percy worked out a better method for unburdening himself. He went into bankruptcy. And he is managing himself with the assistance of the Dodge City wife. Which, some may say, proves that the career of personal manager and/or agent is highly non-essential. As I said earlier, I don't agree. I think a good personal manager is essential. It's just that being one is difficult sometimes.

Jeremy Johnson certainly found it difficult to manage Percy Songbird. I had an occasional problem with a Bobby Darin, a John Gary, even an occasional one with an Eddy Arnold or Jim Lowe. Johnson and I talked about Songbird one day. He, too, said he wondered what Tom Parker would have done with Percy.

I think I've made it plain that your break-in point as an agent or manager can be almost any career, anywhere. I've also mentioned one key organization, the Conference of Personal Managers, you should attempt to join once you launch a career in this area. An agents' organization you should join is the

Artists' Representatives Association, Inc., 1270 Avenue of the Americas, New York, N.Y. 10020. In the meantime, probably the most important thing you can do is get as much background and experience in as many phases of the music/record business as you can. It'll all come in handy.

# PART III

## SECTION THREE

### Administrative

*Zeus does not bring all men's*
*plans to fulfillment.*
Homer

# 61. THE MEN WHO DECIDE DESTINIES

In an earlier part of this book I pointed out that the arbitrary categorization of careers into Creative, Business, et al was necessarily imprecise. It is surely an advantage for a so-called creative practitioner to have good business sense. And by the same token it is a tremendous asset for a person pursuing a so-called music/record business career to be creative. And many are. Many of the most creative people in the industry are in the "business" area.

And make no mistake about the vast influence the industry's business leaders have on the destinies of everyone in the business, in any area. A good deal of the shape and form of today's record business, for example, was determined by a long feud between two of the shrewdest, proudest, most aggressive business leaders I have ever known: The late General David Sarnoff of the Radio Corporation of America and William Paley of the Columbia Broadcasting System.

In the early 40s, the General's National Broadcasting Company was clearly the number one radio network. Paley's CBS consistently ran second. Then one day Paley took Jack Benny, Edgar Bergen and some of NBC's other top comedians from NBC by the simple expedient of making them capital gains deals they couldn't refuse. (Capital gains, of course, is the device whereby a person or organization selling a property pays a 25% tax instead of the normal income tax which may run as high as 90%.

This was one of the earliest applications of the Capital Gains gambit in showbusiness, and it is one indication of the potential and real importance of accountants and attorneys in management, about which more in the appropriate section. At any rate, when Benny, Bergen, et al transferred their audience pulling power to CBS, Paley's network replaced NBC as the number one network in radio virtually overnight.

"Leadership," said General Sarnoff in his usual states-manlike manner, "is no laughing matter." And he proceeded to dedicate himself and Radio Corp's billions to beating Paley's brains out whenever and wherever he could, in television (a monumental battle ensued over color tv); records, etc.

Paley and CBS proved worthy foes. While Sarnoff was urging Elmer "Shorty" Engstrom and RCA's engineers to come up with a superior tv color system, new recording techniques and other technological miracles, Paley was pushing people like Peter Goldmark in similar directions. It wasn't too long after the Federal Communications Commission approved the RCA color system and rejected CBS's color wheel approach that Columbia introduced the twelve inch 33 1/3rd rpm long playing record to replace the standard ten inch 78 rpm disk. And Sarnoff's answer was a 45 rpm record.

The two new playing speeds represented the first significant technological changes on the consumer level in phonograph records since Emile Berliner introduced the flat disk to replace Thomas Edison's cylindrical disk. (I'm excepting, of course, the introduction of studio recording on tape, and other internal technical changes.)

There is obviously no way of telling how great an effect, for better or worse, the introduction of these new physical record forms had on the careers of how many people in the music/record business. One thing is certain: The changes created temporary chaos on virtually every level of the industry and countless careers were dramatically influenced.

I was Editor in Chief of *The Billboard* at the time the two new speeds were introduced, and shortly after the introduction of the 45 rpm record by RCA I went to work for the Radio Corp. My original job was as executive assistant to the late John Wilson, familiarly known as Joe. Wilson was executive vice president of the Radio Corporation of America, second in command to the late Frank Folsom, who was then President of RCA. Both RCA and Columbia were spending millions of dollars in every conceivable form of advertising, promotion, publicity, merchandising and general propoganda. Each, of course, was trying desperately to establish the new speed it had introduced, as the exclusive new standard for the entire industry.

I felt this was wasteful to a large degree, and that there was a legitimate need for both the speeds. I suggested this to Joe Wilson, and further suggested that I might be able to hold quiet meetings with the heads of the other major record companies and attempt to persuade them to adopt both 33 1/3rd and 45 on an equitable, but firm calendared schedule.

Wilson told me to go ahead and see what I could do. I called the late Ted Wallerstein, who was then head of Columbia; Milton Rackmil, head of Decca (who recently retired as a key executive of MCA, Decca and Universal Pictures); and the late Glenn Wallichs, head of Capitol Records.

After a series of long, involved meetings we arrived at a program, whereby Capitol and Decca would adopt both new speeds and RCA and Columbia would follow. Joe Wilson and I were elated over what we considered to be a major coup. We felt we had put together a program, which would not only save RCA and Columbia millions of dollars in extraordinary propaganda costs, but would bring stabilization back to an industry, which sorely needed it.

We saw Folsom that night and told him the news.

"That's out!" he said, "There will be no deal of any kind. It's going to be 45!"

And that was the end of that. Again I make the point that I do not know how many careers were affected, nor to what degree, by the introduction of the new speeds. Nor do I know how many careers were effected by the long delay in the stabilization of the industry which followed upon Folsom's rejection of the program the other industry leaders and we had worked out. I know the effects were enormous on countless careers.

And just so, through the years, the introduction of stereo, tape, cartridges and cassettes, quadrasonic sound, video-cassettes, etc. will have great bearing on the careers of many people in the industry today. One of the most recent of the newer inventions was auditioned for the press recently. It is Disco-Vision.

Disco-Vision is a twelve inch plastic record, recorded on one side only, with a maximum playing time of forty minutes. It may be played on a playback unit, which attaches to the antenna input terminals of any standard VHF television set. There is no needle or pick-up stylus on the unit. It utilizes an optical system with a low-powered helium laser, and throws both the picture and sound on the television tube, just like any other program.

MCA is not saying exactly when the playback unit and disks will be on the retail market, but they expect the unit to sell for about $450, and the disks, depending on playing time, for approximately $2.00 to $10.00

Of course a number of other companies have also introduced video disk and video cassette systems.

The president of MCA is Lew Wasserman. When I knew Lew in the mid 30s he had just come to work for MCA in New York as head of their publicity and advertising operation. Lew had been a press agent in Cleveland. He got the job with MCA by writing Jules Stein, founder and head of what at that time was a huge booking agency, telling Stein that the MCA publicity material on its bands was atrocious. Stein wrote Lew and told him that if he thought he could do better, to come on to New

York and try.

Lew did, and did indeed do better. Today he is President of MCA, and has been a major factor in the past forty years in building the company into one of the true giants, not only of the music/record industry, but the entire entertainment industry - - - and American industry in general. Men like Wasserman, Sarnoff, Paley, Wilson and Folsom do indeed have a great effect on the careers of thousands upon thousands of people in every phase of an industry.

Let's take a look at some of the other men at the top of the music/record business ladder and see what it takes to attempt to join the club.

## 62. GARMENT MAKERS, INDIANS & OTHERS

A recurring theme in this book is that the origin, training
and background of people who have been successful in almost
all careers in the music/record business are extremely varied.
There seems to be no basic pattern. And this is particularly true
of the complex top jobs. Record company executives are certainly no exception.

Quite a few of them (as is further detailed in the Attor-
ney/Accountant section) are attorneys and accountants. Clive
Davis,head of Columbia, is an attorney; Rocco Laginestra at
RCA, an accountant; Milton Rackmil, whom I mentioned in
the last chapter, was a graduate of the New York University
School of Commerce and certified public accountant. He had
his own private practice before he became chief comptroller of
the Brunswick Radio Corporation in 1929. Glenn Wallichs,
whom I also mentioned in the last chapter, operated a small
radio repair shop in Hollywood before he talked Johnny Mer-
cer, one of music's all-time great songwriters and the late
Buddy DeSylva, film producer to join him in forming Capitol
Records. They pooled $10,000 to start Capitol.

Berry Gordy, Jr. of Detroit did even better. With a

loan of $500 he started Motown Records, which today, of course, is not only a major record company, but one of the fastest growing entertainment complexes in the industry. Berry was a song writer in 1958 when he started Motown. He wrote some of Jackie Wilson's and Etta James's best tunes.

Another of the great recent record company successes is A & M Records. A is Herb Alpert, who was a trumpet player and singer when he joined M, who is Jerry Moss. Jerry grew up in New York, majored in English at Brooklyn College, was briefly in television production before he set up his own independent promotion operation on the West Coast, and then joined Herb Alpert in forming A & M in 1962. Their first record was *The Lonely Bull,* featuring Herb and the Tia Juana Brass.

Mike Curb, probably the youngest major record company president in the industry, as head of MGM Records is primarily a producer/performer. He still has an act called The Mike Curb Congregation. And the current president of Capitol Records is an Indian, Bhaskar Menon. Capitol, of course, is owned by the London-based world-wide record conglomerate, Electrical Musical Industries (EMI) and Menon was head of the EMI record operation in India. He was educated in England.

Menon's predecessor at Capitol was Stan Gortikov. Gortikov joined Capitol shortly after I did, in 1960. I was vice president in charge of Eastern Operations and Stan came in as Director of Corporate Development. Stan's exceptional administrative talents are clearly evidenced by his rapid rise in Capitol. After four months in the Corporate Development job he was made Director of Merchandising, Advertising and Market Research. Shortly after that he was given the further responsibility of heading up the entire manufacturing operations. Shortly thereafter he was made president of Capitol Distributing Corporation, which in plain English is the sales wing of Capitol Records. Then he was elected a vice president of Capitol Records, in charge of Marketing and Advertising. From there he became president of Capitol Records, Inc. and then moved up to the presidency of Capitol Industries, which is now the parent company of Capitol Records, Inc.

Stan came into the record business straight from the garment industry. For eleven years he had been in total charge of design and production for one of the largest ladies' coats manufacturing companies in the industry, a firm with four manufacturing plants. Prior to going into the garment business he had been copy chief for a small West Coast advertising agency named Dunn and Fenwick. The Dunn of the pair was a Capitol vice president, who eleven years later brought Stan into the company.

Stan was a graduate (1941) of the University of Southern California, where he had majored in Journalism and was editor of the school paper, as he'd been in high school. He went into the Army straight off the campus and moved up during WWII in the same way he moved up at Capitol. When the war ended he went into the advertising agency business as a copy writer.

Stan Gortikov today is president of the Recording Industry Association of America (of which incidentally Milton Rackmil was the first president). And it is fortunate for the industry, for it is faced with a number of very serious problems, not the least of which is the bootlegging and piracy of records, tapes, cartridges, etc. Incredible as it seems, a number of pirates are taking the position that it is perfectly legal for them to duplicate and sell hit records and tapes without authorization or payment to anyone excepting the royalty to the artist and the mechanical royalty to the publisher. There is even an Association of these duplicators. The battle is being fought in various State courts, and if the pirates are upheld you may be exploring the possibilities of a career in still another new phase of the music/record business - - - Bootleg/Pirate Enterprises.

Since I consider Stan Gortikov one of the best executives I have ever known in the music/record business I had a long talk with him about the training, background and qualifications needed by people who aspire to top administrative positions. Stan's feeling is (as is mine) that every and any kind of training (formal and informal) is desirable. For example Business

Administration, Marketing, Advertising, Merchandising, Journalism, Research courses could all be of great help. I have already
pointed out how many successful executives (and will say more
about this later) are attorneys and accountants.

Stan points out, too, that in today's business world it's
more vital than ever for a top executive to have a complete
awareness and a mature and sophisticated concept of social and
economic elements in our society. Thus a liberal arts degree
would be useful. Another qualification Stan puts high on the
list is the ability to communicate. On an eye-ball to eye-ball,
one on one level; to communicate with small groups or large
assemblies. And not only to communicate, but to communicate
persuasively. Yet conversely to be able to listen, and to learn
continually.

And the ability to communicate with and listen effectively to the most widely divergent group of characters ever thrown
together in any single industry. Within his own company, it
goes without saying, that the top administrator must be able to
communicate effectively and inspire to maximum heights his
own department heads and other colleagues. And in the record
business a record company executive has to deal daily with an
incredible range of personalities of the artist, manager, agent
and other levels. Everyone from a top selling speed freak to a
temperamental septagenarian concertmeister; everyone from
ex-carnival showman Tom Parker to ex-mail room boy David
Geffen.

There was a time when only a person who had a good
deal of formal training and long experience in structured business practices could be an effective record company head. Today, to a degree far greater than ever existed before, that is no
longer true. There are severely structured companies run by
administrators with traditional formal training, and some such
companies are highly successful. But there are also companies
run in a most informal, non-structured, almost ad-lib fashion.
And some of these are also highly successful.

It should prove encouraging both to budding careerists

who choose to follow the formal path, as well as to the non-conformists to know that both styles can work. Let's review a few of each.

A *learned fool is more foolish*
*than an ignorant one.*
  Moliere
  (Jean Baptists Ponquelin)

## 63. FORMAL & FREE-FORM APPROACHES


In my time as Vice President in Charge of Eastern Operations at Capitol Records the company was a severely structured and formally operated one. Key junior and senior executives were urged to attend American Management Association training courses, for example. And there's nothing wrong with this if a balance is maintained between genuine, uninhibited enthusiasm, openness and straight talk and the plastic, frequently pointless psychotricks of the formalists.

Great concentration is focused by the formalists on such ingenious psychological devices as this:

As an executive never say to a subordinate, "Joe, it's important we get this done by tomorrow, so please get off your fanny and do it."

Always say, "Joe, I *suggest* you do this as soon as you possibly can."

Tomorrow, if it's still not done, you day, "Joe, I *suggest* you try to expedite this."

The poorly managed formal, severely structured operations also have a tendency to put total dependence on numbers and none at all on market conditions as they exist and change in the field from day to day. At one point in my Capitol career I took over the Singles Record operation in addition to my other duties. I took it over only on the condition that I would have complete authority in every phase of the operation: Artist & Repertoire; Sales; Promotion, etc.

I discovered that one of the major reasons the company's single sales were not what they should be was that its Sales policies were unrealistic and completely out of tune with market conditions. Almost all record companies at that time were giving their own distributors, one-stops (about whom more later) and other influential elements in developing hit records various bonuses and discounts. A record company might, for example, give a one-stop one free record for each record the one-stop bought on the first five hundred records, as an inducement to persuade the one-stop to "push" the record with his juke box operator and retailer customers.

A knowledgeable and experienced record man was head of sales, actually president of Capitol Records Distributing Corporation, at that time. His name is John K. (Mike) Maitland, and today he's head of MCA Records and highly successful. In my investigation of Capitol's problems in the Singles area I went to have a talk with Mike. He explained that, of course, he was aware that all of our competitors were giving special discounts and bonuses to promote single hits. But the key administrative officer of the company at that time was a man in Finance, who had figured out that the company must show a profit of 14.5% on every single record sold. And he had turned down every one of Mike's requests for permission to extend discounts and bonuses, on the grounds that it would reduce the percentage of profit on each record sold. This financial genius, of course, is no longer at Capitol.

Mike (about whom more later) left Capitol, took over as head of Warner Bros. Records, built it into one of the most successful new operations in the industry, and as I've said, is now head of MCA records.

Clive Davis, Columbia president, on the other hand, is

an example of a man, who heads a company that operates with every bit of, if not more dependence of numbers in market research, profitability projections, budgets, chains-of-command and all the other elements of the traditional, severely structured corporations. (It's a truism, of course, that when an organization reaches a certain size - - - record company or otherwise - - - it's almost impossible to operate without some rigidity and formality.) Davis, however, leavens the structured operation with a good deal of expertise in human behavior, enthusiasm, etc.

One of the best of the young tradepaper reporters, John Gibson of *Record World* asked Davis in an interview:

" . . . you conceive of Columbia as a free-wheeling, well-lubricated company and you don't believe the size hampers efficiency?"

Davis said, "I think Columbia is a very unique company. Obviously I'm not totally objective in that there are problems in any company becoming a large company. But you never hear about the special challenges and rewards connected with being with a large company. For example, the challenge of breathing life and spirit and warmth and camaraderie into what otherwise can be an impersonal organization. I think we've done that and frankly, it's a great feeling. What shocks people on the outside when they first come into contact with us is that when they expect to see General Motors, they find a kicking, alive and spirited group of dedicated people who work endlessly and tirelessly for the artists they're involved with."

Davis also sets the pace for this structured giant operation by personally working twelve hours a day.

Perhaps at the opposite end of the poles of administrative styles is the approach of Marshall Chess, the young man who is head of the Rolling Stones record company. Marshall comes from one of the most knowledgeable and successful families in the record business, a family which pioneered in the rhythm and blues field, among other accomplishments with Chess Records and other labels.

John Gibson also did an interview with Marshall shortly

after Marshall replaced Allen Klein as head of the Stones' record
operation.

"Is it working out like you thought it would when you
started this company?" asked Gibson.

"I never thought," said Marshall. "Part of the reason I
love it, that I do it, is because it is free-form and when you're in
a free-form type business situation you don't plan your life that
way. You couldn't run this operation structured. You could,
perhaps, but it wouldn't be half as effective as running it free-
form."

Even the Stones' company's basic studio is free-form
and unusual. Here's what Marshall told Gibson about it:

"I think our truck, our mobile recording unit is better
than anything in America. We call it The Mighty Mobile. The
Rolling Stones designed it. Their records sound good. They've
been recording and producing for eight years. Glyn Johns helped design it, a lot of people who know what they're doing
really helped. It's a very successful truck. Lots of people use
it, the Zeppelin, Elton John, Neil Young."

Possibly the best example of a company in transition
from extreme free-form as described by Marshall Chess and a
Columbia or RCA or Capitol is WEA. That today is the complex
of companies now owned by the Kinney conglomerate, consisting of Warner Bros., Elektra and Atlantic. The latter, you'll recall from my mention of Jerry Wexler in the Producer section
of this book was the highly successful operation owned by
Ahmet and Nesuhi Ertegun and Jerry. The three produced
practically all the companies records from 1953 to about 1959.
They were always deeply involved in every aspect of the company's operations.

Jerry, apart from being a producer, is one of the best
promotion men in the industry. He probably knows more disk
jockeys more favorably than any record man in the business.
Along the way Jerry and the Erteguns sold several publishing
companies they owned; they acquired Elektra Records, and then
sold the whole shebang to Seven Arts-Warner Bros. WB, in turn,

was acquired by Kinney. And Kinney, as mentioned, is a giant conglomerate. John Gibson also did an interview with Jerry, during which Jerry told him:

". . . we've never had a recording budget, an advertising budget or a promotional budget. If Ahmet wanted to make a record, he'd make a record. Same with Nesuhi or I. We would discuss it many times if there was enough money involved, and if somebody really wanted to do something the others never said no. So we worked without a budget. Of course this gave a big case of the faint hearts to the Warner Brothers accountants after we merged, first with Seven Arts and then with Kinney. They came in and said what do you mean no budget? That's like saying you're existing without oxygen or something. Now as I understand it there are some pro forma budgets submitted to a delegation of gentlemen at the main office, sales projections, budgets, anything they'd like we provide them. We don't want to get them unhappy or irritated unnecessarily."

Jerry was equally frank when Gibson asked him about the various mergers:

" . . . these days when you merge in the industry, there are certain cliche reasons that are always sent up, that are floating like balloons out of cartoon peoples' mouths. OK, so official reasons for merging: 1) to have global facilities at your disposal; OK, that's a cosmic reason; 2) to have the wherewithal to continue expansion. Well, that's good because the NAM would dig that, it's very American to expand; 3) to utilize the technological synergy that will emerge when we put these things together. But the real reason is C.G., Capitol Gains, the American Dream. That's the real reason every time. Everytime for everybody. But I guess you're not supposed to say that."

So free-form or structured you, too, can get to be a record company administrator, maybe even achieve a C.G. or two. But on the business side, there are any number of other careers, which will be useful to you, and which may lead you to the top.

# PART III

## SECTION FOUR

### Sales & Marketing

*An epigram is only a wisecrack*
*that's played Carnegie Hall.*
   Oscar Levant

287.

## 64. STRUCTURES & BACKGROUNDS

Just as there have been many drastic changes in musical styles and in technology, so have there been changes in the channels which take the record, cartridge or cassette from the manufacturer to the ultimate consumer. In the 30s and the early 40s, the lines were beautifully simple: The manufacturer sold his records to his distributor; the distributor to the dealer; the dealer to the consumer.

Today the manufacturer sells a substantial amount of product direct to the consumer through record and other mail order clubs. And he sells not only to the distributor, but also to rack jobbers and one-stops. Sometimes the distributor/rack jobber/one stop are all one firm. In any event, all three operations frequently sell to dealers. The rack jobber generally sets up racks in outlets such as drug stores and supermarkets, and also operates leased record departments in outlets like department stores. The one-stop sells to the juke box operator, but also frequently has dealer customers.

All of which expansion and development, of course, is greatly beneficial to people who want to get into the sales, marketing, advertising or promotion areas of the business.

Virtually every city of any size has a rack jobber or one-stop, and a young person going to work for one of these operations acquires many advantages. To begin with there is probably no better way to learn the music/record business than at the rack jobber-one stop level. Here one gets a consumer's view of the product, what is successful and what isn't and why? A view impossible from almost any other vantage point.

Additionally a person working in a rack jobbing or one stop operation will have frequent opportunities to meet influential people from many record companies. Personnel from the record companies' local distributing branches, whether owned by the manufacturer or independent, will be in all the time. And quite frequently key sales, marketing and other people from the headquarters' offices of the record companies will visit. An alert, ambitious person will soon find an opportunity to move on into the distributing or manufacturing end of the business if he or she chooses.

I mentioned earlier that at one point I took over the Singles Record operation at Capitol. At that time I put together a national sales and promotion organization. The chart which appears on the following page is from a book, called *The Capitol Singles Handbook* which I issued to the staff in all offices at the time. Even though this was issued in the summer of 1962, the structure is quite valid today.

It shows the table of organization of a record company sales staff and the cities which constituted Capitol's seven Regions of the country. It also shows the regional and branch city managerial functions. Naturally under each branch sales manager, there were one or more salesmen.

The Operations Manager in each branch, of course, was in charge of order fulfillment, inventory, etc.

A number of the branches also had their own promotion men. These are indicated in a similar Organizational Chart which I developed for the Promotion operation, and which appears in the Advertising, Promotion and Publicity section of this book. There is nothing sacrosanct about the city composition

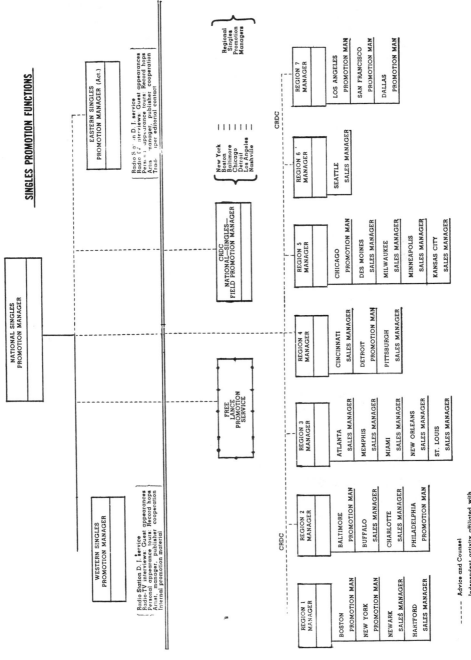

SINGLES PROMOTION FUNCTIONS

of the regions, nor is it significant that Cleveland and Indianapolis, for example, merely had City Managers and not Sales and Operations Managers as did most of the other cities at this time. The reasons for this were peculiar to the Capitol operation at that particular moment. A look at a similar organizational line-up of Columbia, WEA or any other record company would have its own variations.

Sales and marketing personnel, again, comes from many backgrounds and fields of experience. Many of the top sales executives with record companies, naturally enough come up through training in the field. I mentioned Mike Maitland, who I believe is one of the ablest sales and marketing executives in the industry. Mike started as a salesman in Capitol's Detroit branch, became branch manager and worked his way up to the presidency of Capitol Records Distributing Corp., then president of Warner Bros. Records and currently is head man of MCA Records.

Under Mike at MCA as Director of National Sales is Vince Cosgrave. Cosgrave was originally a disk jockey in San Francisco. Before joining MCA he was promotion director for a leading distributor, Chatton Distributing Company in Oakland.

Another highly effective top sales executive comes out of the tradepaper field, another alumnus of *The Billboard*. This is Joel Friedman, who in my time on *Billboard*, was a member of the West Coast advertising staff.

Joel is now President of WEA Distributing Corporation, the sales operation handling all Warner Bros., Elektra, Atlantic and affiliated labels product. He recently undertook one of the most difficult jobs in Sales and Marketing: Setting up and staffing company owned and operated distributing branches in key markets throughout the country. As this is written the operation has over 500 employees in eight major metropolitan areas.

Training? Ambition?

While working as head of sales for Warner Bros. Joel Friedman studied law at night, and got his law degree. He told me he did this not because he wished to be a practising attorney, but simply because he felt it would make him a better sales and merchandising executive.

You don't necessarily have to go that far to make a career in sales and marketing. There are a considerable number of training and educational opportunities in this area. However, since most of them apply to the other business careers as well, let's review the backgrounds, experiences and techniques of some practitioners in the other fields and cover the educational aspects in an all-inclusive subsequent chapter.

# PART III

## SECTION FIVE

### Advertising, Promotion, Publicity

*When a man is wrapped up in himself* 293 .
*he makes a pretty small package.*
John Ruskin

## 65. INSEPARABILITY AT WORK

It may seem even more arbitrary to lump advertising-promotion-publicity into one Section than it is to categorize careers as *Creative, Commentary, Business* and *Educational.* However I think a look at a recent typical highly professional campaign for a major network television music special will clearly demonstrate the essential inter-relationship of the three career areas.

The special was *New Year's Rockin' Eve,* produced by Dick Clark's organization and hosted by Three Dog Night. Also starring on the show, which was taped in the Grand Ballroom of the Queen Mary in Long Beach harbor, were Blood, Sweat and Tears, Al Green, Helen Reddy and Billy Preston. The 90 minute show was carried on 186 stations of the NBC TV network. Not only did the campaign involve advertising, promotion and publicity people and organizations, it involved those departments of all the participating companies, namely:

1. Dick Clark and his organization;

2. The NBC Advertising, Promotion & Publicity Departments; many, if not all, of the 186 stations carrying the show also participated in all three areas;

    3. The Dr. Pepper Advertising, Promotion & Publicity Departments;

    4. The Advertising, Promotion & Publicity Departments of each of the record companies for which each of the artists appearing on the show record;

    5. Independent promotion and publicity organizations working for the participants such as Don Rogers Enterprises, Clark's Los Angeles public relations firm; Los Angeles press agent Jay Bernstein's organization, which was commissioned by Dr. Pepper to do national publicity on the show, etc.

    *On the advertising side here are some of the campaign's elements:*

    At its October convention of franchised Dr. Pepper bottlers, Dr. Pepper announced it was buying the show, and initiated local radio, tv and print advertising campaigns by each bottler in his own area;

    NBC ran a saturation radio and television spot campaign for ten consecutive days leading into showtime.

    *On the promotion level here's what was done:*

    Clark prepared personalized public service announcements, featuring people on the show, and subliminally pitching the show, for 56 radio stations. Each station had the spots on an exclusive basis for its own area;

    Don Rogers and members of the Three Dog Night called top disk jockeys all around the country from Los Angeles, while Clark and members of Blood, Sweat and Tears called jockeys from New York.

    *On the publicity side here are some items:*

    Clark did almost 50 phone interviews with music writers for the underground press and other papers;

    Each of the acts on the show did interviews with uncounted scores of newspaper and magazine writers, all promoting the show;

    Kits containing a copy of the latest LP record of each of the acts on the show, plus photos, biographies, stories about the acts, Clark and the show were sent to over a thousand entertainment editors on newspapers, to teen age magazines like *Flip, 16* and *Star;* to more than 100 college newspapers.

While this campaign is comprehensive, it is not unusual. It is impossible to say how many individual advertising, promotion and publicity people of all kinds participated, probably forty or fifty.

But it clearly demonstrates the inseparable nature of the three functions - - - and consequently the careers in those functions.

Again it will be helpful to have a look at the background, training and experiences of some of the leading people in each area.

*A bore is a person who talks when
you wish him to listen.*
Ambrose Bierce

## 66. AD, PROMO, PUBLICITY
PEOPLE & PROBLEMS

Advertising and publicity for Atlantic Records is
handled very capably by a man named Bob Rolontz. Bob
worked for a small record company, I think it was Bibletone,
before he joined *Billboard* as a music reporter. He worked
many years on *Billboard,* and a few on a now defunct music
paper called *Music Business* before taking charge of Atlantic's
advertising and publicity. George Parkhill, who was RCA's
advertising manager and Herb Hellmann, that company's
public relations director both came out of the field, i.e., they
worked for distributors before moving up to their RCA headquarters offices.

In the music/record business, particularly in record
companies, possibly one of the most difficult problems is
balancing effective advertising practices with keeping the label's
artists and managers happy. Stan Cornyn, who began his record
business career many years ago at Capitol, is one of the brightest men in the industry in a number of creative areas. He's now
vice president of Warner Bros. Records, and here's what he told
*Record World's* John Gibson about that advertising problem:

" . . . Let us say that Elvis Presley records for Warner Bros. Records, and his manager, Col. Parker, comes in and says, 'Well, contract time is just around the corner and you'd probably like to have Elvis for another five years, but we really think before we start talking contract with you that we'd like to have seven billboards on Sunset Strip this month.' *(Ed. note - - - These are a very expensive form of advertising, which many record companies have utilized in recent years).*

"All right, there are three ways of approaching that problem: 1) you can tell Col. Parker that he is an idiot, which he probably would not appreciate too much, 2) you can say, 'baby' you've got it. I love it!' or 3) you can try to make sense. I find the natural tendency has been to take one of the first two alternatives, either cave in or tell somebody to fly a kite, and those are easy ones to do, but the truth is in the middle somewhere. And taking the time to deal with artists and managers as human beings who also have their fears and their problems is the most important thing happening in this business."

Then Stan gave Gibson a specific example of how Warner's worked with a specific artist:

"Alice Cooper, a few years ago, taught Warner Bros. Records some pretty good lessons. Alice's management was deeply interested and had a career plan for the group. We, on the other hand, didn't know much about the group because they were not directly signed to Warner Bros. at that time. They were on Straight Records. We knew something was going on, but that something probably added up to 20,000 albums per release. Alice Cooper's management was quite restive, feeling they weren't getting action out of this record company. That management was correct. We turned around, bit by bit, but what we did was match that management, faith by faith. If they said trust us for seven billboards on the Sunset Strip, which they didn't, it's the correct way to go we said OK, we don't understand what you're doing right now, but you've got it, we're with you. We still may not be cognizant of everything they're doing; it's not our job to have total management

function, and be involved there, but they have strong management, they know what they're doing, we're fully cooperative
and we fund much of what they do."

Otherwise the basic expertise required for a successful
career in advertising in the music/record business is largely the
same as in any other business. The more soundly that advertising expertise is supported by a knowledge of the music and recording industry itself the more effectively will a music/record
advertising man be able to operate.

 ⋅ Promotion, too, has problems unique to the music/re-
cord business as opposed to promotion in any other field. In
record promotion this derives primarily from the handiwork
of Todd Storz, Gordon McGlendon, Bill Stewart and others
responsible for the top 40 format in radio, which development
I treated in some depth in the Commentary section of this
book. Recently this particular problem, basic to getting records
played, tended to become greater than ever, which is to say
that not only are more and more stations limiting the list of
records they'll play to 40, but many stations have cut the lists
to 30 and sometimes less.

Promotion men today, indeed, have taken on a number
of functions other than the primary one of getting records
played by radio stations. The best promotion men make it a
point to maintain regular contacts with rack jobbers, one-stops,
key dealers and other outlets, and frequently work with Sales
department people to coordinate their promotional efforts
with those of the sales force most effectively.

Promotion men have also become an impⲟrtant factor
in artist relationships, since they are generally the record company persons who take artists on the rounds of the most important disk jockeys and help cement the artist's relationship
with the jockeys.

A rather profound change has taken place in the basic
qualifications of promotion people in the past ten years or
more. A decade ago the average promotion man was a clown,
whose main approach to getting his records played was to keep

disk jockeys, music librarians and other radio station personnel amused and to "service" them in a multitude of ways.

The change is admirably commented upon in this recent editorial from the tradepaper *Cash Box:*

"The record promotion man is no longer the character whose depth of intelligence was once measured by his one-liners. That image, thank goodness, has been shed by not only the bright newcomers, but many of the veterans, who have picked up on the no-nonsense (not meaning lack of good-humor) approach that establishes credibility and awareness.

"Yet, we have been told lately that promotion — the basic link (and image) between the recording industry and broadcasting — is a misunderstood function, one that is costing many companies dearly in terms of hit product and others in terms of a low morale factor among its promotion force. One key promotion man puts the roots of the problem at the very top of label executive suites: "The promotion man may be talking to the president or other execs of a non-promotion-minded company, but no one is listening. They are taking the narrow view of 'how come you can't get that specific record played?' No other factors, such as the record itself, tight play lists and the long-range relationship between the promotion man and his radio contacts, are taken into account."

"What is discouraging about this front-office commentary is that it eradicates at one swipe all that is supposed to have evolved in promo man functions in recent years: an honest relationship between him and the broadcaster, thus bridging the credibility gap. A broadening of promo man activities to include regular contact with wholesale and retail establishments so that a proper level of inventory is maintained on successful product and that he gain a proper "feel" of the type of product flow in his territory.

"We have no intention of downgrading the concept of getting play on records. But, won't undue pressure on that "one" record or, for that matter, *every* record on release damage that hard-won credibility relationship? We think labels and their promo force can do a better job by understanding the role of promotion within a broad context, one that does not rise or fall on one release. More airplay on deserving product will come of it. And naturally better communications between the home office and its promo force."

Yet another indication of the new stature of the promotion man in today's music/record business is the fact that Claude Hall in connection with *The Annual Billboard Radio Programming Forum* conducts a competition to determine the best national promotion director; the best record promotion man in each of four districts of the country; the best independent record promotion man and the best national staff promotion man.

The ballot printed here not only shows the structure of the Competition but gives a good idea of how many promotion jobs there are.

# RECORD PROMOTION MEN'S CONTEST

## VOTE:

This is your chance to honor the nation's record promotion men. In each division, vote for first, second and third place by placing a number out beside the man's name. Then send this ballot to: Claude Hall, Billboard Magazine, 9000 Sunset Blvd., Los Angeles, CA 90069.

Those votes will be tabulated by the Billboard staff and winners will be announced at the awards luncheon during the fifth annual Billboard Radio Programming Forum at the Century Plaza Hotel, Los Angeles, Aug. 17-19. Plaques will be awarded to the leading national promotion director in the nation, the leading record promotion man in each of the four districts, the leading independent record promotion man, and the best national staff promotion man.

### SOUTHEAST

| | |
|---|---|
| Johnny Lloyd, Buddah ___ | Jim Harper, Target ___ |
| Donal Gibbons, | Stan Chaison, Atlantic ___ |
| All South ___ | Don Byrt, Ind. ___ |
| Walt Moorehead, | Marty Lacker, Ind. ___ |
| Atlantic ___ | David Esell, A&M ___ |
| Bobby Hurt, CBS ___ | Eddie Lambert, London ___ |
| Peter Nashick, Kinny ___ | Ken Van Durand, RCA ___ |
| Jack Fine, Ind. ___ | Gary Schaffer, |
| Joe Galkins, Ind. ___ | Tone Dist. ___ |
| Eddie Pugh, Kinny ___ | Gary Tanner, Polydor ___ |
| Mike Craft, UA ___ | Bob Holiday, Ind. ___ |
| Charlie Minor, A&M ___ | Leo Carter, Mercury ___ |
| Mike Martin, MGM ___ | Bob Riley, King ___ |
| Marty Kuppe, ABC ___ | Robert E. Lee, |
| Ernie Phillips, Ind. ___ | Rec. Sales ___ |
| Wade Pepper, Capitol ___ | Tom Moore, Campus ___ |
| Larry Bannach, Dot ___ | George Cooper III, Ind. ___ |
| Ed Mascola, Polydor ___ | Bobbi Byrd, SSS ___ |
| Chuck Chellman, Ind. ___ | Philip Rouls, Atlantic ___ |
| Biff Collie, UA ___ | Al Monet, MCA ___ |
| Larry King, Southland ___ | Don McGregor, |
| Dave Mack, RCA ___ | Warner Bros. ___ |
| Tom McEntee, MGM ___ | |

### NATIONAL PROMOTION DIRECTORS

| | |
|---|---|
| Pat Pipolo, MCA ___ | Frank Mancini, RCA ___ |
| Larry Douglas, singles, | Mike Kagan, Epic ___ |
| RCA ___ | Jerry Sharell, Buddah ___ |
| Red Schwartz, Avco ___ | Dick Kline, pop, |
| Stan Bly, Mercury ___ | Atlantic ___ |
| Long John Silver, singles, | Henry Allen, Atlantic ___ |
| Mercury ___ | Ron Saul, |
| Bob Mercer, Fantasy ___ | Warner Bros. ___ |
| Danny Davis, SG/Col ___ | Harold Childs, A&M ___ |
| Vince Faraci, custom labels, | Al Cory, Capitol ___ |
| Atlantic ___ | Buddy Blake, SSS ___ |
| Joe Medlin, soul, | Larry Cohen, |
| Polydor ___ | Jamie/Guyden ___ |
| Cy Warren, London ___ | Gordon Prince, Motown ___ |
| Lenny Meisel, London ___ | Mike Becce, Polydor ___ |
| Steve Rudolph, Scepter ___ | Eddie O'Keefe, |
| Boo Frasier, Perception ___ | Vanguard ___ |
| Freddie North, | Fred Ruppert, Elektra ___ |
| Nashboro ___ | Al Riley, Chess/Janus ___ |
| Pete Bennett, Apple ___ | Gordon Bossin, Bell ___ |
| Mike Sheppard, | Herb Gordon, |
| Monument ___ | Paramount ___ |
| Marvin Helfer, | Jerry Fine, Chelsea ___ |
| ABC-Dunhill ___ | Ben Scotti, MGM ___ |
| Steve Popovich, CBS ___ | Chester Simmons, Stax ___ |

### NATIONAL PROMOTION STAFF

Write-in vote for two candidates. An award will be presented to the best staff national promotion man who is not a director.

1. _____ Company: _____

2. _____ Company: _____

---

## LOCAL & REGIONAL RECORD PROMOTION MEN

### MIDWEST

| | | |
|---|---|---|
| Bob McLain, Capitol ___ | Dick Colanzi, | Ron Els, Capitol ___ |
| Jim Sala, A&M ___ | Poison Ring ___ | Dick Ware, CBS ___ |
| Gene Dononovitch, CBS ___ | Paul Galis, Ind. ___ | Bud Murphy, Atlantic ___ |
| Tom Gilardi, Ind. ___ | Don Markus, | Pat Bullock, Big State ___ |
| Kelvyn Ventour, RCA ___ | Bedno/Wright ___ | Ernie Phillips, Ind. ___ |
| Ken Benson, Buddah ___ | Dave Remedes, | Don Miller, RCA ___ |
| Arnie Leeman, | Kent Beauchamp ___ | Pete Gideon, MCA ___ |
| WB/Elektra ___ | Richie Johnson, Ind. ___ | Steve Dunn, A&M ___ |
| Merlin Littlefield, RCA ___ | Frank Mull, Mercury ___ | Frank Chively, London ___ |
| Luther Wood, Capitol ___ | Jack Hakim, Buddah ___ | Dave Johnson, Motown ___ |
| Richard Taub, Dot ___ | Roger Blund, UA ___ | Dick Bethel, Capitol ___ |
| Bill Heard, CBS ___ | John Rogers, | Julie Godsey, Epic ___ |
| Bill Davis, Atlantic ___ | Big State ___ | Doug Lee, Kinny Group ___ |
| Jim Jeffries, Bell ___ | Chet Miller, CBS ___ | Bud Stebbins, UA ___ |
| Irvin Woolsey, Atlantic ___ | Tom Amman, RCA ___ | Tom Benjamin, UA ___ |
| Mike Gusler, CBS ___ | Danny Ingel, Ind. ___ | Roy Wunch, CBS ___ |
| Bill Cook, Ind. ___ | Al McNutt, MCA ___ | Bob Wurker, Capitol ___ |
| Mike Dragus, Kinny ___ | Gordon Anderson, Epic ___ | Dave Vaughn, Ind. ___ |
| Cy Gold, TDA ___ | Paul Diamond, London ___ | Tim Kehr, CBS ___ |
| Jay Cunniff, ABC ___ | Roy Chievari, WB ___ | Charley Salah, Motown ___ |
| Mel London, | Mike Conwisher, ABC ___ | Gary Lippee, A&M ___ |
| United Records ___ | Mike Levitton, A&M ___ | Lou Sicarass, Atlantic ___ |
| Ed Keely, Capitol ___ | Howard Bedno, Ind. ___ | Perry Stevens, Ind. ___ |
| Don Doublas, Capitol ___ | Frank Anderson, Kinny ___ | Larry Mangiaracino, |
| Russ Yerge, CBS ___ | Al Mathias, RCA ___ | Polydor ___ |
| Nick Hunter, CBS ___ | Norris Green, WB ___ | Wes Hayna, Heilicher ___ |
| Steve Evenoff, Decca ___ | Tex Schofield, | Ted Cohen, WB ___ |
| Bob Shoals, Capitol ___ | Record Ser. ___ | Rob Hegel, |
| Irwin Barg, London ___ | Kerry Knodle, Heilicher ___ | A&I Supreme ___ |
| Paul Diamond, London ___ | Glen Bruder, Roberts ___ | |

### WEST COAST

| | | |
|---|---|---|
| Mike Atkinson, Epic ___ | Terry Powell, CBS ___ | Tony Richland, Ind. ___ |
| Mel Turoff, London ___ | Ron Middag, Elektra ___ | Bill Chappel, UA ___ |
| Mike Kilmartin, Fantasy ___ | Barry Mitchell, UA ___ | Barry Mitchell, UA ___ |
| John Carter, Atlantic ___ | Bill Roberts, UA ___ | Jerry Dougman, |
| Dan Holliday, A&M ___ | Mike Leventon, A&M ___ | Buddah ___ |
| Donna Savedo, UA ___ | Lou Fields, Ind. ___ | Randy Brown, Epic ___ |
| John Fisher, Atlantic ___ | Jan Basham, | Mike Alhadeff, ABC ___ |
| Otis Smith, Invictus ___ | Rec. Merch. ___ | Dennis Morgan, MCA ___ |
| Ernie Farrell, MGM ___ | Chuck Meyer, MCA ___ | Wayne Arnold, Capitol ___ |
| Don Whittemore, RCA ___ | Jack Shields, Stax ___ | Steve Feldman, A&M ___ |
| Eddie deJoy, A&M ___ | Stan Najolia, Buddah ___ | Jeff Traeger, Elektra ___ |
| George Jay, Ind. ___ | Julio Aiello, | Dick Forrester, Ind. ___ |
| Abe Glaser, MGM ___ | Metromedia ___ | Lenny Luffman, MCA ___ |
| Clive Fox, MGM ___ | Ben Wood, CBS ___ | Rich Paladino, Elektra ___ |
| Larry Karp, MGM ___ | Sue Kesick, ABC ___ | Bob Busiak ___ |
| Lou Galliani, RCA ___ | Steve Fischler, Kinny ___ | Jack Ross, Chess ___ |
| Bud O'Shea, Epic ___ | Mike Borchetta, Ind. ___ | Don Graham, Chess ___ |
| Pete Marino, WB ___ | Jim Harper, Target ___ | Jim Benci, Ind. ___ |
| Pat McCoy, ABC ___ | Les Anderson, WB ___ | Ray Anderson, RCA ___ |
| Dave Urso, WB ___ | Sydney Miller, Capitol ___ | George Furness, |
| Joe Gregg, ABC ___ | Jerry Morris, | Atlantic ___ |
| Paul Rappaport, CBS ___ | Fidelity Dist. ___ | Don Carter, Capitol ___ |
| Freddie Mancuso, Stax ___ | David Krause, Elektra ___ | |

### NORTHEAST

| | | |
|---|---|---|
| Buck Reingold, Buddah ___ | Buddy Scott, Ind. ___ | Joe Senkiewicz, CBS ___ |
| Herb Rosen, Ind. ___ | Moe Schulman, Alpha ___ | Ray Melanese, Kinny ___ |
| Bob Ebson, Capitol ___ | Mike Kienfner, CBS ___ | Don Colberg, CBS ___ |
| Earl Rollison, CBS ___ | Zim Zemarel, CBS ___ | Tom Kennedy, |
| Steve W. Rudolph, | Tony Montgomery, | Universal ___ |
| Scepter ___ | RCA ___ | Ron Moseley, Sussex ___ |
| Dan Kelly, Atlantic ___ | Sol Handwerger, MGM ___ | Nate Chacker, RCA ___ |
| Gary Lippe, A&M ___ | Danny Davis, Mercury ___ | Red Richards, |
| Joe Bilello, Buddah ___ | Joe Cash, Ind. ___ | Schwartz Bros. ___ |
| Jim Taylor, A&M ___ | Fred Horton, | Ron deMorino, Kinny ___ |
| Matty Singer, | Best & Gold ___ | Bill Harper, Universal ___ |
| David Posen ___ | Jack Perry, CBS ___ | Dave Marshall, London ___ |
| George Collier, MCA ___ | Barbara Harris, | Steve Rudolf, Scepter ___ |
| Chappy Johnson, | Atlantic ___ | Joe Baldnell, Ind. ___ |
| Chips Dist. ___ | Stan Herman, Ind. ___ | Jerry Ralston, |
| Fred Edwards, | Bill Beamish, Kinny ___ | Best & Gold ___ |
| Stereo Dimension ___ | Tracy, Seaboard ___ | Maury Bloom, MCA ___ |
| Bill Spitalsky, Ind. ___ | John Allen, MCA ___ | Bob Zenter, CBS ___ |
| Cecil Holmes, Buddah ___ | Bob Greenberg, | F. Nestro, Ind. ___ |
| Logan Westbrook, CBS ___ | Warner Bros. ___ | Tom Klimanski, UDS ___ |
| | | Frank Berman, Alpha ___ |

To further clarify the dimensions of the promotion areas of the business, I reproduce my organizational chart from the *Capitol Singles Record Handbook,* which I mentioned earlier. Note that in addition to staff promotion personnel we also employed free lance, independent promotion services on occasions and in territories where it seemed advisable.

Also please remember again that there is nothing sacrosanct about the structure of regions, cities within regions, as shown. They simply represented the soundest alignment for Capitol's specific purposes at that time. Also please note that in many cities a Sales Manager rather than a Promotion Manager is listed. This simply means that we had not appointed a Promotion Manager in that city at that time for one reason or another, and the Sales Manager bore the responsibility for handling promotion as best he could. Another mark of the interchangeability and interrelationship of the careers.

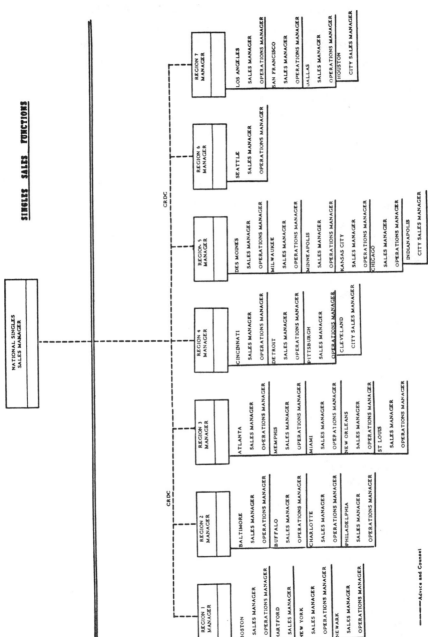

SINGLES SALES FUNCTIONS

------- Advice and Counsel

* Temporary

303.

The major qualification for being a good promotion man really is to be an extrovert, to enjoy "visiting" with people day in and day out. A knowledge of the broadcasting business is desirable. As a matter of fact such top promotion people as Johnny Rosica, formerly head of RCA's promotion department, head of Bell Records West Coast office and now with Creed Taylor Records is an ex-radio man; Jim Jeffries, now with Bell and many other good promotion men come out of radio.

Many, if not a majority of promotion people with major record companies come out of the field, having served either in sales or promotion or both in branch offices, with independent distributors, etc. Many, as previously indicated, get their training in one-stops or rack jobbers, some in retail stores. Obviously, again, the more knowledge of music and records the promotion man has the more effective will he be.

Publicity people in the music/record business, too, generally have the type of training, which competent publicity people in almost any industry have (journalism, English majors; newspaper or tradepaper experience etc.) and, of course, again the more music/record experience the better.

Herb Hellman, RCA's publicity chief, as I've mentioned came straight out of the record field. Two of the best press agents in the music/record business are Jerry Franken, who handles numerous accounts at McFadden, Strauss & Irwin, top Los Angeles public relations firm, and Gene Shefrin, who has his own publicity business. Jerry was radio-tv editor of *Billboard* for many years, during my time there. He also previously worked as a reporter on *Variety*.

Shefrin worked for one of New York's most successful publicists during my *Billboard* days, a man named Dave Alber. They handled many top big band accounts, and today Gene runs his office in Hollywood and handles people like Vic Damone and other singers and entertainers. He also handles literary characters like Irving Wallace, and is one of the West Coast's more successful independent press agents.

In connection with the advertising and publicity phases

of music/record careers I must mention one specific area which holds great potential for people with an artistic bent. That area is Graphics. With the possible exception of books and magazines, the music/record business probably offers more opportunity for photographers, artists, designers and the like than any field I know. The thousands of albums produced each year, in themselves present great opportunities for people in the Graphic Arts, and the millions of advertisements, promotion pieces, catalogues, etc. add to the sum total of opportunity.

Training in the Graphic Arts, of course, is quite standard.

But let's take a look now at the music/record educational opportunities available to those seeking to build careers in the Business areas.

*The object of teaching a child is*
*to enable him to get along without a teacher.*
Elbert Hubbard

## 67. AVAILABLE TRAINING & A NEW IDEA

Virtually every college and university around the country, even some high schools, have courses in Business Administration, Economics, Marketing, Merchandising, Sales, Advertising, Journalism, Publicity, etc. Like everything else in life they vary from poor to excellent, and it is up to you to check out the educational institutions which offer the Courses in which you are most interested.

Obviously the same thing applies to the multitude of correspondence courses covering these general business areas, and to the literally thousands of books, magazines, tradepapers, etc. which deal with these subjects. The point is that there is an abundance of educational material, a vast number of institutions through which you may acquire the expertise which will help you in any of the business careers in the music/record field. Ideally, as I've said in connection with all careers, an ambitious person should get into the field in any way he can, and then study as he works and accumulates practical experience.

In addition to formal training, books, etc. I have also mentioned throughout this book that some music/industry organizations conduct seminars and employment programs. If you live in one of the five cities in which the National Academy of Recording Arts and Sciences has chapters (Los Angeles, New York, Chicago, Nashville and Atlanta - - - and they are planning to set up one or two new chapters in the near future) you will be able to gain some knowledge by attending their annual workshops, some of which cover the business areas we are discussing in this section.

United Artists (to name one record company/entertainment complex) has a college promotion program. Martin Cerf of the company's Creative Services department makes road trips to interview college students for promotion jobs with the company. Five students were selected for the program in its first year, and three of these wound up with full time jobs as promotion men with the company. Among the cities Cerf has visited are New York, Washington, D.C., Boston, Detroit, Pittsburgh, Denver, Seattle, San Francisco and Los Angeles.

Last summer a high school music educator, whom I've not met, made a recommendation to his State Music Educators' Association, which I consider to be one of the most promising I have ever heard. If the obstacles in the path of this kind of a project can be overcome, I believe it holds the potential for creating important career opportunities for untold numbers of young people at a point in their lives when they are most subject to the temptations of drug addiction and other mind and body destroying activities.

The teacher is Albert Carr of Madison East High School. He made his suggestions through the State Educator publication, *The Wisconsin School Musician*.

Here's what Mr. Carr said:

"I hope to share with my colleagues in music education an idea, a positive response to the demands placed on music education in a contemporary society.

It occured to me in the Spring of 1971 that we at East High School should strive to incorporate within our school music curriculum an area of concentration that would help us involve a greater number of students in our program, particularly those not interested in performance or music theory, etc. It is not suggested here that this type program function as a substitute for those course offerings, but as one solution that might help us acquire additional students (those with the interest and desire), or, help us retain those students that might otherwise drop out of our program. At the same time it could very well generate an attitude from administrators and taxpayers, that would be more complementary to our profession and the various endeavors that we might undertake during our careers.

To afford you additional insights, we surveyed the entire incoming (1972) class of sophomores at East High School and found that a total of 23% of this entire class of 540 would be interested in one of the eight areas as outlined in the "Careers in Music" program. Besides this, the music staff through various means, found that there was a very favorable response in the juniors and seniors in our various classes.

However, I'm sorry to say, our excitement was soon dispelled. We found ourselves having to apply for federal funds and this in-the-end was our downfall. In a letter from the Wisconsin Department of Public Instruction dated January 17, 1972, we received the following reply. "Although we recognize the potential job market in the area of music, it is our understanding that music is exempted from qualifying for vocational education funding under the regulations which accompany the Vocational Education Act of 1963, amended 1968. If the field of music should become a consideration for funding, we would be happy to reconsider your application for funding."

Serious educators (administrators) are constantly upon us to further our causes, to advance ourselves and our programs, to seek new and innovative "solutions", etc. It seems that when we do, there are many, many obstacles before us, either locally or by some unknowing agent or agreement.

What I am offering here in the "Careers in Music," program, is only a suggestion. Perhaps it will serve as a point of departure for those who can afford implementation.

*Course Description and Content*

A course of study (a minimum of two semesters in length) designed for students interested in vocations in music that do not require extensive advanced training at the college, university, or conservatory level.

Students would survey musical careers such as: 1) music, 2) instrument repair and upkeep, 3) piano tuning, 4) organ repair, 5) church organist, 6) pop group management, 7) retail sales in — a. recordings, b. sound reproduction equipment, and music stores of all types, c. sheet music, d. instruments, 8) music librarian.

Following the introduction to these areas, every possible effort would be made to place the student in a work situation in the area of his special interest and needs.

Students would be admitted by permission of the instructor. Some experience in music department courses is desirable as an indication of the student's background and interest in the field. Careers in music may be repeated a second year.

*Objectives*

1. To allow the student to explore musical occupations not requiring college, university or conservatory training.

2. To allow the student to work in a situation that is related to his own vocational interest in music.

3. To allow the student to grow as a mature individual, asking him to evaluate his own progress with his instructor on a regular basis, and when feasible, with his employer in attendance.

4. To provide situations and work experiences that will encourage the student to develop desirable character traits such as competency, cooperation, self-esteem, initiative and reliability.

5. To allow the student to make a meaningful contribution to his community by the quality of his work.

6. To help students decide whether they want to stay in the paraprofessional music areas or seek a professional level of work.

310.

*Procedures for instructor*

     1. Survey employment opportunities in musical careers in Madison.

     2. Talk with prospective employers in the various fields, to know what will be available for the students.

     3. Counsel with students to determine if the Careers in Music study would be a benefit to them and select young people for the course.

     4. Survey various careers in music (for students) by lecture, discussion, guest speakers, class reports, and field trips.

     5. Place students in jobs and act as coordinator between "employer" and "student", school counselors, administrators, and other teachers.

     6. Visit student and employer on the job.

     7. Meet with student on a regular basis to help work out problems and difficulties in his work.

*Evaluation*

     At the end of each nine weeks, instructor evaluates student by discussion of his progress with him in a personal interview. The employer will enter into the evaluation by being present or presenting his appraisal to the instructor, and if feasible, to the student. At the end of the year, the instructor will evaluate the success of the course "Careers in Music" in terms of the aims that were sought and how completely they were attained."

     Any number of suggestions might be made insofar as changes, omissions, additions in the detail of Mr. Carr's plan are concerned. At this point the details are unimportant. The basic idea for a program on the high school level, which would enable young people who are not interested in the so-called creative side of music (writing, performing, etc.) but who might well be interested in the business careers is admirable.

     I hope Mr. Carr and his colleagues keep at it. And I hope that other high school educators around the country make the effort to inaugurate similar programs. I, personally, and First

Place Music will be more than happy to help in any way we can.

And let no one deride the notion as being unrealistic or impractical. On the university level a unique program of this kind has been operative since September, 1965. It is the Music Merchandising Degree Program at the University of Miami in Coral Gables, Florida, the one I mentioned earlier in the Music Publishers section of this book.

*Education makes a people easy to lead,*
*but difficult to drive.*
William Hazlett

## 68. THE FINEST FORMAL MUSIC/RECORD BUSINESS COURSE

Early in 1968 I was co-producing the John Gary 90 minute syndicated television program in Miami. One evening my old friend, Fred Fox. head of the prestigious, old-established music publishing firm, Sam Fox Publishing Company took my wife and me to dinner with Fred's wife and another couple, Dr. and Mrs. Bill Lee. Bill was then and is the Dean of the School of Music of the University of Miami in Coral Gables. Today he is also president of the National Association of Jazz Educators.

Before coming to Miami in 1964 Bill had been at Sam Houston College in Huntsville, Texas for seven years, the last six of which he was Director of Music at the school. Texas, I might insert here, is probably the most progressive state in the union in so far as contemporary music education is concerned. While in Huntsville, Bill also was music director of the Little Symphony Society of Houston.

At Miami he had set up programs in five new fields: Conducting, Jazz, Sacred Music, Studio Music and Music Therapy. Bill holds Master of Music and Doctor of Philosophy Degrees from the University of Texas, Bachelor of Music and

Master of Science Degrees from North Texas State University, and took advanced study at the Eastman School of Music in Rochester, N.Y.

About a year after Bill took over as Dean of the School of Music at Miami, he brought in Alfred Reed as associate professor in the Department of Theory-Composition and Music Education. Reed had been editor-in-chief of Hansen Publications in New York and Miami Beach for some 13 years. In those years he frequently became desperate in his search for competent help in the far-flung Hansen publishing operation. (Hansen is by far the largest distributor of song folios, method books and other such publications in the music industry.) Reed discovered the hard way that there is literally no such animal as a professionally trained music publishing and distributing operative.

Reed and the progressive Bill Lee got together, and despite considerable odds, finally got approval for a Music Merchandising Degree Program to be given at the School. The Program is approved and accredited as a regular Bachelor Degree program in music by the National Association of Schools of Music.

At dinner that night Fred Fox and Bill told me with great enthusiasm about the first "intern" the new program had turned out. He was a 25 year old man named Robert Rogell, and he had spent the final semester of his senior year working at the Sam Fox Publishing Company, 1841 Broadway, New York City. Fred said he was the finest new employee the firm had ever had the good fortune to find. It was his intention to use Bill Lee's and Alfred Reed's students to the full limit his firm could absorb them.

The evening was all too short, but several years later when I decided to do this book, I wrote Professor Reed and he was kind enough to send me the complete story of the Program. As I said in the Music Publisher section of the book, the Course is so unique that I set forth here all the pertinent detail concerning it, which Professor Reed passed on to me:

## OUTLINE OF MAJOR COURSE
## IN MUSIC MERCHANDISING, MED 373-374

The general aim of the Music Merchandising degree program leading to the B.M.M.M. (Bachelor of Music and Music Merchandising) is to prepare properly qualified personnel for positions in all areas of the music industry . . . at every level, including that of top management. In order to accomplish this within the usual four-year undergraduate University program, the course schedule has been carefully structured to include a representative selection of basic courses in general education, music and business; together with the major course in Music Merchandising itself, whose purpose is to tie together all of the individual music and business courses into a unified whole, and at the same time prepare the student to make a reasonable and informed choice as to his or her particular career in a specific area of the music industry. *(This choice obviously becomes important in view of the possibilities of interning during the second semester of the Senior year.)*

This major course of the entire four-year program is MED 373-374, which is normally taken in the Junior year. It divides the entire music industry into ten main areas, each of which is studied in turn, after which the many connections between them are traced and laid bare for further discussion.

These ten areas are taken up in the following order:
1. *The U.S. Copyright Law*
2. *Published Music*
3. *Books and Magazines dealing with music*
4. *Teaching of Music*
5. *Recorded Music*
6. *Performed Music*
7. *Musical Instruments*
8. *Musical Reproducing Instruments*
9. *The Music Store*
10. *Non-Commercial Music and Musical Promotion*

Before proceeding to a detailed listing of all of the main

points to be discussed in each of these ten basic areas, it is important to understand the meaning of the word "merchandising" itself . . . especially in terms of contemporary musical and business practice.

The most important precept is to consider "Merchandising" in its true aspect, since merchandising and selling, although related, are not one and the same. The true merchandiser of any article or service today must be a person with wide practical experience as well as basic background, not only in the product or service he may provide but also as to its place in our present day society, the demand for it, and the means of supplying it in such a way as to render the highest possible quality at the most competitive price.

To merchandise is to sell, but in the widest possible meaning of the term, similar to the English expression "to purvey". Successful merchandising, as opposed to mere selling, demands far more than a grasp of sales, promotional and advertising techniques. The relationship between merchandising and selling is similar to that between strategy and tactics in war.

Even today it is possible for a first-rate salesman to have little or even no actual knowledge of music itself, whether he is selling sheet music, books on music, performed music, musical instruments, or anything else. The true music merchandiser, on the other hand, must have at least some first-hand knowledge of music, PLUS a fairly widespread knowledge of the place of music in our society at the present time. Values, judgments, methods and materials of even 10 years ago are no longer valid in some areas, and only partially so in others.

The merchandising of music, in any of its various forms, is dependent on the grasp of changing times, fashions, tastes, and other personal and group factors which, in turn, create demand, and which the merchandiser supplies in such a manner to remain competitive, while at the same time offering the best value he can.

The *business* of music is the *merchandising* of music, and even decisions taken in the area of so-called "free" music, whether sponsored or underwritten by large corporations, foundations, or some form of government agency (at the city, state or federal level), will be found, on close inspection, to be based on much the same factors as those which determine the commercial merchandising of music in this country.

Therefore, no amount of purely *business* study can make the *strategic* decisions that underlie the purely business side of the enterprise, whether in music, automobiles, textiles, real estate, etc. And the basic foundation of successful *music* merchandising is to grasp and understand the place of music, *all* kinds of music, in our contemporary society.

The ten main areas and the principal points to be discussed in each during this course are:

1. *The U.S. Copyright Law*
   Domestic and International protection
   Revisions and changes
2. *Published Music*
   Acquisitions of musical properties
   Individual and folio publications
   Production Line:  Composer - Writer - Arranger
                      - Editor - Engraver - Proof-
                      reader - Printer - Binder
   Distribution - Jobbing - Retailing
3. *Books and Magazines dealing with music*
   Books about music and general classroom music books
   Magazines
4. *Teaching of Music*
   The Private Teacher
   The School and College Teacher
   The Studio Teacher tied in with Retail Music Stores
5. *Recorded Music*
   Mechanical Rights and Royalties
   Records and Tapes, the Recording Industry
   Production - Manufacturing - Distribution - Retailing

Record Clubs - Tape Clubs - Tape Cartridge Clubs

6. *Performed Music*
Public Performance Rights and Royalties
Synchronization Rights and uses
"Grand" (Dramatic) Rights and Licenses
Live and Recorded Music
Records, Radio, TV, Video Tape, Motion Pictures, Theater, Opera and Concerts (including Recitals)
The Juke Box
Performing Rights Societies: ASCAP, BMI and SESAC
EVR (Electronic Video Recording)
CATV (Community Antenna TV - "Cable" TV)

7. *Musical Instruments*
Manufacturing - Distributing - Retailing - Servicing

8. *Musical Reproducing Instruments*
TV - Radio - Hi-Fi - Stereo - Records - Tape (Reel, Cartridge, Cassette); singly and in combinations; home, car and business uses

9. *The Music Store*
Large - small - full-line - specialty
Types of customers and lines of business: individuals, schools and school systems, direct mail ordering

10. *Non-Commercial Music and Musical Promotion*
Foundation Grants - Government Subsidies
Developing the present and future audiences
Music Education programs in the school system

TEXTS USED IN THE COURSE ARE:
A. *Required Texts:*
THE COPYRIGHT HANDBOOK, Howard Walls, Watson-Gupthill, 1963

318.

THIS BUSINESS OF MUSIC, Shemel-Krasilovsky, Billboard, 1964
MORE ABOUT THIS BUSINESS OF MUSIC, Shemel-Krasilovsky, Billboard, 1967

B.  *Supplementary Texts:*
PERFORMING ARTS, THE ECONOMIC DI-LEMMA, Baumol-Bowen, 20th-Century Fund, 1966
THE LANGUAGE OF THE MUSIC BUSINESS, Leston Huntley, Del Capo Publications, 1965
MUSIC IN MODERN MEDIA, Robert Emmett Dolan, G. Schirmer, 1967
THE BUSINESS OF MUSIC, Ernst Roth, Oxford University Press, 1969

C.  *Supplementary Magazines and Trade Journals:*
BILLBOARD - CASH BOX - STEREO REVIEW - HIGH FIDELITY - THE SCHOOL MUSICIAN - THE INSTRUMENTALIST - MUSIC EDU-CATORS' JOURNAL
And other magazines and trade journals

In addition to regular classroom lecture sessions, there are prominent guest speakers from the music industry, as well as field trips to firms in some of the areas to be studied.

The Course structure requires 16 hours in each of the first and second semesters of the Freshman year; 18 hours in each of the 1st and 2nd semesters in the Sophomore year; 17 hours in the first semester, and 18 in the second of the Junior year; 15 hours in the first semester, and 6 hours plus interning in the second semester of the Senior year.

If you want a career in any part of the Business side of the Music/Record industry, I can't recommend the University of Miami program too highly. I hope similar programs will be adopted by schools in every section of the country. If you want to know the qualification requirements and other details write Professor Alfred Reed, University of Miami, School of Music, P.O. Box 8165, Coral Gables, Miami, Florida 33124.

# PART III

## SECTION SIX

### Attorney & Accountant

*A lawyer without history or literature
is a mechanic, a mere working mason; if he
possesses some knowledge of these, he may
venture to call himself an architect.*
Sir Walter Scott

## 69. KEY ATTORNEY/ACCOUNTANT FUNCTIONS

This section deals with the practising lawyer and accountant in the music/record business as opposed to those people who,
although lawyers or accountants, perform functions completely
unrelated to their former professions. Allen Klein is an accountant
but acts as a manager and general entrepreneur; Rocco Laginestra and Norman Racusin are accountants but both are record
company executives, Racusin having been the former head of
RCA Victor Records, and Laginestra the present head.

Lee Eastman practices law but he is known primarily
for his music publishing catalogs and his management activities;
Clive Davis is a lawyer but spends his time as president of Columbia Records. Interestingly enough, recently the triumvirate
at RCA Victor, i.e., the president, the vice president in charge
of artists and repertoire and the vice president in charge of business affairs were an accountant, a lawyer and a lawyer respectively, while over at Columbia the two top men were a lawyer
and an accountant. Indeed there was a time when you walked
into a record company's executive suite, if you couldn't get a
record contract you could at least have a will drawn.

It's not just a coincidence that the front offices of

music and record companies are so well populated by professionals. The music business, as this book tends to demonstrate,
is big and complicated. At its heart is creativity, but without
the legal and accounting brain, the phonograph record could
go the way of the old songplugger.

My own idea of the perfect music/record/general entertainment industry attorney is a man I've mentioned in previous
chapters, Richard Jablow. Despite the fact that he is my own
attorney and friend I am not at all reluctant to cite Dick and
his background as a general model young attorneys desiring to
get into the music/record business might follow with profit.
Dick got his B.A. from the City College of New York in 1944
and his LLB from Columbia University in New York in 1947.
He immediately went to work for one of the finest law firms in
New York City: Hays, St. John, Abramson and Shulman.

While there he was assigned to the Author's League and
to the Versailles night club, among other clients. The Versailles
was the source of Dick's earliest professional relationships with
people in the music business. Among the performers, producers
and composers who worked for and with the club were George
White, Edith Piaf, Irving Caesar, Jack Yellin, Howard Dietz and
Arthur Schwartz (all giants in their own field of music endeavor)
In the mid-fifties the Authors' League separated into the Authors' Guild and the Dramatists' Guild in one organization and
the Writers' Guild (television, motion picture and radio writers)
in another.

In 1954 Dick formed his own firm (now Butler, Jablow
and Geller) and represented, among other clients, the Writers'
Guild of America. The National Academy of Recording Arts
and Sciences, which organization I've mentioned in earlier
sections, was formed on the West Coast about this time. Jim
Conkling, one of the key figures in building Capitol Records
into an important record company, and the first president of
Warner Bros. Records was one of the major forces in the creation of NARAS. When NARAS decided to form a New York
chapter, Conkling asked his friends in the Writers' Guild of

America hierarchy on the West Coast, who they would recom-
ment as a New York attorney. Dick Jablow was the unanimous
and enthusiastic recommendation.

Thus Dick formed the New York NARAS chapter and
has been most active in the expansion and development of the
organization ever since. In NARAS, of course, playing the
vital, day to day role he has played for almost twenty years,
Dick not only made the acquaintance of literally hundreds
of key music/record people on every level and in every area of
the country, but many of these people realized that Dick was a
rarity among professional men: Thoroughly capable and with
thorough integrity.

I could fill the next ten pages with the names of Dick's
clients (singers, composers, producers, managers, music publishers, record company executives, et al), so rather than omit
any, I'll mention none. The point is that Dick's expertise derives from getting into the business at an early age, working
hard at it in every phase.

In the music/record business a mass of legal and accounting talent faces the artist from the company side, so he
must have his own battery of professional help, as soon as he
is able to afford it. Ideally, the practising music attorney is as
much a business man as a lawyer. He must know the economic
trends of the business, which change as rapidly and as radically
as music styles themselves.

He must be aware of technological changes that are
hovering on the horizon so that when he advises his client to
sign a five year contract in 1972, he is protecting the client
from the use of his material by some media which may be in
vogue in 1974. He must protect against such usages as cassette,
cartridge, videotape, and Lord knows what other employment
of the material or performance at a disproportionate royalty
rate.

He must keep abreast of new distribution outlets, record
clubs; bonus record practices; premium record merchandising;
plastic records used in periodicals or direct mail, etc. In short

he must try to get the best deal he can for his client in the areas in which there is some experience factor, and also provide that if any other use not presently contemplated is made of his client's product or services, such use will be properly paid for or negotiated at the time of the developing usage.

These functions obviously overlap to a great degree with the functions of a manager. But the attorney, if he is conscientious, has the responsibility of seeing to it that the deal, as it appears on paper, is a reflection of both his and the manager's foresight. There is certainly nothing more effective than the well-coordinated team of manager and attorney.

Nor should the attorney and the manager be the same person - - - although some attorneys have made the dual function work. The manager works on a percentage commission, and the attorney generally works on a flat fee basis. Thus the attorney should have no reluctance to tell his performer/writer client to pass up a deal, while the manager might be inclined to hesitate to pass up 15% or more of some lush project on which he has spent a good deal of time.

Then too the attorney is really the only buffer between the performer/writer client and his manager. The creative client should entrust the manager with the administration of his business life. Most do exactly that to the point of vulnerability. The attorney is often, and I think should be, the only link between a creative client's check book and the client's manager.

The third member of an effective music/record team from the creative client's standpoint is the accountant. Almost all royalty statements an artist receives (as an example) whether it be from a record company, a music publisher, BMI or ASCAP look something like a Chinese laundry list and make about as much sense to the non-Oriental artist.

It should be up to the accountant to "break the code"; to find the bits of "vigorish", legal or otherwise, that a company sometimes appropriates for itself. It's up to an accountant working with the attorney and manager to stem the tide - - - and roll it back if possible - - - of the many charges, "customs" and "account-

ing methods" many companies use and perpetuate solely. Let's
see what some of these are.

*The law is a jealous mistress, and
requires long and constant courtship.*
Joseph Story

## 70. WHAT LAWYERS/ACCOUNTANTS LOOK FOR

Many of the peculiar practises against which the responsible music/record business accountant working for a
creative performer and/or writer client must guard cannot be
changed except by a Presley, a Streisand, a Tom Jones or
someone with vast bargaining powers.

Look at these:

1. Almost every record company contract provides that
royalties be paid on 90% of the records sold, on the theory that
10% of the records sold will be returned, damaged, etc. Frequently, in specific cases, this turns out to be nonsense;

2. Almost every record company contract provides that
only ½ royalties be paid on sale of cartridges. Why? The profit
to the company is equal to that of records, perhaps more.

3. Almost every record company contract stipulates
that no royalty at all will be paid on bonus records "given
away" by book clubs, record clubs, etc. But the company, of
course, is making money on the bonus records. Many record
companies will remove this clause if the manager or attorney
insists on it, and the artist has any bargaining power at all.

4. Some record companies pay royalties on the wholesale

price (price to the distributor, rack jobber, etc.) rather than on the retail price of the records. Of course the royalty percentage rate then is higher, but nevertheless, in some situations the record company will still retain more of the profit than if the standard royalty based on retail were paid. For example, a royalty based on the wholesale price (in most circumstances) should be a shade more than double the royalty based on retail. So if the artist would ordinarily get a 5% royalty on the retail price, he should get between a 10% and 11% royalty based on the wholesale price.

I wonder how many young artists (for lack of proper managerial, attorney and accounting advice) are walking around boasting that they get an 8% royalty - - - of wholesale, dummy!

5. Every record contract will provide that the company will record a minimum number of sides during each year of the contract. Great! The company has guaranteed to record 12 of the artist's sides during the first year. That means they've got quite an investment in the artist.

Hold it! The conscientious attorney and accountant will discover that a couple of clauses later the contract says the company does not have to release the sides if they choose not to. But still if they laid out the money to record 12 sides why wouldn't they release them and try to earn their money back.

Well, for one reason, because a couple of clauses later the contract says the company will have fulfilled its obligation with respect to the guaranteed sides if it doesn't record any of the sides at all, provided it pays the artist the session fees for the sides it didn't record, which could equal approximately the cost of a ten pound turkey.

So these are a few randomly selected areas of a more or less typical record deal, of which the conscientious attorney and/ or accountant representing the performer/writer/manager client must be aware.

Here is the place to take up how an attorney or accountant becomes aware of these matters, and other requisites for becoming a music/record business attorney or accountant.

## 71. PROTECTORS OF THE STEPPED-UPON

Let's concentrate on becoming a music/record business attorney. First of all, of course, you pass the bar examinations. I know this sounds a little like the first step in a French recipe which tells you to kill, bone and smoke a two pound pheasant. But if you want to be a music business attorney, a brain surgeon or a French chef you know there's a minimum amount of effort that must be expended.

Once you've passed the bar you can expose yourself to many post-graduate courses given on many aspects of the entertainment industry. Such courses are given at the University of California in Los Angeles, Vanderbilt University in Tennessee; New York University and virtually every other university in the country which doesn't specialize in Animal Husbandry. Particularly noteworthy are courses given by the Practising Law Institute. Their schedule can be obtained by writing to them at 1133 Avenue of the Americas, New York, N.Y. 10036. A subscription to a monthly periodical known as the *Bulletin of the Copyright Society of the USA* can be obtained by writing to Fred B. Rothman & Co., 57 Leuning Street, South Hackensack, New Jersey 07606. It costs $25 a year and contains up to date legal decisions in all areas of the entertainment field, articles of interest and current bibliographies of "must" reading for the music lawyer.

Two of the best books in the field are *Nimmer on Copyright* by Professor Melville Nimmer, published by Matthew Bender & Co., 235 East 45 Street, New York, N.Y. 10017 and the book I've previously mentioned in other sections, *The Business of Music* by Shemel and Krasilovsky, published by Billboard Publications.

This latter book, as I've indicated, is also invaluable for laymen in the music business and contains many practical hints, business trends and forms. I might add that no one should undertake to use a form unless he's an attorney and familiar with the field. Unless he's the type of person who would perform an appendectomy on himself.

Also, as I've indicated previously, an aspiring music business lawyer should know what the business is about. There are many symposia given by the Television Academy, the National Academy of Recording Arts and Sciences, the National Music Publishers' Association. Most of these are free, or may be attended at a nominal charge. Join some of these organizations; whichever ones seem most appropriate to you. Only by mingling with people who work in the field can you find out what and where the problems are; what the trends are; what economic factors will shape your practice, etc. In brief, as I've urged in connection with every career, get into the business. And again, as I've urged previously, read the tradepapers listed in the earlier chapters of this book.

In short, the music/record business is a unique and private world - - - but everyone is welcome. Musicians, and many other people in the business, creative and otherwise, as earlier chapters have shown, are frequently neurotic but very nice, friendly, warm and helpful.

And from an attorney or accounting standpoint most of all, musicians, composers, singers, artists as a group, are almost always looking for help. In a sense they constitute the largest non-racial, non-religious minority that was ever stepped upon in the history of mankind. So if you have the background and the interest, you won't want for clients.

One point to keep in mind, however: Not too many people in the business make it as stars. So if what you want is a steady income perhaps you'd best stick with a corporation, such as some of the wise lawyers previously mentioned have done. The same advice, of course, holds true if you like to get to bed early.

The route up the music/record business ladder is made much easier by a legal or accounting degree. You can stick with practising law or accountancy with an entertainment corporation or you may just use your professional knowledge as an adjunct to your creative business career with the corporation. And many, many different types of corporations, of course, are involved: The record companies with their long history of utilizing professional men in creative positions; the talent agencies (Nat Lefkowitz, president of the William Morris Agency is an accountant; Marv Josephson, president of International-Famous Artists is a lawyer, etc.) The networks and local radio and television stations, music publishers, unions (Sanford Wolff, national executive director of the American Federation of Television and Radio Artists is a lawyer, as is Mike Franklin, executive director of Writers' Guild of America, West, and so on and on and on.

Opportunities for professional men who know the music/record business from every angle are many. But you must *know* it: The forms, the contracts, the economics, the people who perform in every area, and what they perform. And, by the way, attorneys and accountants successful in it, will tell you there's one prerequesite:

You must *like* it - - - and that's an acquired taste.

# PART IV

# THE EDUCATIONAL CAREERS

Contemporary Music Educator in
Universities and Colleges
Community Colleges
Senior High Schools
Junior High Schools
Elementary Schools

Music Administration

Miscellaneous Educator Areas

*You can lead a boy to college*
*but you cannot make him think.*
Elbert Hubbard

329.

## 72. NOT $$$, BUT OTHER REWARDS

As I said in the early Chapters of this book, one of the
few areas of the music/record business into which my own
career has not taken me in great depth is that of contemporary
music education.  In the past two years, however, as vice president, general manager and co-owner of First Place Music Publi
cations, Inc. and as Editor/Publisher of the Pro/Ed Review, I
have been involved in the contemporary music education scene.
In that time I have met a number of talented, dedicated music
educators.

Among these an outstanding teacher, a musician-writer
who has devoted his young life (and plans to devote his future)
to music education is Jack Wheaton. Jack currently teaches at
Cerritos Community College in Norwalk, at Cal State at Long
Beach and at Saddleback College in Mission Viejo (all in California). He is also currently working on completing his Doctorate, and on a new book called *The Decline of Jazz as an Art
Form in America.*

He was a past president of the National Association of
Jazz Educators, formerly music director of *Jazz Internationale*,
and chairman of the American Collegiate Jazz Festival. He is

also committee chairman of the College Band Directors' National Association and serves on the Committee on Jazz in Higher Education. He is director of the Stan Kenton Collegiate Neophonic Orchestra and has been a member of the Stan Kenton Clinic faculty for the past six years. Additionally Jack maintains an extremely busy schedule serving as Adjudicator, Clinician and Lecturer at scores of Schools, Festivals and other events.

I am most fortunate in being able to have Jack contribute the Section of this book which deals with Contemporary Music Education as a Career. I think you will find his suggestions and guidance as realistic, practical - - - and I hope, helpful, as my own counselling in the other careers.

Here's Jack Wheaton —

If you are planning to go into Music Education to get rich, forget it. A modest living is all you can expect, unless you are lucky enough to own a music store, publish a widely-used textbook or lecture regularly on a national scale. However there are compensating rewards. For instance, teaching, particularly public school or formal higher education teaching, usually has strong job security, once you receive tenure. Sometimes this works out to be a negative factor, since many music educators obviously go to sleep once they know that they cannot be fired easily.

Another compensation is the joy of teaching music to young people. Don't knock it. After playing for years in front of jaded, half-gassed audiences it can be a real thrill to help some young person create beautiful music; or to watch young people respond, gradually open up like a flower to the many worlds of musical sound.

There are roughly 2660 colleges and universities; 1505 junior colleges; 245 Catholic colleges; 21,110 senior high schools; 9200 junior public high schools; 2290 Catholic high schools; 4575 preparatory private high schools and 68,000 elementary schools in the United States. Except for the smallest rural schools, there are music teachers at almost every level.

At least there were until 1957, when "Sputnik" (Russia's earth-orbital satellite) forced many districts to abandon or cut back on their music programs and develop "crash" science programs so we could all catch up with the Russians. We had barely recovered from that mistake, when economic restrictions in public schools around the U.S. forced many schools into making the tragic mistake of cutting back on their school music program, the cheapest, most efficient way of getting artistic, creative involvement, closer community-school relations, and a real purpose to life in the school program.

This tragic mistake has sent music specialists, particularly at the elementary school level, looking for work in other fields, and has resulted in cut-backs in intermediate and high school level programs as well. Many positions of music supervisor for a large school district have simply been eliminated.

Naturally the colleges and universities have felt the pinch, with decreasing numbers of students from the high schools enrolling as music majors, and alarming drops in the size of performing groups. However the interest in music among the young is at an all-time high. Record sales, sales of pianos, guitars, and other instruments keep climbing constantly.

What has happened?

For one thing, the public schools are left, for the most part, with a program of instruction that is geared to a pre World War II society; a society that only exists in old "Andy Hardy" flics and nostalgic films like "The Summer of '42." There are some places in the country where music educators and school districts have got with it.

There are new, hard-type of music educators, who are trying to reach students on a different and much broader basis than in the past. Up till now, most music educators have been working with less than 8% of the student body (past the elementary school level) in choral or instrumental performing groups. Many music educators and lecturers, like Sid Fox, internationally-known expert on music education for the "Now" generation, are pleading for a concern and program for the disenfranchised 92%.

If you're looking for a place to go and lie down, stay out of music education, at least for the foreseeable future. Things are heating up fast. If you like a challenge, and don't mind championing your beliefs before administrators, parents and children, you may enjoy your work. If you really want to see the power of music at work, you can only see it through the eyes of a ghetto child, who finds his or her only reason for *being* in your music class; or a hard-working mechanic, who attends faithfully, one or two nights a week, a guitar class for adults, where his large, scarred fingers grasp the neck of a six-string guitar, desperately trying to bring alive the sound of some simple song; or possibly the thrill of leading a high school or college choir, marching band, or jazz band before an audience thrilled with the musical excellence that can be achieved through training, dedication and hard work.

We will examine the music education scene from top to bottom. We will take a look at what it takes to teach music at the university, college, community college, high school, intermediate school and elementary school level. We will examine music education in the areas of administration, private studio teaching, music therapy and other highly specialized roles one might play as a music educator.

# PART IV

## SECTION ONE

### University & College
### Educator

*Universities are full of knowledge; the freshmen*
*bring a little in and the seniors take none away*
*and knowledge accumulates.*
Abbott Lawrence Lowell

333.

## 73. THE UNIVERSITY/COLLEGE PICTURE

"Ivy-covered professors, hiding behind ivy-covered walls". That's the gist of one satirical song about the ostrich-like propensities of college profs. Today things are "swingin'" behind those jivy ivy-covered walls.

Leon Breeden at North Texas State University has eleven jazz ensembles this fall. He could have had sixteen. There are over 400 jazz majors at his institution. Berklee School of Music, Boston, Mass. has over 1200 students, all studying jazz, rock, motion-picture and t.v. writing.

Bill Lee at the University of Miami has a complete commercial music program, including on-the-job training in New York Music Publishing companies for his grad students. David Baker at the University of Indiana lets Henry Mancini use his musicians when he tours the mid-west. John Garvey at the University of Illinois has taken his award-winning jazz ensemble on two State department tours, one to the Soviet Union.

Chuck Mangione, graduate-assistant and former student at Eastman, received so much acclaim for his work (seen nationally over NET TV) that he has gone professional with his own combo and has recently returned from a tour of Europe.

These are just some of the things that are happening in jazz and modern music education at the University level. For instance, Duke Ellington just gave his entire library to the music department at Yale, while Leonard Bernstein has returned to the classroom at Harvard; to help "stem the tide of growing mediocrity," according to the maestro of the New York Philharmonic.

There are many college and university orchestras that perform as well if not better than all but the top four or five professional orchestras in the U.S. The Opera productions at the University of Texas, University of Southern California and elsewhere rank with anything done at the Met, except for the high-priced and sometimes over-stuffed prima-donnas.

Of course the college and university marching bands have created an art form all their own, and command larger audiences via TV than even the top professional groups on the tube like Lawrence Welk.

The University Music Department is a college of its own. Its various departments usually look something like this, depending on the size and budget of the institution:

1. Dean of the School of Music (2 - 3 secretaries)
   a. Assistant Dean
   b. Director of Graduate Studies
   c. Musicology and History of Music
   d. Music Education and Methods
   e. Choral (including solo voice and Opera)
   f. Instrumental (orchestra, marching band, concert band, jazz band, instrumental ensembles of various combinations)
   g. Theory and Composition (including orchestration and arranging)
   h. Keyboard Instruction (piano, organ, studio and class piano)
   i. Studio Instruction (private lessons) in: voice, piano, organ, composition, brass (trumpet, fr. horn, trombone, tuba) woodwinds (flute, clari-

net, oboe, bassoon, sax); strings (violin, viola,
cello, bass, guitar); percussion (mallets, trap
drums, misc. percussion); electronic music (moog,
multi-vider, oscillator, etc.) conducting; vocal
coaching and interpretation, etc.
j. Librarian (music and/or research)
k. Equipment manager
l. Piano tuner, technician, staff copyist, staff
   arranger.

A large university may easily have 100 to 150 or more
staff members in its music department, not counting any number of graduate assistants. Most universities like their staff members to have a doctorate degree or the equivalent. Sometimes
national or regional expertise will serve in lieu of a doctorate,
particularly with the performing and studio instructors.

A doctorate is academic "blood, sweat and tears." At
least eight years (sometimes seven, if you are lucky) of higher
education. The wash-out rate for doctoral candidates is somewhere between 60 and 80%. Tough sleddin', and not for everybody.

If you play your ax well enough, you might get by with
a Master's Degree, where the washout is more like 40 to 60%.

Less than a Master's Degree - forget it!

Job opportunities are tight right now. The big parade
of war babies has passed through the gates of most colleges, and
now enrollment is dropping in many areas. Economic and social
conditions have changed, making a college degree not such a
coveted goal as it once was. Nam G.I.'s are not returning to
college in anywhere near the numbers that their WWII or
Korean War buddies did.

Salary ranges from maximums of $30,000 for deans of
large schools of music, to $2500 for graduate assistants. Those
not in administration or working in grad assistantship or fellow-
ship programs are traditionally classified in four academic ranks:
1.  Instructor (full time) $5,500 - 9,500 per year
2.  Assistant Prof. (full time) $7,500 - 10,500 per year

3.    Associate Prof. (full time)  $9,500 - 12,500 per year
4.    Full Professor (full time)  $11,500 - 15,000 per year
Department heads and Deans will receive $1,000 to
$5,000 a year more for their executive position.

These figures are an approximate national average. You
will find many better-endowed Ivy League colleges and universities with scales that are much higher. Ditto some eastern, west
coast and urban colleges and universities in the mid west. Some
universities have created "super professorships," for nationally-
known heavies, ranging from $25,000 to $75,000 per year.

Advice on college teaching:  Unless you can cut the
mustard with good grades, above average (actually outstanding)
musical ability on a particular instrument, or in conducting,
theory or orchestration, forget it.

The competition is stiff, the road to success is a slow
and tortuous one; the possible financial rewards are minimal
for the struggle involved in getting there.

Still, nothing can quite cut the thrill of teaching at a
major university or college, and developing groups or programs
that are almost impossible to achieve anywhere else.

# PART IV

## SECTION TWO

### Community College Educator

*The vanity of teaching doth oft tempt*
*a man to forget that he is a blockhead.*
George Savile, Marquis of Halifax

337.

## 74. FAST GROWING COMMUNITY COLLEGES

The fastest growing institution of higher learning is the community college. The average community college offers instructional and training programs in three diverse areas:

1.  *Transfer Programs*
    Two-year undergraduate programs leading to transfer to a four-year college or university.
2.  *Vocational Education and Vocational Rehabilitation*
    Training programs in nursing, auto shop, cosmetology, etc. leading to employment (hopefully) full or part time in industry.
3.  *Community Enrichment*
    Special programs for persons who wish to enrich their lives through learning a skill, or mastering the fundamentals of some musical instrument, etc.

Community college music departments are usually small. Two to five full-time staff members is the average. Seldom are they on academic rank. Most have a graduated salary schedule that works on units and degrees accumulated, plus years of longevity. Often the community college pays the teacher better than the university or college professor.

Usually the number of contact hours per week is more. The average required number of contact hours (total hours spent teaching per week) for community college staff is 15; for colleges and universities, 12. Don't begin to salivate and think that that will be the extent of your time and duties on campus. My wife and I still get hysterical whenever we remember that one of the reasons I went into college teaching was so I would have more "spare time."

Figure in 3 to 5 hours per week in office hour functions; a couple hours in meetings; 10 to 20 hours per week preparing for classes, grading papers, doing arrangements, making up programs, etc.

Music teachers in the community college had better like to teach. Unlike the university, they are hired for their teaching ability first. Also the calibre of student is generally of a little lower I.Q. and less motivated. You have to work harder to get results. If you like to teach, it's exciting. If you are easily frustrated, forget it.

Salaries range from $6,500 a year to $20,000. Often times there are excellent opportunities for hourly over-load teaching and summer-session teaching; both supplementing your regular income.

Teaching in the community colleges requires a much broader area of specialty. Because of the limited staff and the broad range of programs, community college music teachers must be able to teach with authority in at least three divergent areas (within music).

Job opportunities are tight here as well. Many college and university professors are moving to the community college where they can teach with less political (departmental) influence and interference, look forward to better salary schedules, and not have to sweat out the research (publish or perish philosophy) of the university system.

In summary, teaching music in some quiet, ivy covered, college, out of the mainstream of American hustle and bustle, is often an unrealistic dream. After Kent State, no one can hope for colleges to be immune from what's happening in the world.

Also society is beginning to zero in on colleges and universities, often unfairly blaming them for their freaky children. There's no place to hide. If you plan to teach at the college level, be prepared for fireworks. There is a tremendous change going on in American life. College music departments, especially, have often geared their curricula to the techniques and preservation of a quasi-European culture that was transplanted from Europe to the wilds of frontier America. That culture died on the battlefields of World War I.

The best of our European Heritage *should* be preserved by our colleges and universities; but not at the expense of our own culture. If you would like to join this battle, c'mon in, the water's fine! So far, the traditionalists hold the heavy end of the pool, but the young bucks are gaining some ground.

The talent that is entering the doors of our colleges nowadays in music is sometimes awesome. Not everyone is a no-good hippy. There is an incredible amount of talent in this country. If you feel that you would like to participate in the process of training and molding this talent, there is plenty to do.

# PART IV

## SECTION THREE

### Senior High School Educator

*Age is no better, hardly so well qualified*
*for an instructor as youth, for it has not*
*profited so much as it has lost.*
      Henry David Thoreau

341

## 75. THE SR. HIGH SCHOOL SCENE

The United States has almost 40,000 high schools. There are very few small high schools anymore. There has been a tremendous consolidation of school districts within the past ten years, partially due to the increasing costs of education.

Most high schools employ two music teachers; one to teach choral music and music appreciation (sometimes class piano), and another to teach instrumental music; band, orchestra, beginning instruments and, sometimes, theory. Due to a shortening of the school day and an increase in the number of required subjects, often times the music teacher must teach subjects outside of music to fill his or her teaching load; history, math, geography, etc.

Preparation for high school teaching requires at least a Bachelor's Degree and sometimes a Master's Degree. Pay scales range from lows of $5,000 to $6,000 a year in some rural areas to maximums of $18,000 to $20,000 a year in some wealthy communities. It generally takes 15 to 20 years to reach these maximums.

Competition for the high school level jobs has risen sharply in the past ten years, particularly in the more ideal urban communities. Experience is a must for the choicer positions. Many larger districts insist that their high school teachers work their way up; starting with the beginning instrument program in the elementary schools, progressing to the intermediate schools, and then eventually moving into the high schools.

Sometimes it is a long wait. The approximate ratio in urban systems is; 2 - 3 intermediate or jr. highs to each high school, and 10 - 20 elementary schools to each intermediate school. Consequently, there are many more intermediate and elementary positions than there are high school openings.

The high school instrumental teacher must be equipped to teach marching band, concert band, jazz band, instrumental ensembles and sometimes theory, improvisation, vocal or music appreciation. His background should include training in simple arranging for his various ensembles. Dynamic, dedicated individuals, capable of recruiting and holding students to their program are a must for the good high school instrumental director.

He must give, give and give of his time and talent to make his program a success. He has the reward of realizing that his inspiration and influence comes at a time in a young man's or young woman's life that is crucial for their later years. His influence may be the primary factor between turning out a successful and happy student or someone who cannot make it in today's world.

The high school band director is often "Mr. Music" in his community. He has the thrill of furnishing music for most of the important school and civic functions and realizing that he is a very important and influential person in the community. His or her work is meaningful and rewarding; something that cannot be said about many jobs in a technological society.

If you lack the kind of missionary zeal this takes; if you do not like the idea of having this much influence on young people's lives; if you feel that furnishing music for the school and community is an imposition on your time and talent stay out of high school teaching.

The average term in office (before he goes into

administration or classroom or into his own business) for the
high school band director is ten years or less. No position in the
high school usually has as much responsibility or public attention. Yet, again, there are rewards of a deeper sort.

The high school choral person generally has concert
choir, madrigals, school chorus, boys' or girls' choir and sometimes swing choir. Occasionally the choral person will have voice
class, piano class, music appreciation or orchestra as well. More
often the instrumental person handles orchestra where there is
a program for strings.

The high school choral person can reach a larger number
of students in the school community than the instrumental
director. People who have never participated in music before
can suddenly feel the urge to join a large chorus and learn their
part, through diligent drill and rote practice.

The choral program has undergone some traumatic
changes in the past few years. Too often the choral program
was a thinly-disguised attempt to introduce ecclesiastical literature and services into the public schools, weakening the con-
stitutional protection of Church from State. This does not mean
that it is wrong to sing or play great music, regardless of its
original ecclesiastical use.

However, when some choral directors restrict themselves
to Protestant Literature at the expense of great Catholic and
Jewish serious music, they are doing a disservice to their singers
and to their audience. They too often leave the impression that
their selections are the only valid literature in the choral repertoire; something that is not true.

High School Choral Directors, who are really frustrated
Church Choir Directors, too often have ignored their students'
desires to sing and perform non-liturgical literature. Pop songs
and jazz have been ignored, or often even attacked, as being
unworthy of performance. In the past few years the pressure
has been too great. Students, parents and community now demand an opportunity to sing and perform excerpts from *Hair*
as well as tunes by the Beatles, Bacharach, and from Broadway.

Too often this situation has found high school choral
directors with inadequate training and techniques on how to
arrange, rehearse and perform this type of literature. Young,
dynamic high school choral people, with the ability to teach
Bach or the Beatles to their choirs have a golden opportunity
to reach a broad range of students with music. If choral music
is your cup of tea, you should investigate this wide-open field.

General Music or Music Appreciation at the High School
level is something else. Too often it has only taught students to
hate, rather than love serious music. A word to those who are
interested in this field:

First of all, it is not taught in many schools today.
Secondly, unless you start where your students are, (Rock to
Bach, *not* Bach to Rock! as Sid Fox evangelizes) you will only
alienate those students not already turned off to classical music
and good jazz. However, *this* area, because it reaches the 92%
(those not actively involved in high school performing groups),
and because it trains audiences, which is something that we've
goofed with in our public school music programs, it is probably
the most important of all the high school music classes.

It is also one of the most difficult to teach. The teacher
has to learn to understand and appreciate the students'
aesthetic before there is ever a chance of the students' understanding and appreciating the teacher' sense of values.

The greatest natural resource a nation has is its young.
Our generation (adults) are squandering the natural resource of
the young by not bringing our schools and teaching methods
up to date with the rest of our society.

If you want to really help, teaching music at the high
school level can be very rewarding; as long as money, fame or
power is not your bag.

One of the most rewarding experiences you can have as
a high school teacher is to see your former students return successful, sometimes becoming famous names in the musical or
business world, and to have them thank you for your help in
molding their lives. President Richard M. Nixon has mentioned

several times the importance of his musical experiences in the high school orchestra at Whittier High School, Whittier, Calif. in developing his character. The President is also an excellent amateur pianist, and has mentioned several times that he regrets only one thing about his youth; that he did not practice the piano harder and sooner, so that he could enjoy the benefits of playing more advanced literature today.

We hear so much about our high schools filled with dope, sex and violence. We hear so little about the tremendous effort and musical excellence coming from places like Sumner High School, Kansas City Mo. Leon Brady, director of the Sumner High School Jazz Band won the *Jazz Internationale* competition in Paris, France in the summer of 1972. This all-black band from a deprived area of the city, stood Londoners and Parisiens on their ears with their musical excellence and enthusiasm. The members of that band are not in trouble. They are all too busy trying to be the best band in the country.

# PART IV

## SECTION FOUR

Intermediate and
Junior High School Educator

## 76. INTERMEDIATE & JR. HIGH CAREERS

Most intermediate schools are patterned after the high
school. Usually there are two music people; one choral and one
instrumental. The choral and instrumental person will each have
general music classes to teach. In some larger jr. highs there is
a specialist for the jr. high general music program. Some districts offer class piano as well. The instrumental director will
have more emphasis on beginning and intermediate groups
than on advance groups. Usually there is not a marching band.
Until recently neither was there a jazz band, although jr. high
jazz bands are growing like crazy, particularly on the West
Coast.

The same things that were said for the high school program can pretty much be said for jr. high school programs. The
main difference is in the ages of the students. An important
factor to remember is that the jr. high age is generally the age
when boys begin to change into men, and girls into women. It
is a miraculous but frustrating time, for both the students and
their teachers. Some personalities are geared for this age-level;
some are not.

I've known many an outstanding jr. high person, suffering from the Peter Principle (the urge to be promoted or seek advancement beyond their level of competency) who have bombed when working with high school kids. Ditto outstanding high school directors who feel the urge to go on to college level work. This is not always the case, but if you think you are interested in this age level, you should visit your local jr. high and observe; as well as talk to the music people there.

There is one thing to be said for working with children at this age; you get them (musically) before they have been spoiled. This is particularly true if you have had a good elementary school person working with the kids before they are sent to you.

Wonders can be performed with patient, loving and knowledgeable jr. high directors. It is a very rewarding age, because you can see such progress in such a short period of time. That is, if you can handle the fact that you will be performing simpler literature, and dealing with players who are young men and women one minute and pouty children the next.

The pay scale is approximately the same as high school. Sometimes the high school director receives a little extra for his time with the marching band. This bonus is seldom available to the jr. high director.

Again, because of the tremendous budget cuts in large public school systems (we can spend 120 million dollars a day on a foreign war nobody wants, but we cannot seem to keep our public school system from falling apart) job opportunities are not too frequent. The picture may change, and it varies greatly from area to area within the U.S.

Anyone who has good credentials and is determined to find work at this level will find it. You may not be able to select your geographical preference. But you should be able to find your place.

**PART IV**

**SECTION FIVE**

**Elementary School Educator**

*He who hesitates is lost,*
*sometimes; but sometimes it's*
*better to look before you leap.*
    Papa Gyor

349.

## 77. THE ELEMENTARY LEVELS

Elementary music specialists fall into three categories:
1.  *The traveling instrumental teacher;* who usually has
    beginning and intermediate bands and orchestras
    at 7 - 10 schools.
2.  *The music specialist;* who works with the classroom
    teacher as a consultant, bringing in films, records,
    musical games and helping once a month or so
    with the music lesson, sometimes more often than
    that.
3.  *The single music teacher* in an elementary program
    that does not work on the self-contained classroom
    principle. Rather the students take math from the
    math teacher, reading from the reading teacher, etc.
    Such programs are rare, but where in operation the
    music teacher does the whole job; vocal, instrumen-
    tal, general music, etc.

In most school districts instrumental music is not taught
to students below the 4th grade. The only exception is with
special programs like the Suzuki String Program, where a carefully worked out developmental program for parents and students

alike allows string instruction (violin) to be introduced at a pre-school age.

Some districts, such as the very successful Long Beach, California system, under the supervision of Fred Ohlendorf, only allow string instruction to begin in the 4th grade, giving their string program a year head start over their winds and percussion. This has allowed for an outstanding string program in their district, rivalling the best in the nation.

In teaching at the elementary school you are working with the raw product, the child before he is conditioned, positively or negatively by others. In today's society, a child is no longer a child, as far as vicarious experience is concerned because of television. Marshal McLuhan, expert on environment's effect on man, states that the average five-year-old has had more vicarious experience via t.v. and films than his grandparents actually or vicariously had in their entire lifetimes.

Still, you are working with fresh, young minds. It can be a real thrill, watching a young boy or girl progress from fumbling, feeping noises on a musical instrument to the first song. This kind of teaching takes patience and a great love of children. It also takes a certain humility and realism about musical expectations; if you've always dreamed of conducting Beethoven's 9th, you may be disappointed in only getting as far as "Jingle Bells."

Some fantastic things are being done in elementary schools in the area of jazz and improvisation. Dr. Wong, head of the University of California, Berkley Campus experimental school has children improvising readily on instruments and vocally by the 5th and 6th grade. Also, certain techniques imported from Europe, such as the Orff (Germany) and the Kodaly (Hungary) methods are making great breakthroughs in developing musical sensitivity at an early age.

The two basic requisites of any successful musical performance; regardless of the media or material is the ability to sing or play in tune and the ability to sing or play in time. Both of these fundamentals are developed at an early age. This is why the elementary program is so vital to the future of music. This is also where we develop the good habits of listening; something we have ignored in our music programs for too long.

The elementary level is the base of the pyramid. Not much can happen at the top unless things are run right at the bottom. Unfortunately, we do not have much glamour or extra rewards for our primary teachers. This is unfortunate, for truly, the future of the nation literally rests in their hands.

The primary teachers should be the best trained, the best paid and the best quality of teacher available. Too much emphasis has been placed on the top of the pyramid.

If you are a truly humble, gentle person, who would like to do something rewarding, and live to see the results of your efforts, teaching music at the primary level can be a most satisfying experience. Pay is approximately the same as the intermediate, with an extra allowance for gasoline for the traveling instrumental specialist, or classroom consultant.

Visit your local music program and talk to one of the elementary music specialists if you are interested in this field.

352.

# PART IV

## SECTION SIX

### Music Education Administrator

*One has to dismount from an idea and get into
the saddle again at every parenthesis,*
Oliver Wendell Holmes

353.

## 78. THE DIFFICULT TASK OF THE ADMINISTRATOR

Administration in music education is reserved primarily
for:
1. College deans and department heads
2. Public school district music supervisors
3. State supervisors of music

The dean of a large music department at the university
or college level has a tough job. He has to coordinate all the
divergent opinions and experiences of his staff with the needs
of his students and the university at large and put them together with the facilities, equipment and budget available.

He has to have the wisdom of Solomon, the thrift of
Ben Franklin, the insight of Sigmund Freud, the leadership of
Winston Churchill and the foresight and planning ability of the
head of General Motors. His is often a thankless task, faculty
and students never being totally pleased with his efforts.

He must be primarily inner-directed; not easily swayed
by power cliques within his own faculty or among the students.
He must constantly be checking or running follow-up studies
on his graduates to see if there are any basic weaknesses in his
program or department.

The music dean must have a broad range of knowledge in music; able to judge quality in opera, jazz, elementary music, vocal, whatever. His job seldom allows him to practice his own musical expertise, except on holidays or sabbatical leaves. His salary is not often commensurate with his responsibilities.

The salary for most deans is approximately $5,000 a year more than his better-paid staff members. Oftentimes it is less. Still, it is a heady position, and if you like the feeling of being captain of your own ship it is a noble goal to shoot for. Examine your own leadership potential. Unless you can command respect from colleagues, unless you can crack down on close friends when they are wrong, unless you can stand the brunt of any department criticism (the buck-passing stops at your desk) you had better back off.

Music supervisors of large school districts, like John Roberts, Music Supervisor of the Denver Public Schools have large and complex tasks of administration. Their jobs include:

1. Selecting and hiring staff members for all of the music positions within the district.
2. Preparing the budget and fighting it out with school boards and administrators for their fair share of the revenue.
3. Planning an effective curriculum from kindergarten through community college in music.
4. Planning and executing major musical events like All-City Orchestra, Band, Chorus, Music Week, etc.
5. Introducing workshops and special training programs into the schools, such as John's use of the Stan Kenton Orchestra in the Denver Schools for a full week last year.
6. Handling the burdensome details of music instrument replacement and repair, music ordering, piano tuning, facility coordination, etc.
7. Publicity and handling the public are two important items for any music supervisor today. He must get the cooperation and support of the PTA,

music critics of the local papers, the Musician's Union, and other strong and potentially helpful groups to make his program go.

8.   He must supervise and go after special federally-funded programs, such as the Manhattan Project, a special program for music for deprived children in the inner-city (ghetto). Federal monies are available, but the noisiest wheel usually gets the grease. He must be a successful lobbyist at the local, state and national levels.

9.   He must demand and get the respect and cooperation of music teachers in general music, instrumental, vocal and piano. He has to avoid showing favoritism, or of being unduly influenced by close friends.

A tough job. One that many school districts are simply eliminating sometimes along with the entire music program. Such an attempt was made in Chicago last year. Chuck Suber, Editor-Publisher of *Downbeat Magazine,* along with local papers, t.v. and radio created such a stink about the dropping of the music program from the Chicago Schools it reached the state level and special funds were found to keep the program going. It's that kind of threat, the threat of complete removal of your job altogether, along with the other pressures that make this position a tough one.

Some districts *are not* replacing their music supervisors when they retire, just phasing out the job.

Pay varies. Usually anywhere from $20,000 to $30,000 a year. Some districts more, some less. Certainly not enough, considering the responsibility and the work load.

The state music supervisor must travel within his state and see to it that districts are maintaining at least a minimum program in music if they are to receive funds. It is his or her job to develop minimum and maximum standards of excellence in music education at all levels. National norms must be consulted in relation to state programs. Long term planning must be

engaged in in the area of facilities, staff, budget, equipment participation and teacher-training programs.

Frequent appearances before local civic groups, urging
their support for music programs is a must. Ditto appearances
on t.v. and radio, asking for support and pointing out the good
the music can do and is doing for young people of all ages
through the school music programs.

The state music supervisor must constantly try to up-
date modes of instruction. He must be careful to see that music
is reaching the 92% as well as the 8% participating in music performing groups. He must go after state and federal monies as
much as possible. He must be a good lobbyist.

This position is relatively new, and few states have a
state music supervisor. It's a shame, for we need direction and
guidance as well as representation at the state and national
levels as well as the local level.

Salary will run from $25,000 to $40,000 per year. In
some states the salary will be considerably less.

Music educators should really put heat on their state
governments to create this position if it does not already exist.
It has been one of the weaknesses of music educators to fight
their battles on a local level only, forgetting that everything
filters down from the federal and state levels. Unless change is
initiated at those levels the local battle may die whimpering.

# PART IV

# SECTION SEVEN

## Miscellaneous Educator Areas

'f at first you don't succeed, take another
look at the project; maybe it's not worth
doing in the first place. Or if it is, maybe
you're doing something wrong. Check it
·ut, then maybe try again.
                    Papa Gyor

357

## 79. MISCELLANEOUS AREAS

Sid Fox works for Follete Publishing Co., out of Chicago.
Sid lives in Thousand Oaks, California. Sid does over 150 clinics
and seminars a year. He has traveled to Europe, Africa and Asia
as a special consultant for the government and/or national music
organizations like M.E.N.C. What's Sid's bag? Sid's bag is to
teach music teachers where it's at, as far as the kids are concerned. One of his lecture topics is "From Rock to Bach." Sid
pleads with music educators to get their heads out of the sand,
and realize that this generation, the t.v. generation (according
to Marshall McLuhan) are the most musically sensitive and
hungry for music of any generation we've had in a long time.
They just won't buy the old approach. Sid is doing a marvelous
job through his lectures and books in leading music educators
into some kind of understanding of how to reach their students
and how to save their jobs!

Sid is on salary plus commissions and royalties from his
published works. I have never been told, but I estimate his income to be roughly $30,000 to $50,000 a year. Sid has taught
for over 15 years, has been a professional musician, a conductor
of a large army band, and can speak with authority and authen-

ticity. There is only one other man with as complete a grasp of what's happening and how to explain it, and that man is Tom McClusky, music critic for the Denver Rocky Mountain News. Tom is on staff at the University of Colorado and is music critic for one of the local papers, but an increasing amount of his time is going into lectures, clinics and publishing.

Dick Grove is a successful Hollywood t.v. and motion picture arranger. He has also developed the most comprehensive improvisation method and arranging text available for jazz and modern music. Dick is spending an increasing amount of his time as guest lecturer/teacher/performer/composer-in-residence on high school and college campuses. This last summer he was on staff for four colleges as well as a staff-member of *Jazz Internationale,* an expedition of American High School and College jazz bands to London and Paris for two weeks.

Dick is a show stopper with his improvisation presentations. No one else in the country quite has it together like Dick does, although Dave Baker at the University of Indiana does a tremendous job, as well as Jerry Coker from the University of Miami and Jamie Abersold from Indiana.

This field, showing people how to make music, not re-make it, is the fastest growing single development in music education today. Consequently Dick and the others mentioned are doing a real service in making their expertise available around the country.

Wanna buy a band? Stan Kenton and Woody Herman will sell their bands to any college campus or school district for a few days for a nominal fee. This includes multiple performances by the band within the district or on campus as well as brass, reed, rhythm-section clinics, improvisation and arranging seminars to boot. Don Ellis is doing the same thing. So is Don Rader and the aforementioned Dick Grove with their quintettes, and many other top jazz personalities.

This kind of coming together of professionals and educators and students can have nothing but a very powerful positive effect on the whole music education scene.

Want to write for school groups?

Many composer/arrangers have done just that. Frank Erickson, Paul Yoder, Alfred Reed and many others have done quite well in this field. One of the newest and most successful writers (and also educational director for Alfred Music) is Sandy Feldstein. Sandy has his Doctorate from Columbia in Music Education. He has taught at New York University and other colleges on the East Coast. He has played professionally in and around New York. Sandy has taken Alfred Music, formerly a very conservative publishing house and has turned it into one of the most progressive publishing houses in music education.

Sandy's genius lies not only in his own writing ability, but in his ability to select other outstanding modern-music writers (jazz/rock) and to anticipate the needs of the directors and the desires of their students.

Roy Burns plays drums. In fact, Roy Burns plays drums better than almost any drummer alive today. Roy plays not in some smoky, dingy night club, or on the road with his own or some other traveling band. Roy plays with good high school and college jazz bands and some concert bands.

Roy gives an hour drum clinic that is not only educational and informative, but is one of the funniest bits of entertainment you will find anywhere. Roy is the greatest. Roy is in music education. As a clinician for Rogers Drums, CBS Musical Instruments, Roy is traveling constantly, playing, giving clinics for dealers, schools, etc.

Roy publishes his own books. Roy is successful.

How do you get a gig like Roy's? First of all, you have to establish your reputation as one of the best with the pros. Then you have to know how to write, how to teach, how to talk, how to handle difficult audiences and directors, and how to play . . . how to top the best your audience has ever heard . . . time after time.

Roy is an artist, businessman, educator, writer, lecturer. He is also something of a practicing psychologist. How do you get to be like Roy? Like you get into Carnegie Hall: Practice, man, practice.

There are many other jobs along the periphery of music education; being an area representative for a national musical instrument manufacturer like Selmer, King or Conn. Some might be drawn to be instrument repairmen, a much-needed trade that is slowly diminishing in quality and quantity of participants.

Maybe you have an inventive nature. If you do, you might, like Harold Rhodes, invent something like his electric piano; sold through Fender Instruments and preferred by most pros today. There are all kinds of jobs in music education publications.

There are thousands of music educators who make a comfortable living as private teachers. Studio teaching is an art in itself, and can be both lucrative and rewarding professionally. Organizations like the MTA and NATS (National Assn. of Teachers of Singing) offer help and guidance to those interested in this role.

Anyone who plays a horn, sings or writes is a music educator.

Actually, the most powerful music educator in our society is the disk jockey.

The Pied Piper of Hamlin.

If we can ever get our children back from the Pied Piper, we (other music educators) might have an easier time of it.

I'm proud to be called a music educator. It is a noble calling, one that allows the best of both worlds; a devotion and dedication to the practice of music as an art, and the opportunity to influence and help develop young minds through music. A pretty heady combination.

Unfortunately, you will never receive the public attention that some of our undernourished spastic rock singers get, nor will you tap the till for much bread. But you will have the satisfaction of having done something worthwhile for society, for your fellow man and for your art.

With all these rewards, who wants money or fame?

# SOME GENERAL OBSERVATIONS
# AND RECOMMENDATIONS

*Old people like to give good advice, as*
*solace for no longer being able to*
*provide bad examples.*
Francis Duc De La Rochefoucald

## 80. HERE COMES THE PREACHER

It would be unrealistic if not hypocritical to close a book which purports to give practical career guidance without saying something about the sociological atmosphere in which we all live, for it unquestionably has a telling effect on our careers as well as every other phase of our lives.

The times are troublous.

They've always been.

You've got or had Vietnam and maybe Korea and welfare and crime and corruption in high places. We had World War II and Korea and Vietnam and the Big D, the depression and crime and corruption in high places.

We've all lived, since Hiroshima in 1945, with nuclear bombs dangling by what often seem thin threads over our heads.

I was not able to survive it without stimulants and tranquilizers. I drink four cups of coffee to get going every morning, and have two martinis before dinner and two substantial blasts of scotch on the rocks before bedtime. At one point I smoked four packs of cigarettes a day, every day. For years.

We're all addicts.

But the addictions with which you're tempted today
are far more sinister than were ours. When I first encountered
musicians smoking gauge in the early 30s I was not only
horrified, but terrified. No thanks!

Dashiell Hammet wrote violent private eye stories about
brutal killers, crazed by the cannabis indica.

No thanks!

Today you're more realistic, more honest; consequently subjected to greater dangers. Nobody's proved pot's worse
than booze. But lots of people have proved heroin is, or cocaine
or acid or speed or many downers. Where do you stop? How do
you stop?

I don't preach the evils of pot; I make no speeches against
drugs, period.

The means to cope is where you find it. I do say a Brian
Jones, a Janis Joplin, a Jimi Hendrix, a Hank Williams end is to
be avoided at all costs.

If you find yourself driven in that direction, for whatever reason, your past, your lover, apocalyptic visions of today
and tomorrow, duck it, fight it! If you have any talent you owe
it to yourself, if to no one else to develop it. Troublous times
there are, always were, always will be. Stimulate, tranquilize,
do what you have to do, but keep control.

One of the other big differences which has developed on
the sociological front, which may have a bearing on your music/
record career:  The new permissiveness.

Believe, me, there are always groupies. Solo and in packs.
Particularly if your career is in the performing end, but frequently in any part of the music/record business.

Using groupies in moderation and in reasonably normal
relationships is not admirable, in my opinion, but neither is it
reprehensible. Few can resist temptation. It probably won't
hurt you except for a possible case of venereal disease you might
acquire. But a segment (I don't know how substantial) of the
younger music business leans toward more extreme and flam-
boyant sexual activities. Maybe Columbia Records (a respectable

enough music/record organization, right?) flagged it best in a recent rull page trade ad:

*"To a world of mock depravity and make believe perverts, Columbia Records proudly presents the real thing - - -*

"From Shel Silverstain, America's foremost chronicler of lechery and general debauch, there comes an album that's undoubtedly the most daring we've ever signed our name to: *Freakin' at the Freakers' Ball*. Including *'I Saw Polly in a Porny (with a Pony)*, *'Don't Give a Dose to the One You Love Most'*, *'Thumbsucker'* and the climactic *('When They Ask Me How My Life Has Been I Guess I'll Have to Say) I Got Stoned and I Missed It.'"*

If you think freakin' may be fun, read that last title again. Unless you want to go through your life out of it, skip the more extreme forms of debauchery which seem to be gaining favor in so many young circles.

A lot of good young people fell, before the Roman and Grecian civilizations in which they lived fell.

End of preachment.

Good luck with your career.

## A Personal Note to the Reader

The deeper I got into researching and writing this book, the more apparent it became that no matter how hard I tried to answer every question anyone could ask concerning one or more careers in the music/record business, I would necessarily fall short of achieving that, perhaps impossible, goal.

I hope I have answered most of the questions. If a question, or several, occurs to the serious reader, to which he finds no answer, I will be more than happy to undertake a personal answer. Write me at First Place Music Publications, Inc., 12754 Ventura Boulevard, Studio City, California 91604.

## Index to Unions & Other Organizations

Many of these are discussed in the appropriate chapters and sections of the book. They are listed here alphabetically as a convenience. Except where the group's name is self-explanatory, there is a brief note on the functions and/or membership of the organization.

American Composers Alliance (ACA)
170 W. 74 St., New York, N.Y. 10023
(212) 873-1250
Charles Dodge, president; David Cooper
exec. director
FOR WRITERS

American Federation of Television &
Radio Artists (AFTRA)
1350 Ave. of the Americas, New York,
N.Y. 10019
(212) 265-7700
Bill Baldwin, president; Sanford I Wolff,
national exec. secretary
FOR ALL PERFORMERS WORKING
IN TELEVISION OR RADIO

American Guild of Authors & Composers
(AGAC)
50 W. 57 St., New York, N.Y. 10019
(212) 757-8833
Edward Eliscu, president; John Carter,
managing director
FOR WRITERS
Branch: 6331 Hollywood Blvd., Hollywood, Ca. 90028
(213) 462-1108
Helen King, West Coast rep.

American Guild of Musical Artists (AGMA)
1841 Broadway, New York, N.Y. 10023
(212) 265-3687
Cornell MacNeil, president; DeLloyd Tibbs,
national exec. secretary
FOR PERFORMERS IN THE CONCERT
FIELD

American Guild of Variety Artists (AGVA)
1540 Broadway, New York, N.Y. 10036
(212) 765-0800
Penny Singleton, exec. president; Jack Haley,
executive vice president; Russell Swann,
secretary - treasurer
FOR PERFORMERS PLAYING NIGHT
CLUBS, THEATRES, CLUB DATES,
ETC.

American Piano Teachers Ass'n. (APTA)
1739 Randolph Rd., Schenectady, N.Y.
12308
(518) 377-5254
Lora Benner, contact

American Accordionists' Assn.
37 W. Eighth St., New York, N.Y. 10011
(212) 228-7830
Maddelena Belfiore, president; Emily Martig-
noni, rec'g. secretary

American Choral Directors Ass'n.
P.O. Box 17736, Tampa, Fla. 33612
(813) 935-9381
Morris D. Hayes, president; R. Wayne Hugo-
boom, executive secretary

American Choral Foundation, Inc.
130 W. 56 St., New York, N.Y. 10019
(212) 246-3361
Sheldon Soffer, admin. director

American Federation of Musicians
641 Lexington Ave., New Yor, N.Y.
10022
(212) 758-0600
Hal C. Davis, president; Stanley Ballard,
secretary - treasurer
FOR ALL MUSICIANS; THE MAJOR
INTERNATIONAL MUSICIANS'
UNION

American Guild of Organists
630 Fifth Ave., New York, N.Y.
10020
(212) 265-5630
Charles D. Walker, president; James E.
Bryan, exec. director

American Society of Composers,
Authors and Publishers (ASCAP)
full details in songwriters' section

Artists' Reps. Ass'n. Inc.
1270 Ave. of the Americas, New York,
N.Y. 10020
(212) 246-1379
David C. Baumgarten, president
FOR AGENTS

Association of Rec. Dealers.
150 W. 34 St., New York, N.Y. 10001
(212) 239-0561
Mickey Gensler, president

Audio Eng'g. Society, Inc.
60 E. 42 St., New York, N.Y. 10017
(212) 661-8528
J.G. Woodward, president; Jacqueline
Harvey, managing editor; Dorothy
H. Spronck, admin. secretary

Broadcast Music, Inc. (BMI)
full details in Songwriters' section

Country Music Association, Inc. (CMA)
700 16 Ave., S. Nashville, Tenn. 37203
(615) 244-2840
Mrs. Jo Walker, executive director

ALL-CAREER COUNTRY ORGANI-
ZATION INCLUDES PERFORM-
ERS, WRITERS, MANAGERS,
BUSINESS PEOPLE, ETC.

Composers & Lyricists Guild of America, Inc.
6565 Sunset Blvd., Rm 419, Hollywood,
Calif. 90028
(213) 462-6068
Elmer Bernstein, president; Ted Cain,
executive director
Branch: 270 Madison Ave., New York,
N.Y.
(212) 683-5320
PRIMARILY FILM & TV WRITERS

Conference of Personal Managers
9220 Sunset Boulevard, Los Angeles, Ca.
90069
George Durgom, president

Electronic Inds. Ass'n. (EIA)
2001 "I" St. NW, Washington D.C. 20006
(202) 659-2200
J. Frank Leach, chairman; V.J. Adduci,
president; Roger D. Allan, PR director
TAPE, PLAYBACK & ELECTRONIC EQUIP.
EQUIP. MFRS.

Gospel Music Ass'n.
817 18 Ave. S., Nashville, Tenn. 37202
(615) 327-4434
Les Beasley, president; Norma L. Boyd,
executive sec'y

International Tape Ass'n. Inc. (ITA)
315 W. 70 St., New York, N.Y. 10023
(212) 877-6030, 873-5757
Larry Finley, executive director
TAPE, CARTRIDGE, CASSETTE MFRS.

International Ass'n of Concert & Festival
Mgrs.
c/o Donald H. Horton, Dir. of Concerts
& Lectures, Mershon Aud. Ohio State
Univ., 30 W. 15 St., Columbus, Ohio
43210
(614) 422-5785
Donald H. Horton, secretary - editor

International Rhythm & Blues Ass'n.
2630 E 75 St., Chicago, Ill. 60649
(312) 734-1232
William C. Tyson, president

Music Operators of America (MOA)
228 N. LaSalle St., Chicago, Ill. 60601
(312) 726-2810
Frederick M. Granger, executive VP
JUKE BOX OPERATORS

Music Teachers Nat'l Assn. (MTNA)
1831 Carew Tower, Cincinnati, Ohio 45202
(513) 421-1420
William Fahrer, executive sec'y.

Memphis Recording Prod'rs. Ass'n.
1350 Commerce Title Bldg., Memphis,
Tenn. 38103
(901) 525-1671
James F. Stewart, president; S. Knox
Phillips, secretary

Music Educators Nat'l Conference
1201 16 St., NW, Washington D.C. 20036
(202) 833-4216
Charles L. Gary, executive sec'y.
LEADING ORGANIZATION OF MUSIC
EDUCATORS

Music Publishers' Ass'n of the United States
609 Fifth Ave., 4th fl. New York, N.Y.
10017
(212) 752-4300
W. Stuart Pope, president

National Ass'n of Music Merchants, Inc.
(NAMM)
222 W. Adams St., Chicago, Ill. 60606
(312) 263-0679
William R. Gard, executive VP
LEADING MUSIC/RECORD DEALER
ORGANIZATION

National Academy of Recording Arts &
Sciences (NARAS)
Offices: Hollywood, Calif.
6430 Sunset Blvd., Suite 503, 90028
(213) 466-6181
Christine M. Farnon, LA Chapter
executive director
Atlanta, Ga.
P.O. Box 9687, 30319
(404) 233-6703
Mary Tallent, executive director
Chicago, Ill.
505 N. Lake Shore Dr., No. 6505
(312) 329-0949
Charlotte Caesar, executive director
New York, N.Y.
21 W. 58 St., 10019
(212) 755-1535
Nashville, Tenn.
801 16 Ave., S. 37203
(615) 242-5731
Emily Bradshaw, executive director

National Ass'n of Rec. Mdsrs, Inc.
(NARM)
703 Trianon Bldg., Bala Cynwyd, Pa.
19004
(215) 839-7900
Jules Malamud, executive director
PRIMARILY RACK JOBBERS;
SOME RECORD DISTRIBUTORS,
SOME ONE-STOPS

National Music Publishers' Ass'n, Inc.
(NMPA)
110 E. 59 St., New York, N.Y. 10022
(212) 751-1930
Salvatore T. Chiantia, president; Leonard Feist, executive VP

Nashville Songwriters' Assn. (NSA)
P.O. Box 1556, Nashville, Tenn. 37202
(615) 254-8066
Clarence Selman, president

National Ass'n of Negro Musicians, Inc.
6556 St. Lawrence Ave., Chicago, Ill.
60637
(312) 324-2465
Theodore Charles Stone, president

National Ass'n of Organ Teachers, Inc.
7938 Bertram Ave., Hammond, Ind.
46324
(219) 844-3395
Mrs. Dorothy S. Greig, president; Jack
C. Greig, admin. director

National Ass'n of Schools of Music
1 Dupont Circle NW, Suite 650, Washington, D.C. 20036
(202) 296-4925
Dr. Carl Neumeyer, president; Dr. David A. Ledet, executive sec'y

National Ass'n of Teachers of Singing, Inc.
250 W. 57 St., New York, N.Y. 10019
(212) 582-4043
Mrs. Jean Ludman, president; Martha Lee Baxter, executive sec'y

National Ass'n of Television & Radio Announcers
1408 S. Michigan Ave., Chicago, Ill. 60605
(312) 939-5170
Curtis Shaw, president; Lucky Cordell, executive sec'y
PRIMARILY BLACK RADIO TALENT AND PERSONNEL

National Catholic Music Educators Ass'n
4637 Eastern Ave. NE, Washington D.C. 20018
(301) 277-1577
Reverend William A. Volk CPPS, president; Vincent P. Walter Jr., exec. director

National Entertainment Conference
P.O. Box 11489, Capitol Sta. Columbia, S.C. 29211
(803) 253-4635
D.W. Phillips, executive director
COLLEGE GROUP

National Federation of Music Clubs
600 S. Michigan Ave., Suite 1215, Chicago, Ill 60605
(312) 427-3683
Dr. Merle Montgomery, president

National Guild of Community Music Schools
244 E. 52 St., New York, N.Y. 10022
(212) 753-8811
Harris Danziger, president
   Branch: Silver Spring, Md.
   9214 Three Oaks Drive, 20901
   (301) 585-8560
   Charles C. Mark, executive director

National Music Council
2109 Broadway
New York, N.Y. 10023
(212) 799-0100
Leonard Feist, president; James Browning, executive secretary
MUSIC PUBLISHERS/EDUCATIONAL MUSIC GROUP

National Piano Mfrs. Ass'n
435 N. Michigan Ave., Chicago, Ill. 60611
(312) 527-5494
George M. Otto, executive director

National School Orchestra Assn.
330 Bellevue Dr. Bowling Green, Ky 42101
(502) 842-7121
James H. Godfrey, president

Recording Ind. Ass'n of America, Inc. (RIAA)
1 E 57 St., New York, N.Y. 10022
(212) 688-3778
Stanley M. Gortikov, president; Henry Brief, executive director
MANUFACTURERS' GROUP

Recording Inds. (Music Performance) Trust Funds
1501 Broadway, Suite 810, New York, N.Y. 10036
(212) 239-8550
Kenneth E. Raine, trustee
AFFILIATED WITH AMERICAN FED. OF MUSICIANS

Notes

# Notes